CRIME OF PASSION

The hot fury that had possessed Dr. Kenneth Z. Taylor only seconds before was gone. Washed away in a flood of confused feelings. Horror, panic, fear, even terror, all mingled in the chaotic swamp of his emotions.

"My God, she's dead, she's dead," he repeated to himself as he kneeled beside his wife Teresa, staring.

She lay face down, her arms and legs twisted at unlikely angles. Blood was everywhere. He looked away from Teresa's dead face. Blood had splattered the hall floor and the walls.

He shook his head. It had all been so sudden, so swift, so final. He couldn't think clearly . . . but he knew one thing — that it was all over.

"I had killed her. I hadn't divorced her. I hadn't left her . . . I killed her."

COLD-BLOODED MURDER FROM PINNACLE BOOKS

NURSES WHO KILL   (449, $3.95)
Clifford L. Linedecker and William A. Burt
RICHARD ANGELO—convicted of killing four patients
by lethal injection in a New York hospital
GENENE JONES TURK—serving 99 years for maiming
and killing kinfants in a Texas pediatric clinic
DONALD HARVEY—convicted killer of terminally ill pa-
tients in Kentucky hospitals
INGER LEMONT—Florida homecare worker convicted of
hacking an shut-in woman to death in her home
ROBERT DIAZ—convicted killer of 12 elderly residents in
two California nursing homes

This is the grizzly true crime account of such hospital
killers—men and women who abused their scared role to
save lives in order to take them, hideously, coldly, without
remorse and often for pleasure.

SPREE KILLERS   (461, $4.95)
Edited by Art Crockett
    No one knows what triggers it. Maybe it's a look, maybe
a word. But the result is always the same: Innocent people
are wounded and killed.
    They are mass murderers, spree killers. If they escape the
scene of their bloody crime, they may never kill again. Unlike serial murderers like Ted Bundy, these killers claim
lives indescriminately, usually in one mad burst of violence. There's no way to hide from their insane acts once
the killing urge is triggered. (From the files of *TRUE DE-
TECTIVE* Magazine)

*Available wherever paperbacks are sold, or order direct from the
Publisher. Send cover price plus 50¢ per copy for mailing and
handling to Pinnacle Books, Dept. 547, 475 Park Avenue South,
New York, N.Y. 10016. Residents of New York, New Jersey and
Pennsylvania must include sales tax. DO NOT SEND CASH.*

IN A FATHER'S RAGE

RAYMOND VAN OVER

PINNACLE BOOKS
WINDSOR PUBLISHING CORP.

PINNACLE BOOKS

are published by

Windsor Publishing Corp.
475 Park Avenue South
New York, NY 10016

Copyright © 1991 by Raymond Van Over

All rights reserved. No part of this book may be reproduced in any form or by any means without the prior written consent of the Publisher, excepting brief quotes used in reviews.

If you purchased this book without a cover you should be aware that this book is stolen property. It was reported as "unsold and destroyed" to the Publisher and neither the Author nor the Publisher has received any payment for this "stripped book."

First printing: October, 1991

Printed in the United States of America

ACKNOWLEDGMENTS

As with any book, there are always many people who have contributed. But special gratitude must be offered to Peter Maas, for his generosity in allowing me to see his tape of Ken Taylor's sodium amytal interview, and to Arthur Kopit, for taking so much time to talk with me in such depth about his insights into the Taylor case.

There are also all those who deserve thanks (if not a medal) for putting up with having their brains picked during interviews.

I also deeply appreciated Chris Malkovich's expert help from the depths of the *Asbury Park Press* archives.

And, of course, I would like to thank my editor at Zebra Books, Paul Dinas, for his patience and understanding throughout what seemed an interminable process.

Thanks are also due to Zach and Jean Taylor for their help in providing photographs and to Ken Taylor for his cooperation.

Foreword

Every crime, no matter how clear in motivation, brutal in execution, replete with detail, or satisfying in its final legal resolution, has a "Roshomon complex."

Roshomon was a celebrated Broadway play in the 1950s that revolved around a murder seen from a variety of different perspectives. Each character described the murder and its motives exclusively from his or her own point of view.

Ultimately, the Roshomon complex warns us, we will always walk out of the theater shifting through multiple impressions, weighing the differing points of view and the conflicting facts — all in an effort to make up our own minds about the mysteries of why people kill.

In the Taylor case a number of mysteries remain surrounding the details of exactly what happened on November 11, 1984. Here are the undisputed facts of the case:

Dr. Kenneth Taylor, a respected and successful dentist in a small New Jersey town, confessed that in the early morning hours of Sunday, November 11, 1984, he bludgeoned his wife, Teresa, to death.

Initially, there was puzzlement over motive. There was no million-dollar insurance policy, no inheritance, no lover waiting in the wings and coaxing the killer into action, all of which created confusion about what went on during those final climactic moments of violent death.

What could have caused the brutal beating death of a beautiful young mother, still flushed with the excitement of giving birth to her first child only five months earlier, a young woman with a successful, attractive husband, who was just beginning to live the life she'd always dreamed of?

In fact, everyone involved in this odd saga was at one time or another puzzled over the motive for the killing. Nothing seemed to fit. What went wrong in the lives of these two intelligent, attractive people?

Why did a man who apparently loved his wife (and who steadfastly maintains to this day that he loved her then and still loves her now) kill her in a wild fit of anger? Was he simply a clever psychotic killer, as some have maintained? Or was he, as others believe, a confirmed drug addict and sexually deranged killer who managed to live a normal life by holding in his murderous compulsions until they finally burst free? Was he perhaps a bizarre misfit, an intelligent, charming, logical brute, a kind of Ted Bundy masquerading as your local dentist? Or was he a relatively normal man caught up in a lifestyle of self-indulgence, of casual drug use that finally burned away the civilizing controls on his behavior?

Fascinated to find answers to these questions, I started to delve more deeply into the Taylor case only to find myself immersed in my own Roshomon maze. The deeper I probed, the more confusing the layers of facts and differing viewpoints became.

Where was the truth to be found—in Ken Taylor's truth, which was immediately suspect because it was so obviously self-serving? Could we trust in the beliefs and theories of the dead woman's relatives and friends, who saw events through the haze of their own fury and deep personal agony? Could we believe the county prosecutor's carefully constructed version of the truth, probably equally suspect because of his passionate ambition to win the case? Or should we believe the defense attorney's version of the truth even while remembering that he was a paid advocate feeding on information by the killer: weren't his constructions of "fact" also self-serving as he fought to win the freedom of his client?

As the lone survivor of those final deadly moments, only

Ken Taylor knows for certain what occurred between him and his wife on November 11. And because Taylor is obviously not an unbiased witness, the only way to get at the truth is to reconstruct the events as closely as possible, listen to his story, review the trial, and then piece together the most plausible facts in a rational and fair manner — which is what I have tried to do in writing *In a Father's Rage*.

Yes, the process is frustrating, for there always remain those dark Roshomon corners where the "real" stays hidden; but such mysteries are also a fascinating, mind-teasing delight.

Unsatisfactory? Yes, but it is the only method we have to find — or at least to get close to — the truth of other people's lives.

At the end of any mystery there is always the implied statement, "There, this is all you can know."

Raymond Van Over
Washington, D.C.

Chapter One

It was a typical fall day in the Pennsylvania mountains, dismal and overcast. And even though it was after ten A.M., the woods still had that dark, wet smell characteristic of early morning, as if night were struggling to hang on. Mist rolled slowly into the clearing from the heavily wooded slopes of Hawk Mountain as Neil Griesemer walked along the side of the road. He was stooped over, his eyes on the ground.

Neil, a 51-year-old security guard at the Hawk Shadow Feed and Saddlery in Orwigsburg, lived over the feed store and worked as a part-time cook at the Moose Club over in Hamburg. And even though he worked two jobs it wasn't really enough to make ends meet. To bring in a little extra money Neil had developed the habit of collecting beer cans from alongside the road, which he then sold for twenty-two cents a pound.

Neil had discovered that there were never enough cans along the main roads, but there were always better pickings near campgrounds or where people congregated. That was why he preferred to work the Hawk Mountain Bird Sanctuary. All the birdwatchers and picnickers meant that he would always find enough cans to make it worth his time.

But this Thursday morning was different. This morning he would find something that would deeply affect and alter the lives of many people.

The bird sanctuary was in a remote area of Pennsylvania about fifty miles from the New Jersey border, off Interstate 78 and at the base of Hawk Mountain.

As usual, Neil had parked up the road, nearer the entrance, and checked along the south side. But this morning when he walked back along the other side he saw a tan sleeping bag about twenty feet off the road at the far edge of a half-circle pulloff area for visitors' cars.

Neil walked over and kicked the bag. He felt something solid inside. His first thought was, "Someone's shot a deer out of season and tried to get rid of it, covered it up."

He bent over and touched the sleeping bag. It was still wet with night dew. He pulled the edge of the bag back and saw an expanse of gray flesh. The exposed skin looked to him like that of a pig or some other hairless animal. He couldn't be sure. He looked closer and with a sudden shock realized it was part of a human body.

Neil backed off, his heart suddenly thudding in his chest. He ran to his car and drove back down the road to the Hawk Mountain Sanctuary office and told Tom Kerr, the sanctuary's business manager, what he had found. Tom told Neil to calm down, got his coat, and then returned with Griesemer to the spot of the grisly discovery while Dorothy Brett, the sanctuary's secretary, called the state police barracks in Hamburg.

It was 10:40 Thursday morning, November 15, 1984.

At 11:05 Troopers John Bressler and Dale Bonney arrived. They were the first at the scene. They questioned Griesemer and Tom Kerr and began to secure the area to keep it clean for the investigators. A little while later, around 11:40, Officers Joseph Lescavage and Eugene Taylor arrived. They also questioned Griesemer and took photographs showing the victim's body in its "found" position.

It was a young female. The body had been wrapped in gray padding, the kind of material used under carpets. It then had been stuffed into the sleeping bag.

Even in the gray, shadowed light of the dark woods, they could all see that the head and side of the young woman's face had been beaten badly with a heavy instrument. To the officers staring down at her, it looked like her skull had been

12

crushed, bludgeoned repeatedly. There was no doubt that the terrible head injuries were the probable cause of death. There was little blood next to the body or even in the surrounding area, so the conclusion that she had been killed elsewhere was obvious.

Evidence was marked and collected. A black trash bag and two smaller white trash bags tied together were found with the body. Both men were experienced cops and they especially noted a print made in blood on the white trash bag. Could the killer have been so clumsy as to leave his bloody print? No, they thought, that would be too easy. Little in police work was ever that simple. And true to the rule, it later turned out that the print belonged to the victim.

Along with the normal detritus found near public parks (paper napkins, coffee containers, shotgun shells, and McDonald's hamburger boxes), the officers discovered and itemized the following:

"Hairs from the rectal area of female body; rope 9'10½" long with 1'4" knotted loop; large gray carpet padding 14'3" x 6'; black Pulsar watch with black band; wedding ring, 14k gold; a necklace with tooth and toothbrush charm; a necklace with '#1 Sister' pendant, and one six-pronged earring with a diamond inset."

By the time the ambulance arrived and took the body away, the routine police work was already beginning.

Residents in the area were contacted and asked if they had seen or heard anything that might relate to the discovery of the body. An officer visited the Kempton Mobil gas station and none of the young men hanging around had seen or heard anything odd. One resident who walked down the trail to work every morning reported seeing a blue Volkswagen Rabbit parked in the half-circle pulloff area. The car was parked so the rear end was backed into the mountainside—a strange way to park, but the resident said he didn't think any more about it because many birdwatchers were often in the area and strange cars were common. But still, officers tediously collected the registration numbers of the several dozen vehicles near the scene and sent them through the state and federal computers.

Local restaurants, gift shops, and country stores were all contacted, but no one could remember seeing anyone answering the description of the young woman.

A more thorough examination of the body took place at nearby Pottsville Hospital later that day. Pathologists began working a little after 3 P.M. and added to the growing amount of evidence. But there was nothing to identify her and she was tagged as "Jane Doe."

The victim's fingerprints and palm prints were recorded. Hair samples from the head and pubic area were collected, and a vial of blood and samples of lubricant smeared around the victim's anus and vagina were taken. The young woman's fingernails were examined for evidence, but nothing significant was recovered.

On November 16 a man named Lindy Potts, Jr., from Orwigsburg, Pa., appeared at the Hamburg State Police Barracks and said he thought the body might be that of his missing niece, Lynn Ann, who was twenty-two years old, stood five feet seven inches tall, and weighed 150 pounds. He was taken to Pottsville Hospital at 9:30 A.M. to view the body. Potts stared down at the corpse, trying to recognize something familiar in the damaged and broken face. He shook his head. It was not his niece. He left the morgue pale and shaken.

In the search to identify this young woman every angle was covered. Officers visited local jewelers for information on the value, size, trademarks, and general appraisal of the victim's jewelry. The Jewelers' Association of America in New York was contacted. Companies that specialized in selling charms, and the Pulsar Watch Co. in Mahwah, New Jersey, were all canvased for any thread of evidence. Computers began smoking as lists of serial numbers and descriptions scrolled across their screens. Warranty and maintenance records were checked.

And all to no avail. The identity of the young woman remained a mystery. Two days had now passed, and on the record she was still Jane Doe.

On Saturday, November 17, a uniscope message was received by Pottsville from the Manalapan Township, New Jersey, Police Department, requesting any information about the disappearance of Teresa Taylor, a white female, aged 25, reported missing by her husband, Dr. Kenneth Taylor, a New Jersey dentist. The physical description and scars on the body in the uniscope message matched those of the corpse found at Hawk Mountain.

The lifeless body of Teresa Taylor still lay on a stainless steel slab in the Pottsville Hospital morgue, waiting to be viewed and officially identified by relatives.

The police report contains a dry description of a horrific, emotional experience.

"At 1555 hours, Nov. 17, a positive identification was made by the victim's father, Rev. Albert Benigno, and her brother, Philip Benigno. Accompanying them to the hospital Detective Robert Fausak and Patrolman David Visconi, of the New Jersey, Manalapan Township, Police Department."

A note to the report states that Dr. Kenneth Taylor, the victim's husband, had reported her missing to Manalapan police on Thursday, November 15, at 9:14 A.M., at just about the time Neil Griesemer had come upon the corpse. Dr. Taylor had advised the police that on Sunday, November 11, he had taken her to the Newark airport. On Monday, November 12, he drove to Marion, Indiana, to visit his parents. After returning to New Jersey and finding his wife not home, he reported her missing.

The identity of the battered body was no longer a mystery, but how Teresa Taylor got to that isolated, mist-shrouded forest road—and who killed her—was.

Chapter Two

Kenneth Taylor was from a quiet, conservative lower-middle-class family that had settled in Marion, Indiana, at the center of the American heartland. Teresa Taylor was raised in an emotional, voluble working-class Italian family from New York City.

Two more disparate backgrounds could not have been imagined for a couple trying to start a life together. Although by most accounts from friends and neighbors the Taylors were a happy couple, it sometimes seemed a wonder that the marriage could ever succeed.

Both Zach and Jean Taylor had grown up in the Cincinnati area. They had been high school sweethearts but had decided to wait for marriage until after Zach returned from his tour of duty in the Pacific during World War II. When they finally married on Thanksgiving Day soon after Zach returned from the war, they were both twenty years old.

Zach, a large man with an easygoing manner, got a job in a hardware store in Cincinnati and attended Chase Business College at night. He graduated as valedictorian of his class.

As with most couples just starting out, the early period when they were trying to make ends meet and start a life together was hard. Jean worked as a licensed beautician to help support them while Zach worked and went to school. When she became pregnant two years later she continued to work right up to the last moment. But soon after giving birth to the couple's first child, Kenneth, she stopped working and stayed home to raise a family. Their second child, Nancy, was born later the same year, on December 22, 1949. The third and last child, Thomas Clay, came a few years later, on Christmas Day, 1955.

The family worked hard and prospered in Sharonville, a working-class neighborhood on the northwest side of Cincinnati. When Ken was five, the Taylors bought a new home in a suburb ten miles outside the city limits. It was the children's first experience with rural living. The house was set on a hill, fronted by a creek and thickets of blackberry bushes. A steep rise behind the house was a grazing field for cattle.

All the Taylor children, like their parents, had good if not exceptional intelligence. It was the kind of intelligence that succeeded through hard work rather than sheer brilliance. Competition and pride — for they measured themselves by the traditions and standards of middle America — were an important part of their character.

Ken Taylor seems to have been exceptionally competitive even as a young man. Throughout his own descriptions of his early life he takes great satisfaction in his own and other family members' accomplishments. His brother's athletic abilities, his sister Nancy's musical abilities (she played the glockenspiel in their high school marching band), and even the fact that Nancy had come in second in a high school spelling bee were an endless source of pride to him.

Though Zach Taylor sometimes took extra jobs during these early years, both he and Jean tried to stay involved in the kids' lives. When Ken joined the Cub Scouts, Jean became the den mother and Zach the scoutmaster. And Zach was coach of the basketball team in Ken's grade school for a time.

Ken recalls his childhood in almost unrealistic, idyllic terms, so much so, in fact, that suspicions often arose that he was being defensive and protesting accusations that had not been made. In his unpublished autobiography, for example, he wrote, "I had a marvelous childhood, REALLY [capitalization his]. My family life had been nothing less than idyllic."

But perhaps he was being defensive with reason, for as the Taylor case eventually went to trial and became notorious, and newspaper and magazine articles began appearing around the country, one writer began picturing Jean Taylor as a domineering, joyless woman obsessed with cleanliness and social image, a woman who ran her house like a drill sergeant. But like so much in the Taylor case, the facts were not clear and they did not so easily fit into simplistic categories. While Jean Taylor may have been a mother who used discipline in raising her children, from all accounts she wasn't unduly strict or harsh.

The family recalls one day when Ken was playing in the basement "rec" room. He was sixteen at the time and was performing some gymnastic exercises. He would grab the ceiling beam, pull himself up, and then kick his legs out and try to reach the clothesline. Jean, who was watching her son, suddenly grabbed the beam and did one kick, then another. On the second try her hands came loose from the ceiling beam and she fell, cracking her head on the cement floor. She was knocked unconscious. An ambulance was called and carted her off to the hospital, where she was found to have a concussion.

When she came home from the hospital it became a family joke to "forbid" her to "play in the basement" anymore.

This was hardly the behavior of a joyless, demanding harridan.

Ken Taylor later became incensed when writers fascinated with the court case attacked his family. "It seemed to me," he would later comment, "that I had the best of parents, an ideal childhood, a wholesome, solid environment." It was, according to him, one of the best and most memorable parts of his life. "The fact that I became involved with drugs as a twenty-two-year-old dental student was a decision I made on my own, and was not even remotely related to my upbringing."

Throughout his depositions, letters, and biographical writings, Taylor seemed constantly at pains to take full responsibility for the transgressions of his youth and ultimately for the disaster that finally befell him.

In high school Ken took pride in being athletic, an attitude that would stay with him for the rest of his life. And would be a cause of friction in his second marriage.

In fact, all the Taylor children were athletic. Yet even though Ken managed to win an all-conference award in football as a senior, he admitted that his skills could never equal his brother Tom's. "I seemed to have to work harder to master a particular skill," he has confessed.

Tom was not only all conference in both his junior and senior years, his awards were in three different sports — football, basketball, and baseball. But unfortunately, Tom, who was universally expected to go on to college athletics, perhaps even with a scholarship, had his blossoming career cut short by a knee injury during his senior year as the Marion High School quarterback.

In his sophomore year, he dated a number of girls, but it was as a high school junior that Ken began to learn some serious lessons about sex. He began going steady with a friend of his sister's, a thin, athletic classmate named Betty Macdonald. Betty was a pretty girl with shoulder-length brown hair and large emerald-green eyes who stood five feet six inches tall. She was one of the best female athletes in school and beat Ken at golf, a secret she kept even from her parents.

The romance lasted until their first year of college. It was a time when they both learned about sex in the backseat of his grandfather's eight-year-old white Rambler station wagon. Tooling around town in it, one of the few boys who had the use of a car, Ken became near-famous.

One teenage friend is quoted as saying, "That Rambler was the talk of the school. Everyone called it the Sexmobile. It was like Ken needed a daily injection. He'd pick her up at 7 A.M. every day, and he'd always be off somewhere parking with her."

In January 1967, Ken's senior year in high school, a major change occurred.

Zach's job with Jergens Lotion as an engineer and production-line supervisor was going nowhere. He had no chance for advancement. He was again in the exhausting ritual of working two jobs to keep things afloat and he wanted to move on to a better job. When an RCA plant opened up a couple hundred

19

miles away from Cincinnati offering a similar job but with a good opportunity for growth, he decided to take it. In 1967, when he was forty years old, Zach moved to Marion, Indiana, a small town sixty miles north of Indianapolis. Temporarily, the family stayed behind.

Zach drove home to be with his family every weekend. In the spring the family moved to an apartment in Marion while their new house was being constructed in a development just north of town.

Because Ken was only three months away from graduating he stayed behind, living for a while with his grandparents, who lived nearby, and then with one of his friends, Tom Chatham. The Chathams had two sons Ken's age and lived on the same block as the Taylors, so the transition was easy.

In high school Ken was popular enough to be elected vice president of the student body in his senior year. When he graduated, even though he didn't work hard and was by his own words "an indifferent student," he finished in the top 25 percent academically out of a class of some 300 students.

These last few months before graduation were full. Ken gave up baseball and took a part-time job in a shoestore but spent most of the money on gas for the Rambler and dates with Betty. He was in love.

After graduation both Ken and Betty enrolled at Eastern Kentucky, University in Richmond, Kentucky. Then, during their freshman year, Betty dropped him for someone else.

Ken was crushed . . . and for a brief while bitter. But with the resilience of a nineteen-year-old he recovered quickly.

By now Ken was changing physically as well. During that freshman year in college he grew from five feet eleven to six feet one, staying at the same weight of 180 pounds. Suddenly he was no longer a lumbering, gangly teenager but a lean, well-muscled, attractive young man. He had sun-bleached blond hair, a steady gaze, and a slow, easygoing personality that charmed most people he met.

He also became serious about his studies. His first semester grades were among the best in the freshman class. A talent for science was manifesting itself. In his biology course, which involved pre-med, pre-dental, and pre-veterinarian subjects, he had the highest marks in the class.

With Betty's emerald eyes and athletic body no longer holding him in thrall, and with a desire to be closer to his family, he transferred in his second year to Ball State University in Muncie, Indiana, a forty-minute drive from the Taylors' new home in Marion.

The second year at Ball State was equally results-oriented and Ken realized that he was doing better than most of the academically elite students preparing for medical school. His confidence was growing along with his body, and he thought he might have a chance at medical school. At the end of his second year he switched majors from Physical education and biology to pre-med.

This news surprised and elated his parents. A doctor in the family? No one in either of their families had ever aspired to so much.

During those first two years in college he took numerous part-time jobs — selling shoes, framing houses, and working in three different factories. While he was still going with Betty, most of the money he earned was spent on their dates. After their breakup he still tended to squander much of his earnings on dates with women. Sex had developed into a deepening lure, although it had not yet become an obsession. But being attractive to women was increasingly important to him.

In his first year at Ball State he worked at a series of part-time jobs in order to pay his way through college. He worked that first summer in a small steel mill in Marion. One of his other part-time jobs was as an orderly at Ball Memorial Hospital. He found the work fascinating and he committed himself to a career in some area of medicine.

But the commitment didn't last long. As Ken tells it, he was shocked into the realization that he didn't have it emotionally to be a doctor.

Ken worked the 11 P.M. to 7 A.M. shift as the orderly on call, and one night he was summoned to the nursery. The head nurse motioned for him to follow her to an all-purpose linen supply room. She handed him a bundle wrapped in a white sheet inside a white plastic bag. Rather like a large loaf of bread.

"Take this to the morgue, Ken," the nurse instructed him. "And use the service elevator."

By now the realization of what he was holding in his hands struck him. He was stunned. "Of course," he mumbled and walked out of the nursery, carrying the package as if it were glass and would break if he dropped it. All the way to the morgue he walked in shock. He had taken numerous dead bodies to the morgue and, as he said, "didn't really feel too much emotion one way or the other. But a dead baby?"

"Even a few years later in dental school," he recalled, "when in our twice-weekly autopsy sessions as general pathology students, and working over a cadaver in gross anatomy class, up to my elbows in dead human tissue, I did not react emotionally. Except one morning. Stretched out on the autopsy table was a seven-year-old boy. I remember not only having a sick, macabre feeling deep inside, but I became angry, even enraged."

Taylor claimed that this experience so haunted him that it undermined his resolve and convinced him that he couldn't go on. He knew his limitations, he was later to say. Others claimed it was simply an elaborate excuse to cover up the fact that his grades, while good, weren't quite up to the rigors of medical school.

Whatever the truth of these early incidents, Ken still wanted to be in medicine in some capacity and he finally chose dentistry.

He applied to the dental school at Indiana University's medical center. It was the only dental school in the state, and ranked as one of the three best in the nation. The competition was understandably fierce, but Ken was accepted.

Ken attended Ball State between 1967 and 1971. It was a period of wild social upheaval, the Vietnam era. Code words still describe the period: Haight-Ashbury, Woodstock, free love, drug culture, tune in — drop out. But even while his sympathies were with the war protestors (he claims to have voted for Dr. Spock as a write-in presidential candidate) his life was occupied, and sometimes overflowing, with a few basics: music, study, sports, and women. And always an ever-growing number of women. His pleasures were simple—Jimi Hendrix, girls, the Beatles, girls, Janis Joplin, girls, the Dallas Cowboys and the amazing Mets . . . and more girls.

If he didn't take the politics of the period seriously, he made up for it by leaping onto the bandwagon of free love.

Without any sign of modesty, he claimed, "I had plenty of girlfriends, like Volkswagen had plenty of beetles." If he had dated a lot in high school and his first year at college, it was nothing like now. Women passed through his life, in and out of his bed, an endless number of faceless bodies. It almost seemed as if his proper, hard-working, responsible Midwest upbringing was being thrown off with a rebellious vengeance.

Then, as he would recall, there was so much sex that he became bored. "In 1970, after two and a half years of promiscuous sex, I'd grown tired of the 'free love' scene," he said.

Ken was a month shy of his twenty-first birthday when he impulsively asked one of his girlfriends to marry him. He was young, he knew. But his parents had been only twenty when they'd married and their relationship was still strong. Perhaps, he theorized, he was sick of his unstable involvements with women and yearned for the kind of solid relationship his parents represented.

Katherine "Kay" Mitchell was an attractive, shapely, and intelligent blonde from Indiana's farm belt. They had been sleeping together for three months. At the time, Taylor thought Kay was the best choice to settle down with, if for no other reason than that she didn't fit the mold of the steamy but air-headed type that he normally went for.

Even though these were thin reasons for marriage, the couple eloped to North Carolina. Kay, in fact, turned out to be a good wife for Ken. She was a year ahead of him and studying English when they met. She wanted to be a teacher but had found it hard to get a job and took temporary work as a secretary while Ken finished school.

After Ken graduated, the couple moved to Indianapolis where Kay, still disappointed in her search for a teaching position, got another job as a secretary to help support them while Ken went to dental school. Money was tight, but Ken's mother suddenly came to the rescue. Jean had seen an advertisement by the U.S. Navy offering full dental scholarships. In return, Ken would have to do four full years of active service.

If the School of Dentistry in Indianapolis had been competitive, it couldn't come close to the intense battling for position in the Navy program. The scholarships were lucrative, offering not only to pay a student's complete university costs, but also a solid monthly stipend for living expenses. Only a hundred scholarships were being offered nationwide. After an anxious wait, Ken was accepted. The Navy apparently considered him an outstanding officer candidate.

This helped solve the money problems that had been growing over the last year since their marriage. But other problems had been silently developing.

The drug culture that Ken seemed to have avoided for so long was now in full swing. And the intense pressures to keep up with everyone else had slowly sucked him in. Before he realized it, he was deeply involved. "The drug culture I had avoided until 1972 suddenly embraced me," he said. It had become too enticing. It started with a few joints here and a few joints there. His friends were mostly all drugheads. Common dialogue on the campus was always salted with, "Hey, let's do some acid." "Wanna' do some downs?" "You look burned out, want some speed, some uppers? Good shit."

His two or three close friends in dental school were deeply into the drug scene, even dealing some. Ken claimed that he and his "doper" classmates never sold drugs to make money or become dealers; they simply wanted to support their habits. It didn't occur to any of them that whether or not they were making a profit missed the point. They were still selling drugs.

All in good fun, all to keep the social life moving, to help everyone get—and stay—high. The rationalizations were monumental. And, as Ken later admitted, childish and dangerous. (One of his closest college friends, T. J., later died of a heart attack induced by drug abuse.)

Ken later wrote that "Bourbon, beer, and drugs became the essential part of the party dude's repertoire."

During this period his marriage to Kay began unraveling. Kay was frustrated and unhappy not teaching, and Ken was

24

absorbed in his studies and drug-scene pals. Their lives grew cold and they move apart. Communication dried up.

Add the excesses of women (he began dating again), bourbon, pot, acid, speed, uppers, and downers . . . and, as he would say, "Poof, the marriage was dead. Bourbon and pot were my diversions from a failing marriage. Kay was not to blame. She and I had married on impulse."

But in a moment of reflection, he later admitted that he had changed during the marriage. "Reverted. I became weak and hedonistic."

In Ken's second year, Kay finally got a teaching post. But it was in Ohio, and they could be together only on weekends, when she traveled back to Indianapolis.

This was all right with Ken. He was free again and fell even deeper into the drug scene. He became a "party hound." Acid, pounds of pot, and hash from a contact at the Indianapolis airport—Ken and his friends were supplied with everything they needed. This was in addition to the enormous amounts of uncut amphetamines ("speed") that a chemist friend from the nearby Eli Lilly pharmaceutical plant in downtown Indianapolis brought into the "party kitty." A second contact who also worked at the Lilly plant would walk out of the gate at least once a week with his lunchbox stuffed with 50- or 100-mg Seconals (Reds), or 250-mg capsules of Tuinal ("bluetips," in doper terminology). According to Ken, pot, acid, and even cocaine became his generation's "martini."

And there was an extra benefit to having such fantastic drug contacts. "You had the drugs, you got the girls." The girls at the medical center were, according to Ken, especially heavy into downers and uppers. "The dude who has the party drugs gets the women." Women's lib and "the freedom to explore their own sexuality," as the saying went, added to the drug-culture doper attitude and created an explosion of self-indulgence. It was so wild that even Ken was surprised. He said, "women were prompted to spread their legs with nearly alarming ease and frequency." But he didn't mind at all. As he said later. "Lust for sex had become an integral part of my life." And supplying dope was like inserting a key in a lock. "Coke whores were named for a very good reason."

Ken and his doper friends were also derisive, even scornful, toward the other students, "the clones who had short hair, white shoes, and white belts." He and his friends wore shoulder-length hair, Fu-Manchu moustaches, and glazed eyes. "The nerds," as Ken described them, "were also partygoers, boozers, sloppy drunks, in fact, but not dopers." That distinction made Ken and his doper contacts stand alone. They felt they were an elite, a cadre of students that were exceptional — they were more intelligent, more athletic, more talented, willing to take risks, to experiment with life. Special.

Chapter Three

During Ken's junior year at dental school, in November 1973, Kay learned that she was pregnant. His reaction was odd, to say the least. At first he seemed nonplussed, and after a moment merely said, "Congratulations." He wished her well and told her that she could stay with him until she had *her* baby. But then one of them had to split.

His coldness shocked her. During the following months, Kay remembered, he seemed to alternate between being pleased by the prospect of becoming a father and being distant. But despite his hot-and-cold response to her pregnancy, for Kay, in the end it all came down to rejection.

"I believed, and rightfully so," he stubbornly argued later, "that the child Kay was carrying was not mine." (There was no proof at all, however, that this was so.)

Kay couldn't believe her ears when he told her this. And, as expected, their relationship went from bad to worse. Even Ken's parents, who liked Kay and were overjoyed at the prospect of having a grandchild, were disturbed by his attitude.

In early spring, 1974, Ken took a night job at the Ramada Inn. He worked the 10 P.M.-to-6 A.M. shift. The work involved tabulating the hotel's daily business, making reservations over the phone, registering late arrivals, and other such details. But one part of his job was to drive the hotel's limousine to Indianapolis Airport to pick up the various airlines' flight crews who would be spending their "overnight" at the Ramada. He immediately discovered that this was a rich, new source of women. He had again been growing increasingly bored with the "easy lays," with the nurses and other med school students.

He now had a new challenge: stewardesses. "The spice that made my sauce," he called them. They were not the simple college girls he had known, but sophisticated, cosmopolitan women. During his first two months at the Ramada Inn he met a dozen or so stewardesses and enjoyed this "new breed of woman." As he gleefully described it, "I made the most of another diversion."

He would meet the flight crews when they arrived at the airport and chat with the women on the drive back to the Ramada Inn, and then, more often than not, spend the night in their rooms. It was casual, faceless sex all over again, only this time with a patina of worldly sophistication. In the end he came to the conclusion, almost ruefully, that these women "were different on the surface, but to my surprise their wants, needs, and desires were essentially the same as all the other women I'd known." Whatever he was searching for in women had not yet become clear to him.

But the diversion ended abruptly when he met Marilyn Bergman, a 5'7", 115-pound, lean, stunningly attractive redhead of Norwegian and Italian heritage. As Ken described her, she was a sleek, worldly woman with enticing emerald-green eyes and a dancer's long legs. He summed up his reaction in one word: "Gorgeous."

Marilyn was to become Ken Taylor's second wife.

That first meeting was electric and intensely visceral. "I fell hard for her," he said, "hit the bait, and believe me, I was *gone.*" She was twenty-nine, four years older than Ken, and had traveled to Hawaii, London, and Paris, skied in Aspen, and jetted all over the world. When she asked him to meet her for a drink in the hotel lounge after she changed, he jumped at the chance.

While Kay had been an adequate, "normal" sex partner, Ken's experience with Marilyn was explosive. They fed on

28

each other's sexual energies, only rarely sapping their seemingly endless appetites.

Marilyn returned to New York, where she had an apartment, but Ken telephoned her the next week and begged to see her. She agreed to trade flights with another stewardess and return the next week. After that she began a series of regular flights to and layovers in Indianapolis.

The affair burned on and off for several weeks until on one of her trips Marilyn discovered that Ken was married. She told him straight out that she didn't like being involved with a married man. But Ken, talking fast, said his marriage was in name only. As far as he was concerned, it was over and he was getting a divorce.

Marilyn had heard that kind of line before and it just wasn't acceptable. She wanted a serious relationship; in fact, she wanted children and planned to get married before she was thirty. She didn't have time for any more games with philandering married men.

Ken, madly infatuated with her by now, pleaded for her to give him a chance. He wanted children too. He would leave Kay; he'd never really loved her anyway. They had married only on a childish impulse.

In June 1974, when Kay was in her ninth month, Ken finally moved out and into the mobile home of one of his doper buddies.

Kay came home to an empty house. There was no note, no explanation, nothing. He had simply disappeared from her life. She would never see Ken Taylor again.

Soon after Ken's disappearing act, late in June, Zach and Jean Taylor called Kay to see how the pregnancy was coming along. When Kay told them that Ken had left her, they couldn't believe it. They located him at his friend's place, telephoned him, and told him that this wasn't right. To make relationships work you had to try harder, work things out. "Divorce" just wasn't the answer. He wasn't being responsible, leaving a wife in her ninth month like that. This hit a nerve. All his life "responsibility" had been drummed into him. It was a criticism that hurt, and for the first time in his life, Ken became openly rebellious with his parents. He told them, "Mind your own business," and hung up.

Early in July, Zach was in Indianapolis for an RCA engineering conference and called Kay to see how she was doing. He was surprised to hear that she was just going into labor. Zach immediately called Ken and told him that he should at least take his wife to the hospital and help her through the birth.

Ken refused, and Zach, furious with his son, went to the hospital with Kay. And so Zach, along with Kay's mother, was with his daughter-in-law when she gave birth to a daughter early in the morning of July 3, 1974.

Ken filed for divorce soon after the baby was born. He never went to see the child, steadfastly maintaining that "it's not my baby." (Yet years later, when Kay remarried and her new husband wanted to adopt the child, Ken, who was still legally the father, refused to allow it.)

In July, when the university summer vacation started, Ken traveled to Manhattan and moved into Marilyn's apartment. For him, the month-long stay with her was a summer of bliss. The city became a magical place for lovers. Their sex was just as intense as before, and when they weren't in bed, they roamed the city holding hands — visiting Central Park, Coney Island, the Bronx Zoo, and Radio City Music Hall. They toured the art museums, ate at sidewalk cafés, and fell ever more deeply under each other's spell.

When August rolled around Ken had to return to Indianapolis to finish school. Marilyn, who had enough seniority with her airline to commute to her home base of Boston, returned with him.

During this period Ken was honestly trying to escape the influence of his doper friends and they rented a garden apartment in Carmel, a small town just north of Indianapolis. It was far enough away from the temptations of dope and women near the medical center, but close enough for him to get to his classes. He still smoked a lot of pot, and Marilyn, who was not too pleased with either his friends or his drug habits, rarely joined him. She preferred alcohol, and while she would drink freely, she was far from an abuser.

Marilyn also didn't enjoy the "quiet" life-style of Midwest living. She was used to big cities, travel, new sights and experiences. While she felt a bit trapped, she realized that Ken had to finish his schooling, so she waited. And Ken was sure he could get billeted by the Navy to the East Coast after graduation.

That fall, in October, the divorce from Kay became final. The only requirement was for Ken to pay a hundred dollars a month in child support.

On December 14, 1974, Ken and Marilyn were married by a justice of the peace in Carmel. Although Zach and Jean were only a half hour away, they did not attend the ceremony. They were still angry with the way Ken had abandoned Kay and their grandchild. And Jean in particular wasn't too happy at the way Marilyn had moved in before the divorce was final. It appeared to be an unseemly rush, and it gave, in her eyes, the impression of a manipulating, man-hungry woman.

The couple honeymooned in Cincinnati, Ohio, for three days and then Ken returned to school and Marilyn to her work.

After their marriage Ken did try hard to get off dope. And he remained sexually faithful, carefully avoiding the many available women around the medical center. But as he reduced his intake of dope, he turned to alcohol. He had always been just a beer man, but now he switched to the hard stuff and found a new favorite — Jack Daniels sour mash.

One peculiar accident during that July offers hints about Ken that made later events easier to understand. One afternoon Ken dropped Marilyn off at the airport for one of her trips and then went to a local softball game. After the game he had a few drinks and, half sloshed by this time, promptly drove off the road on his way home, smashing into a utility pole. Marilyn's beautiful blue Buick Skylark convertible was badly damaged, the driver's side crushed in. He backed the car out onto the road and made his way carefully back to the apartment. After thinking about the consequences of what had happened, and how furious Marilyn would be, he got

31

back into the Buick, drove to a country lane, and abandoned her car. Later that day the police found the car, and when they traced the ownership back to the Taylors and showed up at the apartment, Ken's story was that it must have been stolen. He explained that he had returned from a ballgame and had spent the rest of the afternoon at the apartment complex swimming pool. He filed a stolen vehicle report.

It was a story that might have flown, except that three people from nearby apartments questioned later by the investigating officer, Robert Smith, said that they had noticed the car, all smashed up, parked outside for most of the afternoon.

It didn't take the police long to figure out that Ken had filed a false police report. He was arrested and hired a lawyer, who explained to the authorities that there had not been any theft. The attorney plea-bargained, and while Ken was found guilty, he was only fined fifty dollars plus court costs for falsely reporting a crime. He later explained to Marilyn that he didn't want to get her angry at him. He was trying to put his life in order and didn't want things to go wrong between them. He begged her to forgive him.

A final, peculiar act of rebellion took place that summer in 1975 when Ken graduated from dental school. After all the hard work, money, emotional stress, marriages, and divorce of the previous five years, Ken decided he wouldn't go to the graduation ceremony. This was a terrible blow to Zach and Jean Taylor, who took great pride in their son becoming a dentist. But Marilyn seemed to accept it—after all, she was a rebel herself. She was an intense advocate of women's lib, and while Ken agreed with her ardent championing of equal pay and opportunity, they had argued hotly over her demand that they reverse the normal procedure and that he change his last name to Bergman when they got married.

When she had first suggested it, the idea was so absurd to Ken that he had facetiously answered, "Oh, sure, that sounds super." He was stunned when he later discovered that she had gone ahead and contacted a lawyer. She had actually begun the procedure to have his name changed.

Ken swore that there was no way it would happen. "I was not going to graduate from dental school as Dr. Kenneth Bergman after being Taylor all my life.

"I honestly thought she had lost her mind," he said later, "if she believed that I would change my last name."

Immediately after Ken graduated (with a specialty in endodontics and oral surgery), he received his orders from the Navy to report to the submarine base in Groton, Connecticut. They took an apartment in a new complex in Cromwell, south of Hartford, that was filled with other young couples. It was close to both the sub base where Ken worked and a small airport at Windsor Locks, where Marilyn could get a plane to Boston.

Except for an occasional drink or smoke, Ken had kept to the straight and narrow. As he said, "I even went weeks without so much as smoking a joint." He had tried, and succeeded, to remain faithful. He had taken his marriage vows seriously.

But by now the sex between them had cooled. And Ken also began to feel that Marilyn had changed immediately after they married. For example, soon after the marriage Ken claimed that she, like Kay, began to protest his participation in sports. According to Ken, Marilyn considered such behavior "bourgeois," and called him "brutish" for even being interested in sports. He now considered her "an ambitious, hard, and neurotic woman."

Within a week after starting duty at Groton, while Marilyn was on a flight, an opportunity arose that Ken couldn't turn down. His dental assistant, "a tall twenty-one-year-old with a pretty face, muscular body, and coarse manners," came on to him. She reminded him of a female mud wrestler type, coarse but attractive, definitely appealing. She invited him to her place that evening after work. Her girlfriend, an equally coarse type, according to Ken, worked down the hall in another office and wanted to come along, if that was all right with him. The girlfriend was short, with wide hips, bleached blond hair, and a pretty face. Ken grinned and said it was nice of them to help him celebrate his arrival at his new job.

After work he followed them to their apartment, where they had drinks and pizza. The pizza was followed by strip poker, and Ken ended up having both women. As he described it, he drove home "wearily" well after midnight.

33

It was the first time he had been unfaithful to Marilyn during their marriage, but it wouldn't be the last. He soon fell into the old pattern, taking the sex where he could find it. There were no end of willing partners. It was just like college again, with available female officers, lonely military wives, dental assistants, secretaries, married or not, constantly around.

At first Ken had accepted the marital discord with Marilyn. Disagreements, he rationalized, could be expected between two powerful, independent personalities. But as time went on, Marilyn's disapproval of his participating in the base sports became especially grating; and her strident manner in criticizing him began to get to him. The fights grew more frequent and she became, in his mind, a harridan who had taken advantage of him and rushed him into marriage. A sophisticated career woman who wanted to get married and have children before her biological clock ran out. He was a good catch, an easygoing Midwesterner with excellent earning potential as a dentist. Or so went his increasingly bitter analysis.

The simmering conflicts came to a head in December 1976. The dental clinic held a traditional Christmas party at the Chief Petty Officers' Club where spouses, civilian volunteers, and enlisted and clinical personnel all came dressed in suits and evening dresses. It was one of the biggest celebrations of the year, and gifts were exchanged through "blind" drawings. When "Santa" was passing out the gifts from a huge box on stage, he called out one for "Marilyn Taylor."

Ken looked over at his wife, who didn't move from her chair. Santa called the name again and still Marilyn didn't move. Puzzled, Ken stared at her. She finally responded, coldly, "My name is Marilyn Bergman and these people better learn it."

"Relax," Ken said, "just take the gift."

"No," she said through clenched teeth.

"For Christ's sake, go up and get your gift," he muttered, growing angry.

"No," she repeated.

"You bitch," he said under his breath. He rose and walked down the aisle and accepted Marilyn's gift, burning with hu-

miliation as he said, "Thank you very much for this gift to my wife, Marilyn Bergman."

He returned to his seat outwardly calm but boiling with rage.

The long drive home was silent, both of them wrapped in a sullen miasma of misunderstanding and hurt feelings. "At that point in time," Ken recalled, "I realized that for two years I'd been trying to see things her way, but that was it. The music died again."

A frigid, impersonal wall built up between them. Sex was almost nonexistent, and Ken secretly harbored the idea that she was "cutting me off" to get even. With an almost paranoid twist, he believed that Marilyn had underestimated his quiet, laid-back style. She had misinterpreted his easygoing manner as weakness and was now trying to manipulate him.

After the Christmas party episode he began leading a blatantly adulterous life. Instead of divorcing Marilyn, he admitted that he wanted to "punish her haranguing" and also "comfort himself" by finding willing bed partners.

"I played the field. With Marilyn away from home three full days and nights every week on her trips, I let the good times roll."

With the women came the bourbon, pot, and new drugs — especially "black beauties," an amphetamine in capsules that users snapped open and snorted like cocaine.

What Ken described as his new life-style was really only an excessive version of the old college days. The difference was that he now accepted it and reveled in it. Ken had always been an addict of rock music. He could listen for hours, especially when stoned. One of his favorite lyrics was from Steely Dan's "Deacon Blues":

He saw himself as "a gentleman rogue," entertaining his dates with lavish nights out, with expensive meals at nightclubs and trendy restaurants, followed by secluded encounters in hotel rooms or even at his condo-apartment while Marilyn was working. It became his Steely Dan ritual.

In June of 1978 he finally left Marilyn, unable, he said, to take any more of her "verbal tirades, her shrewish personality and increasing coldness to me." He packed his bags and moved out, renting a house in Waterford, on the mouth of Niantic Bay, a few miles from Groton, and continued his Steely Dan life-style.

A few months later, in late August, Marilyn called him in tears. Her father had been diagnosed as having throat cancer. It had metastasized and there wasn't much hope for him. Marilyn and her father had always been very close, and Ken, who liked the old man, consoled her as best he could. Slowly they began communicating again and she moved into the Waterford house with him.

Her father's illness helped their relationship for a time, and they even traveled together to visit the old man in Memorial Sloan-Kettering Cancer Center in New York City.

For a few months it seemed like old times and they both felt that maybe they had another chance. It might work out after all.

Then, in December 1978, Marilyn discovered that she was pregnant.

As with Kay, Ken at first seemed happy with the news of the child. But his heavy use of drugs, and especially black beauties, took their toll and his moods would change quickly. He now believed that he needed the drugs to "fuel the fire" to keep him going. With his mood swings and Marilyn's aggressive defensiveness, their marital discord turned malicious.

One argument in April almost turned dangerous when Marilyn discovered that several hundred dollars she was saving for baby clothes were missing from a hiding place in the kitchen. When she asked Ken about it, a shouting match ensued. It finally ended when Ken smashed his fist into the refrigerator. As Ken described it, "I became so enraged I wanted to hit Marilyn. Instead I punched the refrigerator, fracturing my hand."

When Ken stormed out, he went to the sub base hospital to have his aching hand looked at. It was put into a cast and Ken, who was still angry at Marilyn and wanted to hurt her, made a date with the pretty nurse who attended him. They went out the next night.

Bad spiraled into worse as Ken continued his drug habits and whoring. For several months he had had two regular girlfriends, one a married twenty-year-old blonde and the other a twenty-two-year-old from Barbados. He now added another regular to his stable, a twenty-three-year-old married, light-skinned black woman from Texas who worked in the building as a dental assistant.

He basically ignored Marilyn during this period and occupied most of his evenings with his girlfriends. "When I was at the clinic, fishing, playing ball, or with one of my girlfriends I was entirely happy—but not when I was home."

That April one of their arguments was particularly bitter. Tearing at each other verbally, searching for the most hurtful things to say, Marilyn swore that the reason she didn't want him sexually anymore was that she had a lesbian lover. Ken laughed in her face and sarcastically said that it was understandable, because he enjoyed sex with women all the time, so why shouldn't she? Marilyn struck back and screamed that if their child was a boy she hoped he wouldn't be a jock. In fact, she prayed that he would be gay.

This was too much for Ken. "I went berserk," he said, and for the first time in his life experienced a violent black fury that overwhelmed him. He claims to have blacked out, to have gone into a fugue state, and not to remember what happened later that night.

But Marilyn remembered—all too well.*

For a while now Ken had worked in his basement refinishing old jewelry, and sometimes he would even cast new pieces. With his dental engine he would rouge the pieces, using chloroform to create the final patina. Handled incorrectly,

---

*From here on this part of the Taylor saga becomes complicated. After shifting through all the claims and counterclaims, there remain four different versions of what happened that night in April—one from Marilyn's deposition and three from Ken at different times.

and inhaled for even a few minutes, chloroform could be fatal. Ken kept an abundant supply of the chemical available in his basement at all times.

On April 16, around midnight, Marilyn recalled suddenly opening her eyes. She had been sleeping fitfully, worried about her father, who had just gone back into Sloan-Kettering for more chemotherapy. She sensed someone in the darkened room. After a moment, when her eyes had adjusted, she saw Ken standing in the doorway. She watched him as he walked over to the bed and sat down. At first she thought he had come to apologize for the fight, or to comfort her about her father.

Then he put his arm across her chest, bearing down on her.

"You're hurting me, Ken. Please."

Ken didn't answer—and the pressure continued as he bent over her. She felt a rough "thing" over her mouth and face. It stank of peculiar, penetrating fumes that made her immediately feel lightheaded and giddy.

Ken was pressing a kitchen towel that contained a sponge soaked in chloroform against her face.

Marilyn began thrashing on the bed, twisting her head back and forth, trying to break free of the awful pressure. She tried to talk, to plead with him not to hurt her, but the pressure of the towel and sponge held against her face was too strong. She honestly thought she was going to die at that moment, killed by her husband like in "some stupid soap opera." Her head was spinning and she was losing her strength to struggle when they suddenly tumbled onto the floor. But he was immediately on top of her, pressing the cast on his arm against her neck and trying to get the sponge over her face again.

"Oh, God, help me!" she cried out, trying to avoid the sponge, twisting away from the sickening odor. Then, abruptly, everything stopped. The room suddenly blazed with light. Her head throbbing with pain, she looked up and saw Ken staring down at her. He had a stunned look on his face, unbelieving. She wasn't sure whether he was sane or not. His eyes were wild and he seemed in shock.

"What have I done?" he mumbled. "I've got to call the police. They have to take me away."

Trembling, Marilyn stared at Ken, not knowing what to do. Her face was burning as if it had been pressed into an open flame. She stumbled into the bathroom and with shaking hands splashed cold water on her mouth and chin. She stared at herself in the mirror. She looked awful. The chloroform and rough pressure from the sponge and towel had made her face raw. Her mouth and cheeks were already badly swollen.

Ken obviously needed help. This wasn't just another argument. She tried to stay calm, to figure out what to do next. She didn't know if calling the police in was the right thing. She was even frightened that he might try to hurt her again. She definitely needed help and decided to call Sam Baez, the Navy chaplain who lived a half mile down the street. When Sam arrived, Ken was morose. He sat in the living room, immobile, his head in his hands. Marilyn explained what had happened and Sam drove them to the sub base hospital, where Ken was admitted quietly, "a Navy dental officer wired out on booze and amphetamines," as Ken described himself.

Ken was admitted into the care of Lieutenant Commander Ronald W. Wheeler, the psychiatrist on duty that night. The senior psychiatrist for the base, Commander W. F. Pettit, was on leave, running in the Boston Marathon.

An antagonism developed immediately between Ken and Wheeler. Ken recalled that they "had words and then some more words." As far as Ken was concerned, "Wheeler was an arrogant, paunchy, pipe-smoking pseudo-intellectual who began his 'treatment' with a verbal onslaught, calling me names and chiding me for my abusive, assaultive behavior against Marilyn."

According to Ken, Wheeler denied Marilyn the right to see him and encouraged her to report the incident to the Waterford police as "attempted murder." When Marilyn came to the base hospital a couple of days later, Wheeler had done his preliminary examination and considered Ken "a homicidal maniac" who would eventually try to "finish the job."

It was then that Wheeler suggested she contact the police and report the assault as "attempted murder."

To put it mildly, Marilyn was shocked. A "homicidal maniac" . . . it was hard to believe. Yes, they had had more than their share of fights, most passionate and angry, some hateful and bordering on abuse. But was her husband a maniac who would eventually kill her?

Understandably confused and frightened, Marilyn called Sam Baez, who listened sympathetically. Sam wasn't sure about what to do either. But, he advised, if there was any danger to her, perhaps she should go to the police. "What it boils down to," he said, "is you can't take the chance. Whether its cause was drugs, psychosis, or whatever, you have to be concerned about you and the baby."

Marilyn, still doubtful, then went to the Waterford police and told them that Ken had tried to kill her. She didn't want to make a formal charge, but she did want to make it a matter of record. Ken was visited at the hospital a week after he had been admitted and charged with "attempted murder."

At this point the chief psychiatrist, Dr. W. F. Pettit, had returned and took over Ken's case. He immediately rejected Wheeler's analysis as excessive and, after another examination, wrote that Ken was "neither psychologically nor physically dependent on drugs," although he did agree that Ken was an alcoholic and should be put in a recovery program. Further, Dr. Pettit went on, there was no evidence of a general or specific psychosis. Ken, he said, "has difficulty in dealing directly with his emotions and tends to allow things to build up to where he experiences chronic tensions and anxiety." Ken's alcoholism and his recent excessive use of amphetamines and other drugs had led to the sudden explosion of anger and the resulting incident.

Wheeler, on the other hand, in defending his original analysis, claimed that Ken confessed to him that he had attempted to murder his wife, and it was only because he came to his senses at the last moment that Mrs. Taylor wasn't killed. It was only a matter of time, he said, before Ken would finish the job. Dr. Wheeler did not explain how a homicidal maniac comes to his senses at the last moment during a murder attempt.

Further, Wheeler claimed, Ken had actually *told* him that he was drugged out. He admitted that he was a heavy user of pot and amphetamines and that he had taken more than a half-dozen black beauties over the weekend and three more Monday night before the attack. His memory was vague and incomplete about exactly what had happened, but he did remember hearing voices telling him to kill her. Ken accepted that he had a bad drug and alcohol problem. The heavy use of black beauties for the last several days had literally pushed him over a very dangerous line and he knew he needed help.

Later, in a more elaborate explanation of what happened, Ken himself wrote that the chloroform incident was in fact triggered by Marilyn's attempt to poison *him* with chloroform. In this version, Ken theorized that Marilyn had "turned sour on the world in general" and that he "was an easy target [on which] . . . to vent her frustration and anger."

The morning after their argument when Marilyn taunted Ken with her supposed lesbian lover, Ken claimed to have smelled something strange in his coffee. He brought the cup up to his nose and sniffed it. It had, he said, "the definite sweet, aromatic, benzene-like pungent odor of chloroform."

Furious at the clumsy attempt to poison him, he screamed at her, "You crazy bitch!" Marilyn ran from the kitchen and out the back door and fled to a neighbor's home. "I did not pursue her," Ken said. Nor did he report the incident to anyone. But he did get back at her. "When I returned home from the sub base that evening I forbid Marilyn access to the house. I told her to sleep in the garage. The next day I relented and brought my four-months pregnant wife home. Needless to say, our relationship had been harpooned."

In Ken's final, most recent comments on what happened that night, he disclaims any detailed memory of the incident at all. "As I do not recall the exact nature of what happened, I choose *not* to complicate the issue with a 'version' that is based on faulty recall."

Dr. Pettit had suggested that Ken go into group therapy and undergo counseling for alcohol abuse. Ken agreed, but he still had to face the "attempted murder" charge. Dr. Pettit encouraged Ken to get a good lawyer, which he promptly did.

Before the hearing, Ken's attorney showed Marilyn a letter from the superintendent of Fairfield Hills Hospital, a state

41

psychiatric center, who had examined Ken personally. The psychiatrist wrote that the likelihood of Ken repeating his assaultive behavior was "virtually nonexistent." "Further psychiatric treatment on an ambulatory [outpatient] basis would restore this young doctor to his intended role as someone beneficial to society."

Marilyn, who was still hesitant about filing a formal complaint or even taking the issue to court, then decided that the incident maybe had not been attempted murder. The charge was dropped and the case was dismissed as marital discord. Under Connecticut law the whole case was sealed.

After Ken's release from the hospital he moved into a room at the bachelor officers' quarters on the base. Dr. Pettit continued to conduct some private therapy counseling sessions after Ken's release and then enrolled him in a local AA chapter. He also pressed Ken into taking group therapy sessions at the base twice a week for six months. And in an effort to have them work out their marital problems, he suggested that Ken and Marilyn begin therapy with a marriage counselor. They chose a therapist, Dr. Josephine Beebe, in nearby Niantic. Dr. Beebe counseled the couple together and separately, then enrolled them in group therapy sessions.

All this effort seemed to pay off, for by mid May Ken and Marilyn had moved back together again. Ken kept up attendance at the AA meetings until late 1980 and succeeded in staying away from drugs and alcohol. The couple enrolled in natural childbirth classes and, as Ken said, "we were back together, nearly as well as ever, though tainted by the many months of malicious fighting."

Marilyn was pleased by the turn of events and, on September 24, 1979, she gave birth to a daughter, Rhonda. Ken found new respect for Marilyn watching her give birth and take care of their child. When her father took a turn for the worse, Ken was supportive and loving. The marriage was moving in a wonderfully positive direction.

When Ken proudly paraded his wife and daughter around the base and dental clinic, he was stunned to realize that of the five dental assistants hovering around Rhonda, he had slept with every one. The realization, he said, "was like a slap in the face. I was disgusted with myself. I determined right then to remain faithful to Marilyn and give my best to making the marriage work."

His resolution would last—for a time.

Chapter Four

In early November Marilyn's father died. It had been a tumultuous year emotionally and physically, with Ken and Marilyn tearing at each other, and then ending in tragedy. Yet 1979 was the year Rhonda was born. Marilyn and Ken hung on to that reality, focusing their energies on their child, trying to control their volatile temperaments and make the marriage work.

In July 1980, Ken's military obligation was fulfilled. Marilyn had been pressing to return to New York. She felt she had done her part, she had waited patiently while he finished school and his Navy obligations. Now she wanted to return to the city.

They had visited New York in late May and Ken had interviewed for a position as the manager and working partner of a dental center in downtown Brooklyn that would be opening in July. The timing was perfect.

Since Ken didn't want to live in the center of the city and Marilyn didn't want to live in the suburbs, they compromised by buying a house in New York's most undeveloped borough, Staten Island. It was close enough to the city and Ken's dental clinic in Brooklyn, and equally close to LaGuardia and Kennedy airports, so Marilyn could continue to work. Yet the sparsely populated borough, which is basically an island composed of a series of villages and suburban middle-class homes, still had large sections of green and rows of single-family houses. Parts of it were not unlike many of the Midwestern areas dotted with small towns that Ken was used to.

Within a few months, business in the dental center was booming and Ken had to hire another dentist, more assistants, and another hygienist.

In September, Ken interviewed a number of applicants for the job openings. One of them, in Ken's words, a "punkish looking but rather attractive young woman despite her efforts to hide her natural beauty," applied for the job. Teresa Benigno had just graduated from a dental hygiene technical school and, at twenty-one, was looking for her first job. Ken decided to hire her, despite her punk dress and "eye makeup that looked more like war paint," because he sensed something "special" about her.

Special she was. Teresa Benigno, a vivacious, fun-loving, pretty young woman with a round face, flowing brown hair, and deep-set, intense greenish-blue eyes, was to become Ken Taylor's third wife.

After Ken and Marilyn had settled into their new home on Staten Island, they slowly returned to old habits. From Ken's point of view Marilyn again became progressively bitchy, argumentative, and cold. From Marilyn's perspective, Ken was macho, self-absorbed, and sliding back into drug and alcohol use. It wasn't as obvious as in Connecticut, but the signs were there. Whenever she brought it up, Ken would explain that it was nothing more than an occasional joint and a Jack Daniels now and then. He needed them in order to relax from the heavy stress of trying to make the dental clinic successful and an impossible home life.

Marilyn, who was still working as a flight attendant, had found a babysitter, a mother of three who could look after Rhonda when she would be gone for several days on her flights. And Ken, even though much of his time was necessarily consumed by the growing business at the dental clinic, also fell into his former pattern of casual affairs. For Ken, as usual, sex with a number of different women was a comforting emollient for the turmoil in his marriage. By March 1981 he was in full swing with several of his dental assistants and even an occasional patient. "The intimate encounters with other women were purely physical," he would explain. "Me, at the weakest link in my character, still easily seduced."

Then the unexpected: in early October Marilyn told Ken she was pregnant. He could hardly believe it. He bitterly recounted those rare occasions of sex between August and September (four in all). As Ken described his feelings, in the icy atmosphere of their marriage, "Marilyn's pregnancy was as welcome as a case of hepatitis."

And Marilyn, realizing that the marriage was on another dangerous downward slide, didn't like the idea of being a single mother with two children to raise if Ken left her or, God forbid, there was another violent episode like the one in Connecticut. In fact, another child in their tortured marriage would not be a good idea any way you looked at it.

However, the issue was soon resolved by a twist of fate. At the beginning of November an amniocentesis test for birth defects indicated that the fetus was genetically mutated. Marilyn had an abortion the next day.

Slowly they drifted apart again and Ken turned back to his usual crutches of drugs (mostly pot and booze) and sex.

But it was Teresa who made the difference now; she came the catalyst for Ken, just as Marilyn had when his marriage to Kay was winding down.

Louise and Albert Benigno were first-generation Italian Americans, and both had family roots in Sicily. They were hard-working people, basically intelligent, loving, and family oriented. Teresa, their first child, was born on March 27, 1959.

Albert Benigno's father had arrived in the immigrant-choked port of New York City in 1910. He worked hard and raised his family in Brooklyn, where Albert was born.

Growing up in a typical Italian immigrant working-class family, Al, who had a sharp mind but little inclination for school, joined the Navy at the first opportunity. During the Korean War he served as a radioman. The experience seemed to have matured him, and with the GI Bill supporting him, he went back to school and trained to be a draftsman. A quick-minded, intelligent man, he eventually rose to become an assistant architect in the New York City Public School system, overseeing the design and rehabilitation of the city's school buildings. Ten years later he became a drafting teacher at a vocational high school in Brooklyn where he had the thankless job of educating inner-city ghetto kids in the skills of mechanical drawing and drafting. It was hard, frustrating work, and sometimes just getting students to continue coming to class was a herculean task. But he persevered, doing his best, until his retirement twenty years later.

Louise Arico was a pretty, creative, and talented young woman working as a secretary for a shipping line. Louise and Al had known each other since childhood. In 1955 they decided to marry, and for several years the couple lived in a small rented apartment in Brooklyn.

Louise was the creative one in the family and turned her talent for painting and art into considerable skill as a dressmaker — skills that her first daughter, Teresa, would develop as well. But she refused to go into the workplace or use those abilities outside of the home. No matter how talented, she remained the traditional Italian mother to the core. Her place was in the home with her children while the man went out and worked.

When Louise became pregnant with Teresa, they decided it was time to find a new place to live. With prices in most of Brooklyn out of reach, they eventually found a three-bedroom ranch-style house on Staten Island. At the time they bought the place on the south shore, the island was still almost a wilderness, dotted with dairy and vegetable farms and uncultivated woodlands.

In 1960 Staten Island was still good for horseback riding and quail and pheasant hunting, an island with plenty of open space. Four years later the Verrazano Bridge connecting Staten Island to Brooklyn was built and a forest of new homes and developments began to sprout as the overflow from the other boroughs discovered the island's relative peace and beauty. People from Manhattan and Brooklyn desperate for space crossed the bridge in droves so that today the island seems little more than a congested extension of Brooklyn.

A second daughter, Celeste, was born to the Benignos two years after Teresa, and in 1964, their son Philip arrived.

Teresa was perhaps the most gifted and intelligent child, while Celeste was the beauty. "Teresa has the brains and Celeste the looks," was a common family comment. But like all generalities, this was only partly true.

Celeste, while not bookish, had an instinctive insight into people and situations, a quick, intuitive feel for life. Teresa, on the other hand, was not only intelligent but good at school. She had the kind of vitality that infused her pretty round face with additional appeal. In fact, Teresa's soft skin, olive complexion, and wide sparkling eyes made her a striking, almost beautiful young woman.

But Teresa's concern about her appearance was a constant problem. She was particularly obsessed with her tendency toward being overweight. For a brief period when she was twenty-two she even sought psychological counseling for this.

What others might call a typically Italian hourglass

48

figure, which she inherited from her mother, Teresa would term wide hips and "thunder thighs." During Teresa's period of growing up, "slim was in," and like every young girl, she wanted to be desirable and attractive. Dieting was a continuing ordeal, especially with the naturally slim beauty of Celeste a challenge constantly before her.

Some of her friends felt that Teresa was perhaps pushed to become accomplished in dressmaking and designing in order to dress herself and thereby skillfully obscure what she considered to be her physical flaws.

More than any single thing, however, it was Teresa's energy and passion that seemed to define her personality. One of Teresa's girlfriends at Moore Catholic School on Staten Island is quoted as remembering her as a caring person even as a child. "When we were freshmen, my grandmother died, and my mother and father had to go make the funeral arrangements, and I told her I had to stay home and fix dinner for my little brothers and I didn't know what I was going to do. I could hardly boil water then, and around six o'clock Teresa showed up with two pizzas— not store-bought pizzas, but ones she'd made herself from scratch, dough and all. Not many fourteen- or fifteen-year-olds would be that thoughtful."

After graduating with honors from Moore, an elite Catholic high school, Teresa decided to enroll in nearby Brooklyn College, where she graduated with an associate degree in dental hygiene. Teresa possessed a strong, realistic practical streak and she considered being a hygienist the best path to immediate, well-paying jobs.

When Ken Taylor hired Teresa as a hygienist in September 1980, he was already sexually involved with several women, and while he found the young Italian girl funny and vivacious, their relationship at first was strictly professional—if only because Ken's plate was already quite full. He was working at least sixty hours a week at the clinic, Monday through Saturday. He used the few hours he could spare to see his girlfriends. And then there was Rhonda. He tried to spend some time with his little girl.

When Teresa started to work for Ken, she was driving an ancient Pontiac Skylark, a car she had bought as a senior in high school. The Skylark could barely wheeze over the long span of the Verrazano and Ken offered to give her a lift to work. She would meet Ken at the bridge and park the car there, picking it up after work.

It had all happened innocently enough. At least once a month Teresa would call in to say that she'd be late. Her car had broken down again and she had to take it in for repairs. She would get the first bus she could to the clinic.

Teresa was a good worker, but the occasional lateness was frustrating to Ken. Look, he had said, it's dangerous to drive over the bridge at rush hour when the car could break down at any moment. She could drive to his house, which was only about ten minutes away from where she lived, and then ride to the clinic with him.

It was a logical thing to do, but Ken had not considered how Marilyn might react. In fact, Marilyn had already concluded that Ken was back to his old whoring habits, so she immediately suspected that this pretty little Italian girl was one of his "women."

For some time now Marilyn had picked up all the little telltale signs that were so familiar to her. In the past she could tell that he was seeing someone by identifying a specific perfume on his clothes, or even if the scent was lingering in the air. And then, as time went on, there were other more definite signs—whiskey glasses with the remains of lipstick marks, the stubs of Virginia Slims menthol lights with lipstick on the filter in the kitchen trashcan, long brown hairs on the pillowcase; the list was endless.

And then there was the time Teresa left a cigarette in an ashtray which fell onto Marilyn's cherished cherrywood coffee table. Ken spent an hour trying to remove the inch-long burn in the wood surface, but it did no good. Marilyn noticed the burn almost as soon as she walked in the door from one of her trips.

But the final insult was Marilyn's discovery of a light blue 34-C bra stuffed under the bedsheets in the master bedroom.

These signs were nothing new. Jill, one of Ken's old girlfriends in Connecticut, had once left a pair of bikini panties in the bathroom. Another time Jill had left an empty packet of birth control pills with her name printed on the box. And then Brenda, a one-night stand he had picked up at a bar, also left a bra and panties. Ken labeled these "indiscretions that were the result of my amphetamine-bourbon blitzes" while they lived in Connecticut.

Yet the same thing was happening on Staten Island.

Whenever Marilyn presented Ken with these "treasures," he would stare at her and, with an air of indifference, give her one of several stock answers: "No, I haven't seen that before," or, more brazenly, "Well, what did you expect?"

Eventually a gelid detente crept into the house, and Marilyn even stopped bringing the discoveries to him.

Teresa had already been working at the clinic for several months by this time, but the two women met for the first time that morning when Teresa parked her car in the Taylor drive. According to Ken, from the moment Marilyn looked up from her morning coffee at the pretty young girl smiling in the doorway, there was so much tension in the air that it took your breath away. Marilyn turned an icy glare on Ken and walked upstairs to the master bedroom.

Ken followed her. Marilyn was on the bed, sipping her coffee. She was fuming.

"So that's the latest tramp you hired," she said.

"Don't be ridiculous. And there's no reason to call her a tramp. I hired her because I need the extra help."

51

He was more amused than angry. For some reason her jealousy this morning didn't bother him. Normally her irritation and sharp words would trigger his own anger and they would be off, screeching like two cats into another fur-flying argument. But today he simply picked up his briefcase and leaned forward to kiss her good-bye. He had expected her to turn her head away, giving him another little piece of evidence of her coldness. But to his surprise, she kissed him back with a passionate intensity.

Jesus, he couldn't figure her out. Fire and ice. Passionate kisses followed by glacial looks and bitter words.

He didn't understand why she had suddenly become passionate again. They had not touched each other in weeks, perhaps months. Fear of finally losing him? A rush of competition? Anger translated into passion for some peculiarly feminine reason?

Later he would write sarcastically about the incident, "Perhaps I should bring all the girls from the office home. I bet she'd have her legs open again for me in no time."

When Ken hired Teresa he told her exactly what was needed in the job.

Even more than a new hygienist, Ken explained, he needed Teresa to run the office, to organize the billing and paperwork, to schedule patients. "My partners are very demanding. This dental center is their pet project and they watch every move." In effect, her job was to keep the reception room full of patients and make sure everything ran smoothly. Occasionally she would fill in as a hygienist when the regular woman was out or too busy.

The real problem was that his partners were hanging over his shoulder, searching, waiting for something to go wrong. They were presently unhappy about the front desk. The receptionists were constantly losing track of patients.

This was a new challenge for Teresa. Ken liked the confident way she had held his eyes and said, "Just tell me what you want me to do, show me the system, tell me what your partners like and dislike, and I'll handle everything."

"You're very confident," Ken said admiringly, returning her stare. "I like confident women."

She was tougher and sharper than women he'd met who were ten years her senior. Ken prided himself on knowing women, and especially on knowing when a woman showed interest in him. He smiled to himself and inwardly acknowledged that Marilyn was probably right about him and Teresa eventually making it.

But Ken sensed Teresa was not a tramp. She was the kind of woman who was open and direct (even brazen) when she was attracted to a man, but she was also selective and loyal, once committed. He doubted if she slept around much. In this his instincts were correct.

Even on their first ride together from Staten Island to the Brooklyn clinic Ken was aware of Teresa's sensuous femininity. That first morning she wore a tight pair of white slacks, a short-sleeved, powder-blue top, and "pixie" boots with heels. He became conscious of her perfume permeating the car, of her steady gaze held on him, of the way she tossed her head, of her thick hair flowing seductively in the wind. All, no doubt, he thought, intended to impress him. Well, she had. Ken was enchanted. She was quite a package.

On the long rides to work, and as they waited during the interminable traffic jams on the expressway near the bridge, they began to share confidences. They talked about music, about life, about their hopes for the future.

Teresa told Ken about her boyfriend, Jack Lombardi, a tall red-haired young man she had been going with for two years. Jack was working off and on as a Wall Street broker. He was also Italian, and like many of the other men she had dated from the neighborhood, he was very hot-headed and bullish. Once during an argument he had even hit her. They drank too much and did cocaine too often, she said. At first she had thought she was in love with him, but now, as he was pressing her to marry him, she wasn't so sure.

Ken told her about his life with Marilyn, about her coldness and sharp tongue. She argued with him about everything. He couldn't even say the sun was going to rise without her disagreeing. He explained that she had taken advantage of him. He had been a young kid from the Midwest and she an experienced woman who knew all the tricks. She'd seduced him into marriage and then after they were married, he confided, she'd immediately become frigid. He would leave her in a minute if it wasn't for Rhonda. He adored his little girl.

From the time she started at the clinic, Teresa and Ken were together for almost twelve hours a day, five days a week, except for a two-week period when the whole Benigno family went on vacation to Yellowstone Park.

But they had not slept together or even dated until that fateful evening in March of 1981.

Considering Ken's inclination to bed most of the relatively attractive women around him, and Teresa's romantic nature — and the educated, successful professional image Ken projected — it was probably natural that they would become lovers.

Obviously Ken wasn't shy about sleeping with women he worked with, nor was he overly concerned about the moral strictures of adultery. He had long ago accepted that he needed women. Combine that urge with the belief that Marilyn was "cutting him off for her own neurotic reasons" and *that* he was only doing what was

54

natural and healthy, and his attraction to Teresa and her growing adoration of him created a heated tension between them that both realized would inevitably end in sex.

"I sensed that a romantic relationship with Teresa would be volcanic, meteoric, explosive, and probably addictive as well," Ken mused. "That frightened me because I knew how dangerously close I was to leaving Marilyn. But then, so what? I'd been divorced before, had been blatantly unfaithful to Marilyn—but Rhonda would remain with Marilyn and that was what kept me under the same roof with her."

When Teresa's Pontiac finally broke down completely, Ken offered to pick her up at home. Since Ken would now finally be meeting her parents, Teresa confessed that she had told them he was divorced. She didn't know why she had lied. Perhaps she anticipated their getting together and was trying to avoid any future arguments with her parents. Her mother especially, Teresa knew, would not like the idea of her going out with a divorced man. But a married man would be impossible for her to accept. Teresa's father was possessive and concerned about his daughter's boyfriends; he rarely liked or accepted any of them, but he had long ago fallen away from the Church. Her mother, on the other hand, had remained a devout Catholic and would go through the roof if Teresa started dating a married man.

Ken had smiled at her confession; he understood. It was an innocent enough lie, something to keep the peace.

Of course, none of the Benigno family knew that Ken was married at this time (except of course Teresa). But even Teresa had no idea that he had indeed been divorced back in Indiana and had another child. If Al had known this, he would no doubt have been much more concerned over his daughter's involvement with a man who had such a promiscuous, checkered background. He might have even tried to prevent Teresa from seeing him.

Louise's reaction probably would have been much more extreme; even her angina might have flared into a full-fledged heart attack.

But when the Benignos met Ken they were impressed. He was obviously intelligent and charming. He was respectful to them both. He complimented Louise on her paintings and her dressmaking and was sympathetic to Al's problems with teaching ghetto kids. He had good manners and was, after all, a professional man, a dentist with a good practice. He even offered to give the family free dental work if they ever needed it.

Prior to their first date in March, Ken and Teresa would sometimes have a drink together after work. During these evenings Teresa was introduced to Ken's favorite, Jack Daniels, and soon, as Ken relates it, they were "drinking a pint of Jack Daniels most evenings on the drive home from the office."

One morning as they were driving to work Ken asked Teresa to go out with him that night.

"Sure, I'd enjoy a night out," Teresa said, thinking it was just another invitation to an early evening drink or pizza.

"No, think about it," Ken said. "I know you and Jack have something going and I'd prefer you thought it about during work today. Let me know later in the day."

Teresa was stunned. It was something that she had been fantasizing about. That morning she called Louise and said that she was staying overnight with one of her girlfriends. Later in the afternoon she took two hours off and went shopping at a nearby department store.

At 7:30 that evening, when everyone had gone for the day, Teresa disappeared into the ladies' room. She emerged in a black dress, gathered at the waist and with a stylish flare at the hips. The dress was unbuttoned down to her navel, exposing her ample breasts and the edge of a French cut, half-cup, kelly-green bra. It was a tasteful yet sexy arrangement that did what it was meant

56

to—display her best features to advantage and focus Ken's attention.

And it did. Ken couldn't keep his eyes off her breasts all through dinner.

"You look gorgeous, Teresa," Ken said as they left the office.

During dinner at Beefsteak Charlie's in Manhattan, Teresa was unnaturally quiet, even demure. By now they both knew what was going to happen and the tension was electric between them. After dinner, a few drinks, and coffee, Ken asked her, "Care to join me at my place?"

"And look at your sketches, no doubt," she answered with a grin.

"Something like that," Ken replied.

According to Ken, their sex together was "awesome." He had suspected it would be exceptional, but nothing like the reality turned out to be. (Ken seemed unaware that he had used almost exactly the same ecstatic words to describe his sex life with Marilyn when he was breaking up with Kay.)

They then began "a torrid affair that lifted us to the highest plateau that either one of us had ever known," he wrote. "My Love for Marilyn had been intense, perhaps in hindsight a true love, but I had never known the excitement, the absolute fever pitch of love that I felt for Teresa."

For herself, Teresa truly seemed a young woman in love. She became a new woman. She lost weight, her face glowed, and she radiated that particular joy people in love possess.

As Ken later described it, he and Teresa found many ways to indulge their lust for each other. "If Marilyn was at home, we would use the office after work. When she was off on a three-day trip, and with Rhonda staying at the babysitter's, I would take Teresa home at least one or two of the free nights. When Marilyn was away we would also occasionally rent a motel room for several hours before I would take Teresa back to her parents' home."

Then, in late August, Teresa told Ken that she was pregnant.

It was in the evening and they were driving home from work after having had sex in the office. Ken was shocked.

"I thought you were on the Pill."

"I am, but sometimes I forget to take them."

"Is it mine?" he asked.

Shocked and angry, Teresa turned and slapped him—hard.

It was his second surprise of the evening. He immediately realized that he had been stupid. She wasn't that kind of a woman. He had misspoken badly.

"I guess that answers my question," he said, rubbing his face. "You have one hell of a slap, young lady."

He apologized and leaned over and kissed her.

"I'm sorry," she said. "You should know better than to ask me that question."

Teresa felt she had no choice. Ken was still married and her parents simply wouldn't understand. She had to get an abortion.

In early September, Teresa went to her gynecologist. Ironically, and in one of those peculiar twists of fate that occasionally happen, it was the same doctor who'd performed Marilyn's abortion. Out of a dozen or more gynecologists practicing in Staten Island, Teresa and Marilyn had both chosen the same man. At that moment none of them realized that the doctor would perform two more abortions, one each for Teresa and Marilyn, during the next year.

Friday morning Ken picked up Teresa as usual. He drove her to a nearby shopping mall where a girlfriend, Susie, met them and drove Teresa the rest of the way to the hospital. Teresa was drowning in conflicting emotions. She felt dirty, frightened, embarrassed, and loaded down with guilt.

At ten o'clock that night intense contractions began and Teresa passed the male fetus.

Ken paid the hospital bill and Teresa went home the next day. Monday morning Ken picked her up at home as if nothing had changed. Louise and Al, of course, had no idea at all about what had just happened.

The abortion seemed to focus Ken and Teresa's attention on their untenable situation. Teresa in particular was beginning to feel the pressure of being "the other woman," of having to hide and live a life of deceit. They decided that it was time to make a move. Teresa would finally and irrevocably tell Jack that there was no future for them, and Ken would leave Marilyn.

Marilyn had invited her brother and his wife to Thanksgiving dinner. It was a pleasant evening. After dinner the women cleared the table and went into the kitchen to do the dishes and the men moved to the living room to watch a football game on TV. Then Ken put Rhonda to bed and came downstairs. He put on his jacket and left. For Ken it was meant to be the final break. No more Marilyn in his life. From now on it was only him and Teresa. It happened that quickly—but it was not to be all that final.

A few days later he telephoned Marilyn to set up the ground rules for the separation, especially about when he could visit Rhonda. Marilyn was subdued and agreeable. They both were concerned about the impact on Rhonda and didn't want an acrimonious or ugly separation.

Ken rented an apartment a few miles away, in the Huguenot section of Staten Island. Teresa was ecstatic when she saw the new place: no more "quickies" in the office or unromantic, tacky motels. Almost immediately Teresa set about stocking the cabinets and drawers, decorating and supplying the kitchen and bathroom. He and Teresa could be together now almost every evening in their own place.

Louise Benigno immediately sensed a change. Ken had began to spend more time at the Benigno home, including some holidays and evenings. It now became clear to everyone that the relationship was getting serious.

Louise was torn between her protective instincts as a mother and giving her grown-up daughter (who was now twenty-two) the freedom she needed. And it was also true that her religious beliefs nagged at her. It was extremely distasteful to have her daughter so obviously sleeping with a man who was not her husband. Louise, her voice a mixture of anxiety and anger, would sometimes call Ken's apartment as late as two or three in the morning and ask that Teresa come home to her own bed.

Bitter arguments exploded between mother and daughter and they would suddenly find themselves screaming at each other. In one angry moment, Teresa taunted Louise, "Look, before you get all worked up, you don't think I'm still a virgin, do you?"

That spring Teresa lost her job at the dental center in Brooklyn. She had spoken up once too often. One day Irwin Azar, one of the partners, arrived to do his weekly examination of the accounts. This evening he was particularly nasty in his criticism, and Teresa, who rarely pulled her verbal punches, told him he was wrong. An argument developed and Irwin stormed out. The next morning Irwin called Ken and told him he wanted Teresa fired. She had not only been insubordinate but damned rude. Nothing Ken could say dissuaded him.

Teresa didn't really care, she told Ken. She could get another job easily. And she did. She was hired immediately as a hygienist in the office of a Staten Island dentist, Dr. Ron Avis.

Throughout December and January Ken and Marilyn remained friendly but distant. Lawyers had been hired, divorce papers had been filed, and the process was moving ahead slowly. Ken regularly visited Rhonda on weekends, trying to keep up the relationship. Then another messy complication occurred in February—again, mostly due to Ken's inability to resist the offer of sex.

Ken arrived at his old house on Travis Avenue to see Rhonda. Marilyn greeted him pleasantly and led him into the kitchen for coffee. Rhonda was still sleeping, so they chatted for a while. Since their separation the angry tension between them had dissipated and they could both relax more and enjoy each other. Maybe, he thought, that old cliché was true in their case—"You can't live with 'em and you can't live without 'em." But Ken definitely felt he was getting those signals again from Marilyn. Before anything more developed, however, Rhonda came bouncing down the stairs.

Later that afternoon, while Rhonda was taking her nap, the old vibes began again. Marilyn was too close, her ripe body too alluring, and the old electricity was still generating. She was also clearly interested, so when she reached for his hand, he followed her willingly to the master bedroom. "Our 'on-again-off-again' sexual relationship was 'on-again,'" he said later.

After that afternoon, Sundays held a double purpose for Ken—to visit his child and to have sex with Marilyn, usually when Rhonda was sleeping.

Ken often left those Sundays deeply perplexed . . . not enough to change what was an impossibly difficult situation, but enough to wonder who he was cheating on. Was he cheating on Marilyn, his wife, or Teresa, the woman he was seeing regularly? He finally came to the conclusion that he had, incongruously, cheated on his girlfriend with his wife.

And then the role reversals between Teresa and Marilyn began. After one particularly intense liaison Sunday afternoon, he still had a rich amount of Marilyn's perfume covering him. Teresa accused him of being with Marilyn behind her back. He denied it and Teresa accused him. Back and forth it went. But his denials never convinced her.

What she didn't know was that his "occasional" had turned into sleeping with Marilyn two or three times a week.

In late March Marilyn shocked Ken with the news that she was pregnant again. She had already determined that she was going to have another abortion. There was nothing he could say or do that would change that.

Four abortions . . . that was the number of abortions the women in his life had had. Out of five pregnancies, four were aborted. The facts struck him hard. "That's a lousy average, asshole," he argued with himself.

Despite the abortions, and the fact that Ken claimed to love Teresa and wanted to marry her when he was free, he still couldn't resist other women. When the replacement for Teresa at the office turned out to be willing, Ken ended up taking her out to dinner after her first day at work. Ellen was a tall, hyperactive, talkative, not unattractive woman. And though Ken knew that she wouldn't work out as a permanent replacement in the office, they ended up checking into a sleazy downtown Brooklyn hotel for a few hours before he drove her back to her car at the dental clinic.

As time went on Teresa became more and more convinced that he was seeing other women. She rationalized it all away, however, by recalling that he had indeed left his wife for her . . . and that they were just waiting for the divorce to be final before they got married. She didn't want to lose him, so eventually she swallowed her pride and quietly accepted the fact that he was probably still occasionally having sex with Marilyn. And perhaps even with other women, she thought with a sinking heart. She even suspected, rightly it turned out, that his usual Saturday night "poker games" with the boys were just excuses to be with another woman. But as long as it was nothing serious, nothing that would take him away from her, she tolerated it.

The summer months passed and only one major disappointment occurred: Marilyn's lawyer died and the divorce proceedings were slowed considerably.

Some arguments between Teresa and her parents flared up during the summer and winter of 1982. Seeing their daughter carrying on so openly with Ken bothered them deeply. Ken and Teresa would often "play house" Friday nights and Saturdays, a situation that was driving even Al up the wall. But every time the issue came up, Ken would defuse the situation by assuring them how much he respected Teresa and how, once some personal problems were settled, he wanted to marry her. Then, in March 1983, Ken's lawyer called with the good news. His divorce was final. He was a free man.

Immediately after receiving the news Ken called the florist and ordered two dozen red roses. One dozen he had sent to Marilyn, with the simple note, "Love, Ken." The other dozen he sent to Teresa with the note, "It's over. I'm yours. Love, Ken."

Teresa was ecstatic when she received the roses and the note. It was finally over. No more waiting.

Ken bought Teresa an "official" engagement ring, a 1-carat diamond solitaire. Louise and Al were elated. Their daughter would finally be made an honest woman.

The wedding was scheduled for July 10, 1983. The elaborate wedding and reception would be followed by a honeymoon in exclusive resort in Acapulco, Mexico.

Chapter Five

For a number of years now Albert Benigno had not been deeply involved in the traditional church. But while his childhood Catholicism had waned, he still considered himself religious man—in his own way. He had continued to read and study the Bible and had come to some of his own conclusions about the soul and salvation. In fact, he had talked with some of his friends and even written away for information about becoming a minister. Al had no established church, so people who viewed such things cynically, such as Ken Taylor, believed that he became a minister in a weird little self-proclaimed church only for income tax purposes; but that didn't bother Al. Of course, it was true that Al had no love for the IRS, but then, who did? Al believed in his ministry, and if there were tax benefits, that was just what any corporation would call a "write-off"—if they could get away with it.

When Al suggested to Teresa and Ken that he become involved in the wedding ceremony as their minister, Teresa blanched. The argument that followed was finally resolved when Teresa put her foot down: "I don't want him to be the minister, I just want him to be there as my father."

Soon after the news that his divorce was final, when

Teresa turned twenty-four on March 27, Ken sent a huge floral bouquet to Louise, thanking her for bringing such a wonderful daughter into the world. Louise was touched. "That's such a beautiful thought," she said. It was just the kind of Ken Taylor gesture that had charmed people for years.

Ken had thought they would have a simple civil ceremony, perhaps down at the City Hall or at a justice of the peace. But for Teresa and her family, it was a once-in-a-lifetime opportunity for their eldest daughter—and they were going for a traditional Italian wedding.

April was a hectic month. Teresa, her family, and her girlfriends all dived giddily into the wedding plans. As Ken described it, Teresa was determined to "go the whole nine yards." The church was scheduled, along with a reception hall, a band, meals and catering, bartenders, waitresses, gowns, tuxedos, photographers, flowers, limousines, hotel reservations—on and on it went.

After much confusion and haggling, the theme song for the wedding was chosen—from Boz Scaggs' group, "Love, Look What You've Done to Me." The irony of the song's title did not become apparent until months later.

Because Ken was divorced, the priest at St. Charles, the parish church where Louise worshipped, denied them a Catholic ceremony. They had to settle for the Huguenot Methodist Church near Ken's apartment. The church was a charming, quaint old monastic building with rock walls and stained-glass windows. Inside it had high ceilings, and dark bare wooden beams in the sanctuary. The young minister, who was of the Reform persuasion, even agreed to allow Al to co-officiate the ceremony—for an additional fee.

Brimming with excitement, Teresa talked with Jean nd Zach Taylor on the telephone. She told them how happy she was, what a wonderful son they had, and that she couldn't wait to meet them. For their part, the Taylors were delighted that Ken's divorce from Marilyn was final and that he was settling down again with a sensible girl from a normal, hard-working family.

According to Ken's account, two weeks before the wedding Teresa came to him with shocking news. She was pregnant again, and she was going to have another abortion. Since their marriage was only days away, it didn't make any sense until she explained that she had been recently using drugs heavily and was worried about the baby's health being affected.

Teresa scheduled an in-office saline, suction-type abortion with her gynecologist, the same doctor who had performed her previous abortion, for Friday, July 1. That weekend Teresa and Ken went on a short trip to Connecticut, a sort of mini-vacation from the stress of the wedding plans. Both she and Ken used the trip as a forced drying-out period before the wedding. They wanted to start fresh and went off alcohol and all drugs for three days. When they returned to Staten Island Monday evening, they felt that they were "clean." The wedding was six days away.

Ken had wanted his brother to be the best man, but at the last moment Tom canceled. The reason was never made clear, but some suspected it had to do with his own growing addiction to drugs. After Tom had destroyed his knee in a freak accident, his athletic career had ended and he had drifted from one job to another.

Celeste was to be the matron of honor, and to "keep it in the family," Ken asked Teresa's brother Phil to stand in. He agreed and the "best man" crisis was over.

The night before the wedding Al and Louise gave an elaborate cookout. Jean and Zach had arrived from Marion, and even Jean's mother, Annabelle Bearghman, an aging but lively free spirit, had flown up from Florida.

One of Ken's first duties was to take Jean on a subway

ride. It was something she had insisted on, so they took a short hop from the Hoyt Street stop in Brooklyn near Ken's office to Wall Street. The quick trip into the hot and congested, dirty city was enough to satisfy her curiosity and they thankfully escaped back to Staten Island.

As the sun set, the families split up. Teresa spent the night with her family, and Ken drove his parents and grandmother back to his apartment. He had plans for the evening and was anxious to leave. Everyone was tired from their travels and the socializing at the cookout, so nobody objected when Ken said he had to go out for a while.

He got back in his car and drove to Marilyn's. They had arranged to meet that night—their final night before his marriage.

The next morning he left at dawn after a "lust-filled night together." It was, Ken said, an understandable feast for them both, but especially for Marilyn, for she "needed to have me again before I married Teresa."

There were only a few hours left before the ceremony when Ken slipped back into his apartment and fell into an exhausted sleep on the couch. At this point Ken was troubled by only one thing—he felt that he was in love with two women, Marilyn and Teresa (the occasional other women he had sex with were unimportant), and he had no idea about how to escape from the confusing dilemma. As he fell asleep he fantasized about how great it would be to have two wives.

The wedding couldn't have come off better. Even the weather conspired to make it all work perfectly. It was a beautiful, sunny July afternoon. A hundred and fifty guests attended the ceremony, the bridesmaids all in pink and mauve and the men in light gray tuxedos.

Ken and Teresa spent their first night of married life in a hotel at Kennedy Airport. The next morning they flew to Mexico City. Their destination was Las Brisas, a famous resort in Acapulco. Jacqueline and John Kennedy had stayed at the resort on their honeymoon. It was the fulfillment of Teresa's dream ever since she'd read about the exclusive hideaway in Sidney Sheldon's book *Rage of Angels*.

When the plane landed, Ken and Teresa were almost comatose. They had been drinking heavily the whole trip, and the colorful, small two-ounce bottles of Jack Daniels were scattered around their seats like the husks of seeds in a birdcage.

When they stepped off the Eastern Airlines Jumbo jet, the scorching Mexican sun hit them with the power of an open furnace. They were escorted to a connecting flight to Acapulco and were soon in the air again—all on only a few hours' sleep and with aching hangovers.

The noonday sun was no kinder at the small, steaming Acapulco airport where the newlyweds hopped into a van heading for Las Brisas.

Fellow vacationers, middle-aged Richard Peraino, his wife, Sorayda, and their three children were already waiting in the van. Teresa, in her effervescent and cheery way, struck up a conversation with the woman. In her late thirties, Sorayda was a Mexican national who had immigrated to Brooklyn years before, where she had met and married her husband. They had six children and they always tried to take their yearly vacation in Las Brisas. This time it was the turn of the three youngest Peraino children to travel to their mother's homeland.

Teresa and Sorayda chatted amiably on the drive while the men, after a few pleasantries, silently watched the scenery roll by.

Las Brisas deserved its reputation. It was dazzling. The resort and its many small cottages were situated on the side of a mountain overlooking the Bay of Acapulco.

Below and to the right of the resort lay the hotels, boutiques, restaurants and nightclubs of Acapulco city, and to the left the great expanse of the Pacific Ocean. Guests had exclusive *casitas* surrounded by gardens of tropical flowers—red and pink lilies, giant rhododendrons, and ferns with leaves as wide as a man's chest. The cottages dotted the whole mountainside. They were connected by a serpentine road bordered with a high rock wall that wound its way up the mountainside through lush, jungle-ripe vegetation. With the rental of each *casita* came a Jeep for the guests' use.

Every cottage had its own swimming pool, dining area, and patio. The pool, with its own deck, was enclosed by tuge rock masonry walls and more lush tropical flowers and vegetation.

Because they were in the honeymoon cottage, their *casita* was in one of the more private areas—in the first row, about 150 yards above the road that led into town, which was another hundred yards or so above the bay. The *casita* was backed by a high stone wall separating it from an open field.

They were hideaways in an exquisite prison of comfort and beauty.

For the first day Ken and Teresa did nothing but swim and sunbathe at their private pool, eat their meals in bed, and sit on the patio sucking in the clean, perfumed air as they watched the daily ritual of an old, grizzled Mexican man replace the dying bouquet of lilies on their patio table with fresh ones. It seemed an impossible dream that they would have five full days of this perfection.

As they had all planned, the next Sunday night Al and Louise drove to Kennedy Airport to meet the honeymooner's return flight from Mexico. They waited outside the Customs exit, watching, searching for Ken and Teresa. After more than an hour Louise began to get nervous and Al went to the information counter. There was no Kenneth or Teresa Taylor on the flight.

Well after midnight they gave up waiting and drove back to Staten Island, full of anxious questions. No matter how reassuring and logical Al tried to make it sound ("They were having fun and decided to stay longer"), Louise was deeply worried and found it impossible to sleep.

First thing Monday morning Al called Las Brisas and was stunned to find that Dr. and Mrs. Taylor had checked out Thursday, well ahead of schedule — in fact, three days early. The more Al pressed the assistant manager at the resort, the stranger it all became. The man was polite but reticent; Al could sense that he knew more than he was saying.

Worried by now, Al first called the Mexican Consulate in Manhattan, and then, on their advice, the consular agent in Acapulco. The agent, a man named Lambert Jean Urbanek, did know what had happened to the Taylors.

Teresa, he said, was in a hospital, the Centro Medico in Acapulco, and in serious condition. She had been badly beaten. Her husband, Dr. Taylor, had been arrested. He was suspected of having beaten his wife.

Stunned speechless, Al could barely keep a grip on the phone with his shaking hand.

Al and Louise were both close to hysteria and didn't know what to do. After trying to calm her, Al telephoned Celeste and her husband, Jeff. Celeste said they would be right over, but before they arrived the phone rang.

It was Ken.

He explained briefly that they had been robbed and beaten by thieves who had broken into their cottage. He

70

had just come from the hospital where he had seen Teresa. He hid been arrested (but not charged with anything) and had to bribe his way out of jail—for five hundred bucks.

The Benignos didn't know what to believe. It was all happening too fast. One thing was certain: they were going to go to Teresa—on the first plane they could get.

Al called the travel agent who had booked the honeymoon flight. He got them priority tickets. It was now Monday. Al and Celeste would arrive in Acapulco Tuesday afternoon, July 19, nine days after the wedding.

Immediately after leaving Customs, they took a cab directly to the hospital and were given directions to Teresa's room. Ken was sitting next to her bed.

Teresa looked awful. Her face was bruised and swollen. One eye was covered in a bandage, the other was only a slit of discolored, puffy flesh. A large bandage covered half of her neck, near the jugular, where her throat had been viciously slashed. Some of her front teeth were broken into jagged fragments.

Al and Celeste could barely control themselves. Celeste rushed over to Teresa and clutched her hand, tears in her eyes. After Al had calmed down he walked over to his daughter.

"How do you feel, sweetheart?"

Teresa was clearly dazed. She was still receiving Valium through an IV in her wrist. "I don't know," she managed to croak.

"What happened?" Al asked, trying not to stare at his daughter's wounds or show how the sight of her horrified him.

"I don't know," she repeated, barely able to talk through her swollen lips.

The attending Mexican physician appeared and took

71

Al and Ken aside. He explained that Teresa had had many serious wounds around her face, neck and head. But fortunately, his greatest fear had not materialized. There was no damage to her brain or facial nerves. The lid of her right eye, and the brow above it, had deep cuts that had needed stitches. Pieces of glass had also been removed from her eye. But the surgery had gone well and her sight would probably not be affected. She also had stitches on her face and neck where there might be small scars, but nothing that would disfigure her.

After the doctor left, the two men walked out into the hallway Al, still shaken by what he had seen, asked Ken what the hell had happened.

In Ken's initial description to Al, he left out parts of the story, mostly about the drugs he claimed that Teresa had brought along (unknown to him) concealed in the lining of her makeup bag.

It was, Ken later said, Tuesday evening when he discovered that Teresa had brought along the three grams of cocaine. As he described it, he was furious with her for the danger from Mexican Customs that she had put them both in. But he quickly accepted the fact that the coke was already here and he couldn't do anything about it. Teresa wanted to get high and Ken was feeling pretty good himself. The honeymoon so far had been fantastic—so why not continue the party?

"And party we did," he said. "Well into the night and the next morning. We saw a breathtaking sunrise, then finally fell asleep, drained from the marathon lovemaking and partying. It was life in that fast, fucking lane . . ."

Wednesday was spent shopping and sightseeing, and lounging by their pool. That evening they had a brief drink with the Perainos, avoided a dinner invitation, and then headed back to their *casita*. Thursday, Teresa and Ken spent another idyllic day by themselves. On Thursday evening they dressed for dinner, climbed into the Jeep, and headed into town to eat.

This was to be the night that changed a honeymoon into a nightmare.

The evening started off badly. When Teresa, who had ordered a large fruit salad at the restaurant, bit into a mango, she stopped suddenly, her mouth open, and stared at her plate. She turned a pale shade of green. Part of a worm was still wriggling in the open fruit. She had eaten and swallowed the other half. Angry now himself, Ken stood up and took the salad plate to the waiter. He pointed out the still squirming half of the worm and disgustedly dropped the plate on the floor in front of the man. They walked out.

Back in the *casita* Teresa went into the bathroom, shoved her finger down her throat, and vomited.

After she had calmed down they ordered sandwiches from room service, had several drinks, snorted some coke, and made love again. By ten-thirty Teresa was asleep, exhausted from the emotional turmoil of the evening. Ken said he then walked out onto the patio and smoked a cigarette. He was undecided about whether to take a late swim or go to bed. He was tired, so he decided to go back in and join Teresa.

"I was nearly asleep," Ken would testify, "when I heard sound on the patio, a crackling noise at the base of the sliding screen door that led from the *casita* to the pool. I quietly got out of bed and went to the door and turned the porch light on. It illuminated the whole patio and pool area. There was nothing there — probably one of the dozens of damned lizards that were always running about. I went back to bed and was asleep in seconds. In my sleep I didn't hear the door slide open. Then a heavy blow from a bottle or club of some sort cracked against my skull. I felt hands grabbing my feet, pulling me from the bed. My head was ringing. My chin smacked against the slate floor. I was still very wobbly from the blow to the head, but I tried to get to my knees to defend myself when a karate-like kick out of the dark slammed into my temple, just above my right ear. I fell over unconscious.

"Apparently Teresa awoke as I was assaulted. Either she had struggled or was merely a victim of a vicious attack while she was asleep—as I was. Although we never knew for sure, we believed that the intruders smashed the thick glass lamp next to the bed into Teresa's head and face.

"When I regained consciousness I saw Teresa next to me on the floor, facedown in a pool of blood and surrounded by shards of broken glass. The jagged broken glass had cut her eyebrow open down to the bone, her two central incisors were broken, and she had a deep gash on her neck and another on her thigh. The cut on her leg, as with my own cuts, probably resulted from our groveling about on the floor, which was covered with broken glass. I had cuts on my hands, knees, and feet, all probably from crawling around on the floor in the dark.

"She was motionless. Instinctively I checked her pulse and realized that she was alive. I called the front desk and pleaded for help. 'We've been attacked,' I told them.

"After I hung up the phone I noticed the glass shards in my hands, some stuck to the flesh of my face. I staggered to the shower and rinsed the glass from my face and body. The cold water revived me momentarily and I made my way to the patio, where I looked around for any sign of the intruders.

"As I started to descend the stairs my head began spinning again and I collapsed, falling unconscious on the stairs. The next thing I knew I was being examined by the resort's young Mexican physician, Dr. Esteban

Ortiz Pavon, who was taking my blood pressure."

Dr. Ortiz helped Ken to his feet as three men in hospital whites came rushing up the steps carrying a stretcher. There were already five or six men in the room, all in the uniforms of the resort's security police. As Teresa was lifted onto the stretcher the full extent of her injuries became more apparent in the light. She had been brutalized. Her face was already a bloody pulp. Her eyes were swollen completely closed, her mouth was bloodied, and an ugly gash on her neck was open and bleeding profusely.

Ken's description of the scene continued. "The security men were milling around when eight local cops arrived. noticed the resort's security chief conferring with the head city cop. Something was going on. The vibes seemed all wrong to me. I checked under the mattress where I had hidden our money. The thieves hadn't found the stack of bills and I quickly stuffed them inside my pants, down into my underwear. I looked around the room. Teresa's diamond ring was gone. After she had vomited she had washed her hands, taken the ring off and set it on the nightstand. Her gold bracelet and diamond earrings were also gone from the bedside table."

The leader of the local police, a bulky man named Captain Guiterrez, began to direct his men to search the place. When Ken asked what was going on, he was told that they had orders to search the *casita* for drugs.

Of course, the bag of coke was found immediately.

"Qué pase?" Guiterrez asked, holding the bag of coke front of Ken.

Ken was handcuffed and pushed along the walk in and down the stairs and shoved into an old 1972 Ford station wagon. The eight local cops climbed in with him.

Visions of *Midnight Express* danced through his head as the station wagon bounced through town on its useless shock absorbers.

75

They stopped in front of an ancient building, the facade reminiscent of an old American western movie set. Ken was pushed inside the "police department," past a couple of skinny stray dogs nibbling at garbage on the street next to the entrance. Nearby, down the street, the dark hulks of broken-down cars stacked on blocks squatted like giant black beetles. A group of men stood nearby talking quietly and smoking, watching the arrest of the Americano.

"I was *not* booked, charged, or officially arrested," Ken said. "I was taken to an interrogation room where Guiterrez, with the help of the resort's security chief to translate, asked me about the cocaine. I denied, denied, denied, and said nothing except to insist that I be taken to my wife. Instead, I was led to the holding cell area—which was outdoors."

The "jail" was a large square room attached to the police station. It had no ceiling. The roof was solely a matrix of iron bars like those of the cell block door. There were no beds, mattresses, sheets, pillows, or towels. The twenty or so Mexican men already in there were sprawled about on the concrete floor. There was a shower in a corner, but the shower drain, which was simply an open hole in the cement, also served as the toilet.

On Friday night, soon after his arrival, a police official who introduced himself as Jose Milo appeared and told Ken that the prisoners were not fed by the state but by their families. If he wanted to eat he would have to pay for it.

Sensing a shakedown, Ken said he had only fifty dollars. By now he had hidden most of his cash deep in his underwear, securely under his scrotum. But he had kept out some cash so it would be available for just such emergencies as this. Ken gave Milo the money, wondering if he would ever see the man again.

The next morning Milo came into the cell with a

handful of pastries and a shallow pan full of coffee. Ken hoped this wasn't all his fifty would buy him. But Milo was apparently trying to earn his money, for he also brought a note from Teresa. In a shaky handwriting she wrote that she was scared, had no idea about what had happened to them, and that she was in a lot of pain. She wanted to see him.

For the rest of the weekend he heard nothing more. Milo seemed to have vanished.

The Mexican officer did not reappear until Monday morning. By then Ken was furious. The place stank worse than a bus station toilet and was crawling with huge cockroaches and any number of exotic-looking bugs. The few times he was able to fall asleep with his back propped against the wall, he was constantly awakened by the damn things crawling all over him.

He had been in the crowded cell since Friday night, and all day Saturday and Sunday, when the temperature had risen to over a hundred degrees during the days and down to a humid chill at night.

Barely able to control his fury when Milo finally showed up, he demanded to be let go. "Look, you son-of-a-bitch," he spat out, "either you charge me or cut me loose. I'm an American citizen, and I won't tolerate one more minute of this bullshit."

Milo listened to the American's ranting quietly. He was amused. He had heard it all before.

"Okay, Dr. Ken," Milo finally said. "For five hundred dollars you can be released, returned to your hotel for your luggage, and then taken to your wife."

"Five hundred is all the money we have," Ken lied. He didn't trust this Mexican cop for a minute.

"Where is it?"

"At the hotel," he lied again. All their cash was in a tight wad under his scrotum.

"Okay, let's go," Milo said. He led Ken from the cell,

77

but before they left the building Ken asked to use the restroom. He explained that he had been unable to go in the shower hole. Milo grinned at the American's delicacy.

In the toilet stall he removed four one-hundred-dollar bills and two fifties. He tucked them under his belt.

Back at Las Brisas they were led to the manager's office, where the luggage was being kept. Ken slipped out the money from under his belt and palmed it as he rummaged in his luggage. He pretended to open the lining of the suitcase and pull out the cash. He handed the bills to Milo, who counted them carefully before pocketing them.

Ken was then taken to the front desk to check out and pay the hotel bill. Also at the desk was Sorayda Peraino, the woman they had ridden with in the van from the airport.

She was the last person he wanted to see right then. According to Ken's version of the Acapulco incident, he and Teresa had had an unpleasant evening with the Perainos. They had gone to their *casita* for drinks the night after they arrived. Neither he nor Teresa particularly cared for the woman, who seemed emotionally overwrought and aggressive.

"You look terrible," Sorayda said, alarm etched across her face. "What happened to you?"

In Ken's testimony he claimed to have told the woman that "we were robbed and beaten." As he tried to explain what had happened one of the Mexican policemen started talking rapidly to Sorayda in Spanish.

The woman's face went white and her hand flew to her mouth. She stared at Ken for a moment as she listened and then hurried away.

Ken Taylor had no idea how this moment would come back to haunt him.

Accompanied by the resort agent, who needed Teresa's

signature on the hotel's bill, Ken was then taken to the hospital, where he found Teresa still in a daze from her trauma and the heavy dose of intravenous Valium being given her.

Al believed Ken's story. He wanted to believe him. The idea that Ken himself might have beaten his daughter on their honeymoon was too preposterous to accept.

Al and Ken began to plan getting out of Mexico. Ken's description of the blatant extortion by the Mexican police was hard to believe, but to be safe Al was willing to leave as soon as Teresa could be moved.

Ken hadn't eaten a decent meal in almost four days and he was beginning to get weak. Celeste went with him to find a restaurant and Al stayed with Teresa. They hadn't been gone for more than twenty minutes when Officer Jose Milo showed up with three other men.

Milo motioned for Al to step outside. Al identified himself and Milo explained that they were Mexican police and that they wanted to talk with Ken. Al remembered Ken's story of the extortion and was immediately suspicious of the overconfident cop and his three tough-looking companions, He told Milo that Ken was not there. Milo smiled politely and said that they would return in the morning to speak with him.

Al was deeply worried by the policeman's visit. Apparently Ken's problems with the Mexican police weren't over. Maybe the rest of them might become involved in some way. A moment later his anxiety was confirmed. The resort's medical adviser, Dr. Ortiz, arrived to see how Teresa was doing. He had checked with the doctor on her case and was happy to see that she was recovering quickly.

"She was a lucky young woman," Dr. Ortiz said. "When I arrived and saw all the blood, I thought she was already dead."

79

With a nagging suspicion still in the back of his mind, Al asked Dr. Ortiz what Ken's condition had been. A lump on his head and cuts and scratches on his hands and knees, Ortiz said. Nothing serious that required any further medical attention.

Before he left, the doctor took Al aside. A nurse had informed him that she had overheard some police in the hallway talking. Apparently they were planning to "get some more money from the Americans."

"It would be best if you took your daughter out of the country as soon as possible, *señor*," he said.

Al's doubts were suddenly replaced by fear. It looked like Ken's story about the extortion was true.

The next morning they waited anxiously to see if the hospital would release Teresa. Their flight was booked for 2:30 that afternoon . . . and they wanted to get away before Milo returned.

While they waited for Teresa's physician to tell them if they could go, a well-dressed Mexican and an attractive redhead came to the room. They were polite and began questioning Ken about the break-in at Las Brisas. The man seemed to be a lawyer for the resort, but the woman did all the talking.

Ken again told them his version of what had happened. When he finished, the lawyer gave Ken a document releasing the resort from any responsibility for the assault and loss of property. Ken and Teresa both signed it and the man and woman left.

Finally, just before noon, Teresa's physician came by and told them he thought Teresa was strong enough to leave. They quickly packed her bag and organized their own luggage. Just as they were planning to leave, Dr. Ortiz showed up and offered to drive them to the airport. They gratefully accepted.

They waited in the Eastern Airlines terminal for almost two hours, anxiously wondering if Milo was still on their trail, or whether he might suddenly appear with a warrant or some other excuse to keep them from leaving. When the boarding announcement finally came, Teresa, in a wheelchair, was escorted onto the plane by an Eastern agent, who bypassed all the normal boarding rituals. The Taylors, and Al and Celeste, who had purchased coach tickets, were all placed in first class, compliments of Eastern.

On the flight back they rested from their honeymoon ordeal, too tired even to talk about it, arriving in New York just after midnight.

They were met with an emotional homecoming. Louise, Phil, Jeff, and Teresa's lifelong friend Karen Oliveira were all waiting at the terminal. When Louise saw Teresa she burst into tears.

Teresa was taken directly to Staten Island Hospital, where Louise and Phil stayed with her for the rest of the night. Al and Celeste, who were both exhausted, went home to get some much needed sleep.

Ken, who was examined in the emergency room, was immediately released and went home to his old apartment to sleep. The hospital records indicated that Ken was examined at 12:40 A.M. on July 21. "Patient states that he was hit in the head and passed out. No bumps on head noted. Initially patient seemed in a dazed state. Was alert and oriented before leaving."

Chapter Six

Teresa remained hospitalized for a week and was visited constantly by a stream of friends and well-wishers. Ken spent most of every day at the hospital as she slowly regained her strength. The hospital record noted that along with her physical wounds, Teresa was suffering from "retrograde amnesia" and would probably never remember exactly what had happened that night. The report added that she was "very frightened and needed much support and assurance."

When Teresa was finally released, she and Ken moved temporarily into the Benigno home, staying for a week in the same room that Teresa and Celeste had shared at one time.

Even though Teresa was slowly recovering physically, turmoil continued to disrupt their lives.

According to Ken, he had been having financial and professional differences with his two partners for some time, and decided to leave the Brooklyn dental center.

His two partners, Irwin Azar and Edward Sutton, told a different story. They said that during Ken's absence in Mexico they had discovered terrible discrepancies in the accounts. They claimed that he had stolen somewhere between five and ten thousand dollars in cash and checks. Ken, in turn, derided the accusations as merely the result of the growing friction within the partnership. He was not a thief. He was a partner in the business, and how the money was collected, calculated, and used was as much his business as theirs. Any money he took was due him, either as expenses, reimbursement or salary.

For whatever reason, Azar and Sutton did not try to recover the money or press charges (they claimed they just wanted to be rid of him). The two men decided to write off the ten thousand dollars if Ken would just pack up and leave.

Even though money was tight at the moment, Ken gladly submitted a letter of resignation and started looking for work.

Almost immediately Ken began talking with a dentist, Dr Stanley Becker, who had four offices in Staten Island.

Becker had been having problems of his own. The previous summer an eight-year-old boy had died in the office while under the care of Becker's junior partner. The child's parents had filled out the medical history questionnaire, ignorant that the boy was allergic to the anesthetic that would be used. The child was dead before anything could be done to help him. The dental business was, of course, profoundly affected by the boy's death. In fact, Dr. Becker was forced to close the office where the death occurred and another office nearby when business slackened off.

Dr. Becker was impressed with Ken and hired him

to try to revive and operate the abandoned dental practices. One of the offices was located in a mixed neighborhood of hispanics and blacks in the heart of Staten Island's ghetto. The other was about three miles away, near the Goethals Bridge.

Ken's plan was to work for several months in the defunct practices and slowly build them up; then he would negotiate a partnership for himself. But for the moment he would have to work as a salaried employee.

Also, Ken and Teresa debated suing Las Brisas and consulted with a lawyer over their prospects. For a brief while they fantasized about a big settlement — until the lawyer they had asked to look into it advised them that they would have to go back to Mexico to file the lawsuit. They both knew that was impossible. To return to the mercies of the Mexican judicial system didn't appeal to them at all, and the idea was soon dropped.

After their short stay at the Benignos', Ken and Teresa moved into Ken's apartment. Teresa was still very emotionally withdrawn emotionally and easily upset. She tended to stay in the apartment for long periods, rarely going out. Her old spontaneity, her easy joy seemed to have left her. For several months she experienced lingering fears: she would have nightmares in which she heard Mexican voices from the shadows and suffered anxiety about being left alone and unprotected.

Ken claims that at this time Teresa also began using drugs again — including, according to him, cocaine. And while he said that he strongly disapproved of her return to using drugs, he inexplicably still helped indulge her habit by prescribing large amounts of codeine for her. He also testified that

84

Teresa's brother, Phil, was her cocaine supplier. Ken testified that Phil had "connections" with the Italian underworld in Manhattan, where he could get all the coke he needed.* For himself, Ken maintained he kept on with his mild use of marijuana and his occasional drinks.

A break in the pattern of Ken working long hours at his new clinics and Teresa's fearful reclusiveness changed in mid-September. An old girlfriend of Teresa's was getting married, and they decided it was time to get out, to try and live a normal life again. Teresa dressed carefully and began looking like her old radiant, ebullient self. She and Ken went to the reception and, for the first time in weeks, had a wonderful time.

After this Teresa began to experiment more with going out alone, to shop or visit with girlfriends. A few days after the reception, however, she drove their car into a wall, completely wrecking it. Ken received her call at the clinic. She was physically unhurt yet emotionally shaken.

But Teresa didn't seem to let the accident get her down and she continued reaching out, progressing slowly on her path toward complete recovery. She even went back to work at Dr. Avis's office. Ken had already repaired her broken front teeth with root canal and caps. Her facial and neck scars were fading, and her old energy seemed to have returned.

Then Teresa discovered that she was pregnant again. This time they were both mentally and emotionally ready for it. In fact, a child in their lives

*This information regarding Ken Taylor's statements about Phil Benigno was taken directly from Taylor's sworn testimony, recorded in court documents used in his trial.

would be the perfect antidote to their recent harried existence—a renewal, an affirmation of life itself. And when they announced the fact to the family, it seemed that the lingering effects of the nightmare honeymoon and the last few months finally over.

Ken also seemed to be energized by the news. He hung over his wife, attentive and protective. Others who knew the couple well were impressed with his role as a nurturing and loving husband. It didn't seem he could do enough for her.

By early October the dental businesses had improved enough for Ken to open negotiations with Stan Becker on a partnership. Becker clearly needed Ken, and a deal was quickly struck. Ken was given a piece of the action. He would make weekly payments to Becker, and even though the payments would be high, it was a partnership that Ken believed would eventually turn out to make good business sense. The more money he made above the weekly "rental" or "lease" charges, the more he could keep for himself and his growing family.

But he would need a buy-in fee, which was more than he could afford at the moment. Underwritten by Zach, Ken received a loan of $7,500 from a bank in Marion.

That fall the landlord surprised them with a sudden jump in the rent on Ken's three-room apartment, and they decided it was time to move. The apartment wasn't really enough space for a larger family anyway. They would buy a house.

Ken said he wanted to live in the country, and Teresa wanted to be close to her roots. They began searching in New Jersey, where they found two houses that were "possibles" in Manalapan Township, a rural part of Monmouth County. The house they finally chose was $20,000 more expensive than the other they were considering, but it was exactly what they both wanted. The house on Valley Road was eleven years old but still in great shape. It was a wooden-shingled, two-story, three-bedroom house on a corner lot in a quiet, upper-middle-class neighborhood. Surrounded by magnolias, Japanese yew, and junipers, the house had a large backyard with a swimming pool and was within an hour's drive of work for each of them.

They settled on a purchase price of $89,000. On December 3, 1983, the down payment was made. It came from Teresa's savings. They moved into the new house in mid-December.

The months between November 1983 and March 1984 were happy ones. "The happiest months of our marriage," Ken would later say. Suddenly everything seemed to be going their way. The pregnancy was going well, they were happy in their new home, Ken's new dental businesses were thriving, and he had even bought Teresa a new car.

As the year ended Teresa decided to leave her job with Dr. Avis and return to work in Ken's office. She was good at her job, so she would obviously be a great help, and most important in her mind, they could be together more.

One of Teresa's closest friends was also her cousin, Angela Rozak. Both women were short, full of energy, and extroverted, and they possessed a kind of spontaneous joy about even the smallest things. Angela had, in fact, been one of Teresa's bridesmaids. And of all their friends and acquaintances, the Rozaks socialized with the Taylors the most

—especially after their move to Manalapan.

Angela later remembered that Ken seemed to be a considerate and caring husband, although Teresa was obviously the most expressive partner. She was always the one touching and kissing Ken, who was much more low-keyed and reserved with his wife in public.

The two couples, while not strongly compatible, even went to a "couples only" weekend together in the Poconos.

Yet, almost as if fate wanted to remind them that life is never simple—or easy—soon after her birthday near the end of March, on a bright Saturday morning, Teresa went into premature labor. She was in her sixth month —a dangerous time for "preemies" to be born. Ken quickly took her to St. Peter's Medical Center in New Brunswick, New Jersey.

Teresa's obstetrician, Dr. Robert Klein, told Ken that the odds of the child's survival was about 75 percent. That left them only 25 percent to worry about —which was more than enough. The numbers were pointless, anyway. Teresa and the baby were in real danger, and no one in the family cared whether the statistics were in their favor or not.

Throughout the ordeal Teresa tried to remain stoic. But at one point she broke down, pressed her head on Ken's shoulder, and burst out, crying, "I'm going to lose my baby, I'm going to lose my baby," over and over again. She even asked to speak to a nun.

At the first opportunity Ken quietly told Dr. Klein about the saline abortion the previous summer. It was an abortion technique that had involved inducing premature labor contractions. Klein didn't think that the previous two abortions would affect her condition now. She was young and healthy, and the chances were good that she would carry to term.

With a little luck, Klein said, he thought he would be able to stop the contractions.

Ken and the family stayed at the hospital Saturday night and all day Sunday. By Sunday afternoon the contractions began to subside.

On Monday Dr. Klein performed an ultrasound test and amniocentesis. There didn't seem to be any damage to the fetus, which, it turned out, was a boy.

Despair became elation. A boy! A healthy boy. Teresa was ecstatic. She had always wanted to give Ken a son.

Before he released her on Tuesday, however, Klein was cautioning. He warned that Teresa had to take it easy. For three weeks she was to remain in bed. After that, she wasn't to do any housework or even climb stairs. No showers and definitely no sex. She could cook a little, sew, walk to the TV. That was it.

While Dr. Klein found no physical cause for the premature labor, Ken later claimed that the reason was obviously Teresa's drug use. She had, he said, been using both cocaine and codeine steadily for several days prior to the onset of the contractions. Teresa, according to Ken, was so relieved that the child had survived, and so worried about the dangers of drugs to the fetus, that she vowed to him to stay off any drugs or alcohol for the remainder of her pregnancy.

Angela, however, later remembered that in their frequent telephone conversations during her convalescence, Teresa had mentioned that Ken himself was often using cocaine. "Ken smokes pot to relax,"

89

Angela quoted Teresa as saying. "And he does coke. It helps him get through the day."

Angela said that she had been shocked when she heard this. "He treats people when he's stoned?" she asked, incredulous.

Teresa confided to Angela that most of his patients were on Medicaid and it was routine, boring work. And besides, he felt under enormous pressure to have the clinic succeed. He was working killing hours. The bills and overhead costs were high, and he would do a couple of lines when he went into the office. At home, she admitted to Angela, she would also do a few lines with him as well. They had often used it to enhance their sex. But, of course, that had all stopped during this last trimester of her pregnancy.

Angela later told two more interesting stories about life at the Taylors' at this point. Mixed messages about Ken were coming at Angela fast and furious.

On May 20, Angela's daughter's first birthday, Teresa disobeyed her doctor's orders to stay home and went to the little girl's party anyway. Angela was deeply touched by Teresa's gesture, and during the party she observed Ken being very attentive, even solicitous, toward Teresa. He would help her to the couch, get her food, and generally make sure that she was comfortable and happy. She had also already noticed that he seemed to be a good husband. He worked hard around the house, always puttering in his large vegetable garden and among the rosebushes, petunias, and other flowers that he had planted around the house. She had even pointed out to her husband, Peter, that it wouldn't hurt if he could be a bit more like Ken.

In fact, Ken had learned that he enjoyed working in the garden almost more than anything else. He had started a major renovation and planting project in late April, a few months after moving into the new house. He had first begun his flower and vegetable garden by closing off the back portion of the yard by planting a stand of pine trees. And when the garden vegetables and flowers started to bloom, he consistently provided fresh vegetables and bouquets of flowers to Louise, who was touched by his garden "gifts."

Then, on June 3, there was a surprise baby shower for Teresa at the Valley Road house. While Angela was marveling at the many outfits that Teresa had created for her soon-to-be-born son, Ken and Peter went off to play some golf.

On their way home from the baby shower, Peter told Angela that he had had a strange experience playing golf. Ken had hooked a long drive. Everyone hooked shots now and then, but Ken flew into a rage, cursing and screaming, and threw his golf club thirty yards down the fairway. Peter had never seen Ken this way and it had surprised him. To say the man had a temper was an understatement.

Angela also related a conversation with Teresa about Ken that had jolted her at the time. During lunch one day, Angela remembered that Teresa suddenly asked her if Peter liked to "eat you right at your period."

Startled, after a moment Angela said, "God, no."

"Well, Ken does," Angela recalled Teresa saying.

"God, that's gross," Angela muttered.

More than a year later, when Ken finally heard about this conversation, he became furious. After his initial shock, he wrote in a letter that "Teresa

91

and I did have an open sex life, and such an incident may have happened, but it was certainly nothing that either of us waited for or even planned. I have always seen sex as an enjoyable, *mutually enjoyable,* relationship. I consider sex a pleasurable, mutually satisfying experience and *not* some sort of sadistic perversion."

Angela didn't know what to say—or think—about Ken. He seemed a person with such extremes to his personality.

On a warm Sunday night in June, Ken and Teresa were watching television. Angela had telephoned again that evening. In the middle of the conversation Teresa suddenly stopped talking. Then in a voice full of awe and surprise, she said, "Oh, my God, I'm all wet . . . I think my water just broke."

Ken immediately called the doctor and then raced Teresa to Middlesex General University Hospital in New Brunswick. She was admitted a little after midnight.

At the first opportunity Ken telephoned his in-laws, who were attending a wedding on Long Island. Typically, the whole Benigno family piled into the family station wagon and drove to the hospital.

The twelve weeks of little or no physical activity had left Teresa's leg and abdominal muscles flaccid and weak. In this condition her labor would not be easy.

Even though Ken and Teresa had faithfully attended natural childbirth classes, and were practiced in doing all the right things—controlled breathing, relaxation and focusing techniques—Teresa was simply too weak physically to do the hard work necessary. She just didn't seem to have enough energy to complete the exhausting effort of giving birth, and Dr. Klein was seriously considering a caesarian section if her labor went on too long.

Al and Louise and Phil and Celeste joined Ken in waiting out the anxious hours. Celeste was particularly nervous, for she had herself recently become pregnant with her and Jeff's first child.

Sixteen hours later, on Monday, June Il, 1984, Philip Andrew Taylor was born in a final, exhaustive effort on Teresa's part.

Ken, who had assisted Teresa constantly in the husband's "hands-on" role allowed by modern hospitals, rocked the newborn child for the first hour after his birth while Teresa fell into a brief, weary sleep. The nurse instructed him in how to bathe the infant until Teresa was able to take the baby and begin breast-feeding.

Later that day he wrote a short note to Teresa:

"Today you shared with me the greatest gift of all—the gift of life. Your pain, your hurt, your joy and exaltation have motivated me and inspired me more than you can ever realize. I would rather die than see you hurt, ever, at any time. Your love for me is endless and totally giving. My feelings for you run so deep inside me they will forever be a part of me. I must do my best for you and I always will. I love you so much. Thank you for allowing this miracle to transpire. Your husband, with love as always, Ken."

For the next few days Ken worked half a day at

the dental clinic and spent the remaining time with Teresa and the baby at the hospital. When Teresa came home the following Thursday afternoon, her mouth literally dropped open as they turned the corner on Valley Road and approached their house.

The day before Ken had bought rolls of light blue crepe paper and three dozen light blue balloons, He worked all morning the day he was scheduled to pick up Teresa. He covered the trees in the front yard with balloons and strung the blue crepe paper on the shrubs and trees all across the yard in front of the house in celebration of Teresa's and the baby's return home.

Teresa was moved to tears.

The following night, Friday, Jean and Zach Taylor flew in from Marion to see their new grandson and give a helping hand for a week.

A quiet antagonism, or rather an undercurrent of tension, seemed to be developing between the two families at this point — at the very least, there were many conflicting viewpoints about life, and especially about how to raise a baby in the Taylor household. The atmosphere was not made any better by the fact that both groups of in-laws were constantly underfoot.

No single thing pinpointed the differences that seemed to arise between them; perhaps it was as simple as two families from strikingly different cultures — the demonstrative Italian immigrants opposed by more subdued and controlled Midwesterners — finally confronting each other.

One example illustrates the point. In one way, it could almost be called "another mother-in-law" story. When baby Philip failed to bound back from his normal initial weight loss after birth, Ken claimed that Teresa had returned to cocaine use and it was aupsffecting her breast milk. Ken, who still visited his daughter on weekends and continued to have sex with Marilyn after his return from Acapulco, had complained to his ex-wife that Teresa was heavily into coke again. And she was even forging his name on prescriptions for codeine. Codeine, he explained, extended the cocaine high and made it easier to come down. Her drug abuse was the real reason for her premature labor and the baby's lack of weight gain. He hadn't made these complaints openly to the Benignos or to anyone else, not even Teresa's doctors, but, he said, it was driving him crazy with worry.

He told one story about coming home from work on Monday to find baby Philip visibly agitated after his breast feeding. Normally the baby would feed and then drift off to sleep, often with his mouth still attached to Teresa's breast. But this time, Ken claimed, something was wrong. The baby wouldn't sleep and seemed "jumpy." Teresa also noticed the difference, and that the baby seemed upset. As Ken described it, "the awful specter of Teresa's using drugs" rose before him.

When Ken asked her if she had done coke again, Teresa said, yes, she had done some that afternoon.

Ken claims that he became furious and demanded Teresa stop using drugs. He explained to her how the drug was going through her breast milk. "Don't you know that your cocaine is being absorbed into the baby's blood and making him high?"

Ken would later testify that Phil was not only Teresa's steady coke supplier, but a user and dealer himself. Back in April, Ken testified, he had to fire

Phil not too long after hiring him to help manage his two dental offices.

He discovered, he testified, that Phil was using the upstairs apartment of the office to sell cocaine. One afternoon he noticed several young men enter the office and go directly upstairs. He followed one of them and discovered a drug deal going down. Phil, Ken claimed, had a scale on the desk and was weighing out cocaine.

Ken waited for the buy to conclude and then fired Phil on the spot.*

Later, when he heard tand redhe story, Phil denied that such a thing had ever taken place. Sure he occasionally took cocaine. So did most of the people he knew. And yes, he knew Teresa would now and then use coke. But like him, it was infrequent. Neither one of them was an abuser.

From the Benigno point of view, the baby's problem gaining weight was Jean Taylor's fault. According to this interpretion, Jean, who had become a vegetarian after she developed colon problems, was manipulating Teresa by playing a "domineering mother-in-law" role. While not pressing Ken, Tom, or Zach to abstain from meat, she was supposedly insisting that Teresa adhere to a strict vegetarian diet even while she was breast-feeding.

Angela, in particular, recalled Teresa as saying, "I'm starving. What I need is some beer and red meat . . . and all I'm getting is raw carrots and grapes. I can't wait for them [her in-laws] to leave."

But this version didn't account for the baby's

---

*This information regarding Ken Taylor's statements about Phil Benigno was taken directly from Taylor's sworn testimony, recorded in court documents used in his trial.

continuing loss of weight over a number of weeks
. . . or explain how Jean Taylor's vegetarian domina-
tion over her daughter-in-law could occur when she
was visiting with Ken and Teresa for only a week.

After another visit to the doctor and extensive
tests, however, nothing was found to be wrong, but
the doctor thought it wise to put the baby on formula. The weight problem began to disappear at
once, and the issue of whether it was caused by
Jean's vegetarianism, Teresa's drug use, or something more mysterious became moot.

Another area of contention, according to Ken,
was Teresa's difficult relationship with her mother
and sister.

During their week-long visit in June, Jean also recalled that when she asked about Louise and Celeste
helping out with the baby and household chores,
Teresa said that it was difficult having her mother in
the house. "My mom bosses me around all the
time," she said. And as for Celeste, Jean recalled
Teresa saying that the two sisters had always been at
each other, and Teresa wouldn't let her look after
her cats, let alone the baby.

For others who knew them, however, the Benigno
family was close and loving even if they did get argumentative and critical with each other at times.
That was simply their emotional Italian nature,
these friends said.

During this contentious summer of 1984 Ken was
hit with more bad news. Marilyn had decided to sell
the Staten Island house and move to Pittsburgh,
which was her flight base.

Ken was surprised and even shocked by the announcement, for he felt that their relationship had
grown deeper and matured. In truth, he had settled

into a comfortable polygamy: two women, two families, and he was content with the situation even though Teresa still didn't know for sure about his affair with his ex-wife. With a kind of defensive pride, he said, "Since my marriage I have had no other infidelities, remaining faithful to Marilyn and Teresa."

During the previous few months he and Marilyn had spent more time together than they had before he'd married Teresa. In addition to his normal Sunday visits to see Rhonda (and have sex with Marilyn), he would drive over just to have lunch and talk. And at least once a week he and Marilyn would quietly go out to have dinner together. He had, he later said, even confided to Marilyn his great secret, his growing apprehension and disgust with Teresa's continuing drug use. He swore that he himself had stayed off hard drugs, that he had learned how dangerous they were in Connecticut. Now he only indulged in an occasional joint of marijuana to relax and a few drinks.

As he later described their conversation, "Marilyn and I even discussed the possibility that should Teresa continue to abuse drugs after the baby's birth, a divorce was possible."

According to Ken, however, once Marilyn learned of his concern, she had constantly pressed him on the issue of Teresa's drug use and his unhappiness with the situation. She was obviously, Ken believed, trying to "win him back." But since she knew he "was more interested in Teresa's drug rehabilitation than a separation" (especially now, since there was baby Philip), it seemed to Ken that Marilyn was trying a ploy on him. By moving to Pittsburgh, he theorized, she was trying to force a decision on him to leave Teresa. Well, he decided, if that was her plan, it wasn't going to work. He watched his ex-wife and daughter move with a heavy heart.

It was also during July that Teresa and Ken returned to what he called their "normal, extremely active sex life." Teresa's transition from exhausted mother to wife and lover was a relief to him. In his words, "Teresa's renewed insatiable lust allowed me to more easily tolerate Marilyn's move, but obviously did nothing to ease the hurt of not seeing my daughter."

Chapter Seven

On July 6, with Teresa's knowledge and understanding, Ken took out a $100,000 Equitable life insurance policy on her. He paid the initial $247 premium in cash. Teresa agreed that it was a wise thing to do. She had had a difficult birth; and if anything ever happened to her the insurance would make things easier for Ken and the baby.

That August, over the Labor Day weekend, Ken and Teresa traveled to Marion to be with his mother, who was to have colon surgery. Teresa then surprised Ken when she asked Jean and Zach to become baby Philip's godparents. They had never really discussed religion in depth, but it was obvious that their backgrounds were quite different. Ken had always assumed that Teresa was deeply committed to her Catholicism, but when her priest had rejected her request to be married in the Church, she'd started to become disillusioned.

The elder Taylors were flattered by the request, and it was all arranged with their pastor, Darrel Parris, at the Marion First Baptist Church. Little Philip was "dedicated" at the church that Sunday in preparation for eventually being baptized into the Protestant faith. It was a baptismal "dedication" because in the Baptist faith no one can be actually be baptized until they reach the age of reason.

Little Philip's becoming a godchild and being "dedicated" would normally be a relatively uncomplicated spiritual act in most families; but within a year these simple ceremonies would come back to bitterly haunt both the Taylors and the Benignos.

Perhaps Teresa was just being polite, but Reverend Parris remembered her commenting to him in a private meeting how much she enjoyed attending church in Marion. Everyone seemed to really want to be there, not at all like her stuffy and formal church in Staten island, where attendance was compulsory.

Teresa openly admitted that she was still angry with the Catholic Church over their refusal to marry her and Ken. She wasn't sure that she would ever forgive them. In fact, she was even seriously thinking of converting to the Protestant religion. Jean had been enthusiastically supplying her with brochures and information about their Baptist church at every opportunity, but Teresa still wasn't sure. She was leaning toward the Presbyterian denomination because their local minister in New Jersey was "extremely nice."

After they had returned to New Jersey, however, Angela recalled that Teresa had said life in Marion was dull. It wasn't the kind of place she'd like to live in, she confided. And Angela quoted Teresa as saying she thought that Jean Taylor and her younger son Tom were both "nut cases": Jean because of her vegetarianism, her stiff Midwestern code of living, and her ardent religious beliefs, and Tom because —well, just because he was Tom, lost and wandering through life.

101

Two other memories from two different people later came to light; both of them related events occurring late in September. Together, and with no corroboration, they indicate just how confusing are the facts in the Taylor case.

Ken claimed that in late September he received a disturbing phone call from a local pharmacist. The man had called to ask him about a number of prescriptions he was holding—prescriptions made out to Teresa Taylor for codeine. The pharmacist explained that Teresa had been bringing him the prescriptions for some time now, and he had noticed a difference from Ken's normal prescriptions. He had called to make sure that Ken was aware of what was going on.

According to Ken, both Teresa and her brother Phil had been apparently doing the forgeries for some time.* The result of this revelation, and of Teresa's growing drug use during the previous summer, Ken said, was her becoming progressively unstable, and eventually even losing control and throwing a wild tantrum in Ken's dental office that ended in an argument between them.

In order to save money, Teresa had come back to work with Ken as a hygienist only a few months before. She would drop off the baby at her mother's and drive to the office. But because of her drugs, she was no longer the efficent hard worker she once was, Ken said. When she became hysterical in the office that day, he fired her on the spot. Ken said that he was sure her emotional outbreak was caused by her drug abuse, and his firing her, he believed, shocked

*This information regarding Ken Taylor's statements about Phil Benigno was taken directly from Taylor's sworn testimony, recorded in court documents used in his trial.

her back to reality. She suddenly realized that her drug habit was indeed out of control, and she immediately promised Ken that she would try harder to break free of her drug dependency.

When Teresa's lifelong friend Karen Oliveira later heard Ken's repeated claims about Teresa being heavy into drugs, she couldn't believe it.

"I've known Teresa all my life," she said, "and we've exchanged secrets nobody else ever heard. If Teresa was doing cocaine at all, it was because of Ken. She'd do anything for him."

Ken's story about the forged prescriptions, while possible, raised several questions. Assuming that the prescriptions were truly "forged" and not simply another example of a doctor's sloppy handwriting, it seems odd that the pharmacist would put his job on the line by accepting illegal prescriptions—even for a dentist he knew who worked nearby.

Far more likely, either the pharmacist would report the forged prescriptions to the proper authorities, or sternly warn Dr. Taylor that if there were any recurrences he would report him and Teresa. In any event, simply to protect his professional standing, and indeed his job, any reasonably intelligent and responsible man would have informed Ken that he would no longer take his prescriptions if he couldn't be confident that they were genuine.

None of these things, however, were ever said or even hinted at. According to Ken, the pharmacist simply accepted his lame excuse that it was a matter of convenience for him to have Teresa do this and had gone right on filling the bogus prescriptions—at least to the point that he had to make several phone calls over a number of months to Ken about the problem.

103

In addition, the police would later investigate these claims. They were unable to find any pharmacist who recalled the forged prescriptions and were therefore not able to confirm Ken's charges about Teresa and Phil getting drugs this way.

Another confusing story that supposedly occurred around this time eventually came to light.

A few days after her birthday, on September 29, Angela Rozak had a post-birthday celebration. She was not only a year older, but pregnant again, with her second child. Teresa had invited Angela to the house to measure her for some new clothes and to give her friend birthday gifts of a pair of gloves and a silk blouse. She had also baked a cake and invited Al and Louise to the small gathering.

During the early evening Angela recalled that Teresa started looking for something (she couldn't remember what) and innocently opened Ken's attaché case and lifted out a pair of earrings. She held them up, puzzled, staring at them.

"Ken," she said over her shoulder, "aren't these my earrings from Acapulco? I thought they were stolen."

Angela remembered that Ken stared at Teresa strangely, his expression intense. "You're mistaken, Teresa," he finally said. "It was a different pair."

Still studying the earrings, Teresa seemed confused for a moment. Then, Angela claims, Teresa said, "Oh," in a soft voice and replaced the earrings.

If Angela's memory is accurate, then several disturbing questions immediately come to mind. Had Ken Taylor actually beaten his wife to within an inch of her life on their honeymoon? And, as incredible as it sounds, had hethen carried around the incriminating diamond earrings in his briefcase for more than a year? Or, equally strange, had he hidden the earrings

104

for all that time and for some reason just retrieved them and put them in his briefcase only to have them unluckily discovered? Was Teresa, fifteen months after the experience, still so hazy on the details of Acapulco that she could indeed remember the "special" earrings that she had taken on her honeymoon, but not identify them with any confidence? Or, as some of Teresa's friends have theorized, was she so intimidated by Ken and his abusive ways that she immediately caved in without asking any further questions?

No one else heard the exchange except Ken, Angela, and Teresa. And despite Angela's clear memory of the moment, Ken claimed that the whole scene never happened. Nothing more was ever heard again about the missing Acapulco earrings.

In mid-October Ken disappeared, or so Teresa's family and friends remember. As they recall, Teresa wasn't at all sure where Ken had disappeared to. One morning he was simply gone. When her brother asked where Ken was, Teresa told him that he'd left. "Right after breakfast, he said he had to get something from the store and that he'd be right back," she told Phil.

Teresa waited and when he didn't return she checked outside. She saw a note under the car's windshield wiper. Phil said that Teresa handed him the note, which read, "I'm leaving for a couple of days. I have to get my head together."

As Phil remembered their conversation, Teresa said that she thought he had probably gone to Pittsburgh. He had often spoken about wanting to see his daughter.

For Ken, his trip to Pittsburgh wasn't a great mystery. As he recalled it, there was no note, no effort to escape from personal or business pressures. It was simply an effort to see his daughter again. He had made plans which, he said, were not secret, to visit his "other family." He had taken "three days' liberty from my dental practice" and called ahead to Marilyn. She and Rhonda met him at the airport. He spent the afternoon with Rhonda at a nearby playground and the evening with Marilyn after shopping for some gifts for his daughter. Their lovemaking during the short trip was just as sexually intense as always. Ken said that when he returned Teresa was, of course, "understandably irate" by his visit to his ex-wife, but she tolerated it because she knew how much he needed to see Rhonda.

Angela and Celeste both remembered everything differently. At this point in their relationship Teresa was, according to her friends, deeply troubled about Ken. She had told her friends that he seemed really disturbed. He was worried and anxious over the dental business, she said, and had even talked of suicide. She couldn't figure out what he wanted and had confided her fears (at different times) to Celeste, Angela, and Karen. She didn't know what to do and was even thinking about divorce.

According to both Angela and Celeste, Teresa told them that Ken had returned from his Pittsburgh trip "with his tail between his legs," pleading for forgiveness. He had explained again how he needed to see Rhonda and begged for Teresa's understanding.

This whole episode, however, adds other confusing elements. Just exactly what was Teresa's state of mind regarding Ken during this period? Was she, as some of her friends described, an abused wife too terrified

106

to speak up, as in Angela's story about the discovery of the Acapulco earrings? On the one hand, she is remembered by some of her friends and family as being frightened and dominated by Ken; then there is the conflicting picture of Ken returning home with his tail between his legs, and Teresa, far from being cowed, is shown as strong and resolute enough to complain openly to her friends and seriously consider divorcing him. Yet while confiding to her friends her most intimate family problems with Ken about sex and money, Teresa never once told any of them that Ken was abusing her. Nor did her friends ever say that they saw any signs of physical abuse.

Teresa's family was also constantly on the alert for any evidence of abuse after Acapulco — especially Al and Phil. Whenever they were over at the Valley Road house and everyone was sitting around the pool in bathing suits, they would quietly but carefully check out Teresa, searching for bruises, cuts, or abrasions. They never saw further signs of physical abuse.

While Teresa and Ken were not socializers, they did see a small group of friends now and then. Often drugs and booze would play a major part during the get-togethers. The reports and testimony about these times, however, often seem self-serving, with each teller putting his or her own spin on the tale.

One weekend Teresa had invited her friend Carrie and her new boyfriend, Jon, to spend the weekend. Carrie had been recently rejected by her former fiancé two days before their wedding. The cause of his canceling the wedding was that he had fallen in love with his secretary. Carrie was, of course, devastated by the sudden collapse of her imminent marriage.

Since she had been left standing at the altar, Carrie had been wild, had drunk too much, and had indulged in several brief affairs — that is, until Jon showed up. Here, at last, was a good man, a serious lover for Carrie, and Teresa wanted them all to get together socially.

As Ken remembers those weekends with Jon and Carrie, they "inevitably led to excessive drinking and drug abuse."

On one particular Friday that fall, November 9, only two days before Teresa was killed, Phil and his girlfriend Kathy came over about nine o'clock and the drug scene became really heavy.

Sometime during the night, lines of coke were spread out on the coffee table for everyone's use. According to Ken's sworn testimony, Teresa, Phil, and Kathy "finished three bottles of wine, and snorted nearly three grams of coke between them." Ken said that he didn't have any coke that evening, but stuck with his bourbon and smoked a joint.

For months after this particular Friday night party, however, Phil would deny even using cocaine. Then, finally, after continued questioning, he admitted to authorities that along with Ken both he and Teresa did use cocaine that Friday evening.

The day after the party with Phil and Kathy, on November 10, Saturday, Teresa had an early appointment with a girlfriend from her high school days, Cindy Diaz, to go shopping for some fabric. When she arrived to pick Cindy up, Cindy's husband, a photographer, began shooting some video tape of

Teresa and the baby to test out his new camera. After this the girls drove to the Brooklyn discount warehouse to look at the fabric. Cindy recalled that Teresa seemed tired, even run-down.

Teresa laughed it off, explaining that she was just a little hung over. Her brother had been to the house last night and they'd all had too much to drink. Teresa didn't mention the cocaine or taking any drugs to Cindy.

After a quick lunch Teresa dropped Cindy off and picked up Ken at his office. He usually worked a half day Saturdays, treating seven or eight patients from 10 A.M. to 1 P.M. They then drove back to the Valley Road house. For November, it was a warm day, and Ken puttered in his garden. Teresa went into the laundry and sewing room that also contained Ken's barbells and weights. She opened the windows and sat at her machine and worked on some clothes for little Philip.

About mid-afternoon, Angela telephoned. She and Teresa had planned to get together later in the day for Angela to try on some maternity dresses. Teresa had also created some clothes for Angela's daughter, Chrissy, a cowgirl outfit complete with skirt, blouse, and matching vest. The maternity dresses, which Teresa had prepared for Angela's growing pregnancy, were ready, but Teresa said that she was tired. She wanted to take a nap. Could they meet later? she asked.

Of course, Angela agreed. They planned to get together that evening at seven-thirty.

It was an evening, Angela said, that she would never forget.

Angela, Peter, and Chrissy, their cute and energetic eighteen-month-old daughter, arrived on time. Angela had brought along two Entenmann's crunch cakes.

Teresa was delighted. She was starving, she said, even though she had already eaten. Ken had made her supper while she was napping and she had eaten a full meal only an hour or so earlier. Teresa put one of the cakes on a plate and the other in the freezer.

Angela later recalled that when they'd entered the house, she'd felt a peculiar tension in the air, as if Ken and Teresa had just had a fight. Peter testified, however, that he didn't sense anything wrong between them that evening.

After a few drinks the two men moved into the living room and watched television while Teresa and Angela went into the sewing room. Angela was ecstatic over Chrissy's cowgirl outfit. It was a perfect miniature Western costume, right down to the pearl buttons, fringe, and studs that Teresa had sewn on.

For Ken, the evening was boring and dragged on and on. He was exhausted and wished only that the Rozaks would go. He just wanted to go to bed. But thankfully the evening was calm, a welcome break from the partying that had been going on over the past weekends.

When Teresa had finished showing Angela the clothes she had made for her and Chrissy, they returned to the kitchen and Teresa put on some coffee. While Angela was chatting on about how much fun it was when they had gone to the Poconos last February and that they should do it again, Teresa served the cake.

Ken had put Philip to bed earlier, and even though it was getting late (it was a little after nine), eighteen-month-old Chrissy was still wide awake and bouncing all over the place. Ken took her aside and whispered that if she was really quiet she could have a peek at her baby cousin sleeping. He took her up-stairs and they snuck into Philip's room. When they came down, Ken paused, sat Chrissy on the stairs, got his camera, and snapped some pictures of her.

Angela and Peter watched the two of them from the living room. Ken really could be so sweet, Angela thought.

According to Angela, one strange thing did occur that evening. As they were having coffee and cake, the conversation turned to sex. Angela commented that while sex was important at first in any relation-ship, other things began to count for more as time went on.

Ken, Angela recalled, suddenly turned to her and said that after the "whopping" he had given Teresa the other night, she wouldn't dare refuse him sex.

Alarmed, Angela looked over at Teresa. There were no bruises on her face and she showed no emotion. Angela relaxed then, assuming Ken had been just making a bad joke, especially after what had hap-pened in Acapulco.

When Ken later heard this story he simply shook his head. "It never happened," he said. "Nothing like that was even brought up."

About 10:30, when Chrissy began acting up again, Angela said that it was getting late and they had bet-ter leave. Teresa and Angela picked up the plates and coffee cups and took them into the kitchen. "Don't bother with the dishes," Teresa said. "I'll do them later."

The Entenmann's cake was only half gone, so Teresa took a roll of plastic wrap and laid it on the counter, ready to wrap the cake and put it away.

Ken helped Peter fold up Chrissy's portable crib and gather up her toys. Then he gave Peter a hand loading up the car. Ken and Teresa waved good-bye as they drove away.

It was the last time Angela would see Teresa alive.

Chapter Eight

Teresa had planned to attend a christening party for the new baby of another of her high school friends, Lorraine Taibbi, that Sunday afternoon, November 11. All of the old gang, a group of girls from school who called themselves the "Glitter Chicks," would be there, and Teresa was eager to see them.

When Teresa didn't show up, the girls were disappointed, but they assumed that something important must have come up. No one was worried about her absence, and so the christening went on smoothly without her.

In fact, no one, including the Benignos, thought it odd that they didn't hear from the Taylors that Sunday. They all had their lives to live and there was no reason to worry.

The family's normal schedule wasn't really disrupted until Monday morning, November 12, when Teresa usually dropped off Philip before going on to work. (Teresa had gone back to helping out at Ken's office recently, as had Phil Benigno.)

Sometime after nine-thirty Monday morning,

Louise began to wonder where Teresa was. She telephoned Teresa at home and there was no answer.

Louise still wasn't alarmed. Teresa was probably on her way.

Phil, who still lived with Al and Louise, had already left for the Grandview Avenue office. Around ten o'clock he began to wonder where his sister and Ken were.

A little after ten-thirty the office phone rang. It was Ken.

Phil was stunned as he listened to Ken's quiet, soft voice telling him that Teresa had gone away. She had a severe drug problem, Ken explained, and she wanted to go away somewhere, isolate herself, dry out once and for all. He had taken her to the People's Express terminal at Newark airport Sunday and he was now on the road with the baby. Teresa had asked him to take Philip to his parents in Indiana, since she knew he couldn't work and care for the baby himself while she was away and it would be too much a burden on Louise.

"Where did Teresa go?" Phil asked.

"She wouldn't tell me," Ken said. "She just wants to be alone, needs to be alone, private time, you know."

"When is she coming back?"

"In two or three weeks," Ken said, sounding a little impatient, anxious to get the conversation over with. "She said she'd telephone in three or four days.

"Listen, Phil," Ken continued. "Teresa doesn't want to upset Al and Louise. And she doesn't want them to know about the drug problem, She asked me to tell them that we went to Indiana for a short vacation, just the two of us."

Then, in a relatively calm voice, Ken instructed Phil to stay on top of things at the office and cancel his appointments until his return on Friday. He'd be in touch.

When Ken hung up, Phil stared at the receiver in his hand for a moment. This was nuts. He didn't know what to do — or even what to think about this confusing and drastic change in their lives.

After mulling over how his mother, with her heart problems and high blood pressure, would react to Teresa's sudden disappearance, he decided to go along with Ken's vacation story. He called Louise and explained, as calmly as he could, that Ken and Teresa had gone to Indiana for a "quick vacation."

Louise sounded doubting to Phil at first, but when he finally hung up, she seemed to accept the story.

As the day wore on, however, Phil began to worry. This just didn't seem like Teresa. She would have called him, or at least their parents, before going off somewhere. Even if she did need rehab, which he didn't believe, she'd arrange it all in a more organized way. It was simply all too abrupt, too strange.

That night, as the family was talking over the sudden trip, Phil told them that he hadn't talked to Teresa personally, and that Ken had telephoned him from the road. As his parents stared at him, their faces pale with surprise and shock, Phil admitted that Ken said Teresa had gone off by herself to get clean of a drug problem she had. He was taking the baby to his parents in Indiana alone.

Louise's face went white and her lips began trembling. Teresa was missing. Gone. With no word. Not even a telephone call to tell her family what was going on. Memories of Acapulco leaped into her mind. The images burned in her, flashing on her daughter's bruised and swollen face. It was all she could think about.

115

Al tried to calm his wife, telling her to take it easy, but when she went pale Al jumped up to get her nitroglycerin. He talked to Louise softly, explaining, rationalizing—maybe she really did have a problem, maybe she had gone off to visit a girlfriend? Let's wait and see, he said, keeping his voice as steady as he could.

After things had settled down a little, Al telephoned the Taylors in Indiana. Zach answered. Yes, they had heard from Ken. He was on his way, but he had run into a snowstorm in Ohio, It would probably be another six or seven hours before he arrived.

Al asked Zach to have Ken call him as soon as he got in.

After midnight, around 12:30 A.M., Ken telephoned the Benignos from Marion. He told Al the same story. Teresa had had a problem with drugs for some time. She was trying to straighten out and had gone to a rehab center. He didn't know where.

Al couldn't believe it. Behind him he could hear his wife crying. She was on the verge of hysteria. He tried to keep his voice calm, to get the truth out.

"How could you just let her go off by herself?" Al asked. "You should have insisted on knowing where she was going."

"Teresa's stubborn, Al," Ken said. "You know how she can be."

"I don't care," Al said, struggling to control himself. "You're her husband. It's your responsibility, You can't just let her disappear by herself. It's stupid, a very bad error in judgment on your part."

For a moment there was silence. Then Ken admitted that Al might be right. It had been a spur-of-the-moment decision.

Al, trying to fight back his own anxiety and panic,

116

said in a clipped, quiet voice, "I want her reported missing to the police."

Ken agreed. As soon as he returned he would report it to the Manalapan police. He just wanted to get Philip settled, and then he'd start back. He'd be home by Wednesday. By then he hoped Teresa would have called in, as she had promised, and everything would be all right.

Tuesday morning Celeste and her husband, Jeff, decided to go over to the Valley Road house and see if they could discover anything. They didn't know what they were looking for—anything that might shed some light on where Teresa had gone, or, God forbid, what might have happened to her.

Memories of Acapulco were sitting like a cancer in everyone's minds, digging roots ever deeper, ready to burst upward at the moment anything hinting at violence was discovered.

For Celeste it was like a shot in the dark. She didn't know what she would find at her sister's house. It was just something she felt she had to do.

Ken's Datsun 200-SX was in the driveway. He must be using Teresa's car. The front door was locked, but Ken and Teresa often left the door leading into the garage open, and it was now.

The door from the garage into the house opened onto the dining room. They walked into the kitchen. The first thing they saw was the Entenmann's cake and the roll of plastic wrap next to it on the counter.

This was really strange, Celeste thought. This wasn't at all like Teresa. She was a fanatic housekeeper. Everything had to be spotless. She would never leave the half-finished cake out like this.

In the living room another odd thing struck Celeste. Teresa's house and car keys were on the coffee table. She wouldn't leave the house without her keys, no matter where she was going.

They checked the other rooms. Everything seemed to be in order, though Jeff noticed that part of a roll of gray carpet padding stored in a spare room being renovated next to the sewing room had been torn away. Or, at least, it seemed somehow different from how it had been the last time he was here.

Celeste noticed the attic crawl space in the master bedroom and asked Jeff to check it out. He stood on a chair, pushed the panel up, and peeked inside. Empty. Nothing.

Outside everything also seemed in order. The pool was covered for the winter, and Jeff looked underneath the tarpaulin. It was also empty. Everything appeared normal.

Celeste telephoned her mother and told her about the keys and the cake, Both of them were almost trembling with growing anxiety.

Tuesday afternoon Al went to the local precinct in New York near where he taught school. He told the desk sergeant what had happened but was advised that they could do nothing for him. Teresa was a New Jersey resident, and besides, her husband should be the one to file a missing-person-report.

Later that evening Al called his niece, Angela Rozak. He knew that she and Peter had been at the house Saturday night. Maintaining his calm as best he could, he explained that Teresa was missing and quietly asked Angela if anything strange had happened Saturday night. Did she know anything about Teresa being on drugs?

Angela was shocked by the news. Nothing odd happened, and she couldn't believe Teresa was spaced out on drugs. Neither she nor Peter had seen anything of the kind. When Celeste got on the phone and told Angela about the keys and the cake left out, Angela almost fainted. Teresa wouldn't have gone away like that. If anything had happened, it must have been right after they left — even before Teresa could finish cleaning up.

On Wednesday there was still no word from Ken. Celeste had learned that Sheri Delile, another close friend of Teresa's, had flown from Newark on Sunday. She had taken a People's Express flight to Michigan. Was it possible that Teresa and Sheri had gone together?

Louise telephoned the Delile home and learned that Sheri had left Sunday to visit her sister. But Sheri's sister had just moved to Michigan, and a telephone had not yet been installed. There was no way they could get in touch with them, but Sheri was scheduled to return Thursday.

That was surprisingly close to Teresa's plan to call in a few days — at least according to Ken.

All they could do was wait, and hang on to the fragile hope that Teresa was with Sheri.

Ken finally called Wednesday night. He apologized for not calling sooner, but he had felt exhausted after the long drive back. He would speak to the police in the morning and then come over.

Al told Ken about their discovery — Sheri Delile was in Michigan with her sister, and maybe, just maybe, Teresa had gone with her.

119

Ken seemed happy with the news. He agreed that it would be a good idea to meet Sheri's plane Thursday morning. He'd go along with Celeste and Jeff and bring a couple of photographs . . . one of Teresa alone, and one of her with the baby.

Early the next morning, Thursday, November 15, Ken called the Manalapan Police. The duty officer listened quietly and then said that he would send an officer to the Taylor house right away.

A little after nine Patrolman David Visconi arrived. He was a short, thick-bodied cop who was developing a noticeable paunch. Ken had seen him a number of times along Route 9 when shopping at local stores.

Officer Visconi declined Ken's offer of a cup of coffee and asked a number of standard questions—a description of Teresa, any reasons that she might have gone away, etc.—all of which Ken answered. Visconi made notes throughout the interview. Ken didn't tell the officer the story about Teresa going away for drug rehab or about any drug problem she might have had. He made the whole thing seem the result of relatively normal personal problems involving stress and work that Teresa had.

A half hour later Visconi left. He assured Ken that a teletype with Teresa's description would be sent out immediately. But he could promise nothing.

It was just about the time that Officer Visconi was leaving the Taylor home that morning that Neil Griesemer was walking toward a body wrapped in a sleeping bag near Hawk Mountain in Pennsylvania.

Later, Officer Visconi filed a report on his conversation with Ken.

120

According to Officer Visconi's notes:

"Husband, Mr. Taylor, reported to this officer he took his wife to Newark Airport (People's terminal) on 11/11/84 because she told him she needed space. Husband related she feels pressure as a result of work and family problems, Mr. Taylor believes his wife may be in Michigan. Her girlfriend, Sheri Delile, from Staten Island, left to visit her sister in Michigan on 11/11/84."

Officer Visconi later that day learned airlines keep their passenger lists for only twenty-four hours. But then, he thought, Mrs. Taylor would probably show up. The police were always getting reports of missing people who would suddenly reappear. Near the end of his report, Visconi noted, "It appears at this point his wife wanted to leave her family. No domestic violence was involved. This case is being closed until such time as it would require reopening."

After the patrolman left, Ken drove to his dental office to pick up Teresa's brother. He and Phil would drive out to People's Express with the photographs and see if anyone recognized Teresa. They were both nervous. Ken particularly looked edgy, Phil thought. But then, so did he, he was sure.

No one at the People's Express counter remembered seeing Teresa the previous Sunday. Ken and Phil tried a restaurant nearby, and a bar. None of the waitresses or cashiers remembered her. At another bar the bartender stared at the photo for a moment and said that yeah, he might have seen her. Or someone who looked like her, the previous Sunday.

The news that she might have been seen didn't help the mood at the Benigno home at all.

Later that evening Ken drove to Newark Airport, where he would meet Celeste and Jeff. They planned to wait for Sheri Delile's plane. But another shock awaited them.

On the "Arrivals" board there was no flight from Detroit even remotely near the time they'd been given.

They called Louise and discovered that Sheri Delile had already arrived home. She had called the Benignos and told them that she had switched to a Northwest flight. Teresa was not with her. And she had not heard from Teresa since she'd left to visit her sister.

On Friday morning Ken received two phone calls. One was from Sheri Delile, worried about Teresa's disappearance. The other was from Officer Visconi. Visconi told Ken that "under the circumstances, police involvement in the case was limited" and that the file was being closed.

Later that morning Ken went to his office and picked up the past week's mail. He told Phil that he was going home to check over the mail; he was too distracted to work in the office. He also told Phil about his conversation with Officer Visconi—that the case was being closed.

Phil was, of course, stunned by the news, and he called home. But Louise had already talked with Visconi, who had called on November 16 to advise the Benignos that the case was being closed. Louise then told Visconi about their suspicions regarding Teresa's having been beaten on their honeymoon. It was the first time Visconi had heard about Acapulco. He im-

122

mediately wrote another report and handed it to his superior. The case was reviewed during the Friday afternoon briefing at the Manalapan station and a detective, Robert Fausak, was assigned to look more carefully into the disappearance of Teresa Taylor.

Detective Fausak, a wiry, energetic, and intense thirty-six-year-old cop, had been with the Manalapan department for twelve years. He was one of only three detectives on the thirty-two-man force. When he was assigned the case he was unimpressed. It seemed routine. He had been a cop long enough now so little surprised him. People disappeared all the time, for any number of reasons. It was one of the lesser problems he had. Crime in the Manalapan Township was generally of the more serious kind— sexual assaults and burglaries.

But Fausak came from a cop family. His father and two uncles had all been cops, and he took his job seriously.

When he received the phone calls from the Benigno family, first from Celeste and then from Al, and heard more of the details about Teresa's beating in Acapulco, he began to sense that this might be something other than a simple missing-person case.

Al had been straight with him, Fausak thought. He admitted that his daughter had always maintained that her husband had not been the one to beat her. And Al had never seen any evidence of further abuse by the husband. But it was precisely Al's honesty and not censoring the story that gave his fatherly concern the ring of truth, so Fausak decided to look a bit deeper.

123

He telephoned Taylor and asked if he could come by the house.

Ken was pleasant and agreeable when Fausak arrived. But he was curious about the visit. He thought the case had been closed.

"Just a few loose ends," Fausak explained. "You know how it is."

The men sat at the dining room table and Ken retold his story. Teresa had been unhappy recently for several reasons: conflicts with her family, work pressures, and maybe even postpartum blues after giving birth to their baby. She had left with her MasterCard and almost a thousand in cash, two hundred of which he had given her.

Fausak nodded and listened, trying to sense any holes in the quiet tale Ken Taylor was telling.

He again got a description of what she was wearing: Calvin Klein jeans, black patent leather pumps, a white sweater, and a white jacket.

Ken explained that he had reported her missing because she had not telephoned in the promised three- or four-day period. That had worried him, for she was normally very good about things like that.

Fausak listened and took notes. Then, before he left, the detective asked if he could look around. Of course, Ken said, and took him on a tour of the house. Fausak asked a lot of questions as they went from room to room. In the bathroom he noticed the toothbrushes.

"Whose are those?" he asked.

"Two are mine," Ken explained, "and the other two are Teresa's."

"Didn't your wife take hers?"

"Of course," Ken answered. "She had many more

124

in the cabinet." Don't forget he was a dentist, Ken added.

Nothing seemed obviously wrong in the house, but as Fausak prepared to leave, he suddenly asked Ken if he had a photograph with both himself and Teresa in it.

Ken gave the detective a large 5 x 7 blowup in a heart-shaped frame of him and Teresa taken in the Poconos the previous February.

Ken later described his feelings during what he considered "this search and interrogation" as proof that he was already a suspect. The photo of him and Teresa together was probably to show someone in an effort to identify him. "I could have run then," he said later. "I should have run . . . and if I knew then what I know now I would have run."

But instead of running, Ken went out to eat at a local diner and then called Marilyn. He told her how much he missed her and Rhonda, and that he would attend a birthday party with them Saturday afternoon.

Back at his desk Fausak wrote out a missing-person bulletin that he sent to police departments throughout Pennsylvania, New Jersey, Ohio, Indiana, and Michigan. In his description of Teresa he noted that her two front teeth were missing. Almost as an afterthought, he added, "Possible foul play involved."

The bulletin was sent over the wire at 11:15 P.M. that evening.

At 5 A.M. Saturday morning the duty officer at the Manalapan station telephoned Fausak. The Pennsylvania State Police had responded to his bulletin. They thought they had a match.

When Fausak arrived at his desk he found three other responses to his bulletin. But they were just requests for more information.

Then he received a phone call that turned a missing-person case into homicide. Corporal Gary Millward from the Reading barracks in Pennsylvania was on the line. A female body had been found Thursday morning by a man picking up beer cans in a bird sanctuary off Interstate 78. The woman was estimated to be between twenty and twenty-five years of age. The body was wrapped in a gray carpet padding and stuffed inside a brown sleeping bag. She had been beaten to death. There were massive head and face injuries.

Everything matched Fausak's bulletin except the clothes. She had a white knit sweater and white pantyhose, but was wearing beige culottes, not Calvin Klein jeans.

The uglier part of it was that it looked like there was something sexual going on. The culottes, pantyhose and a sanitary napkin were pulled down from the buttocks to just above the knees. And the vagina and anus were covered with considerable amounts of Vaseline.

"What about her teeth?" Fausak asked.

Two teeth were missing, Millward said. One upper front tooth was completely gone, another looked like it had the remains of an original tooth that was probably capped.

The jewelry found on the body included a gold Pulsar watch with a black band, a wedding ring, a single diamond earring, a charm necklace with a gold tooth and toothbrush, and another necklace with a gold charm engraved, "#1 Sister." After he hung up, Fausak first notified the Monmouth County prosecu-

126

tor's office Major Crimes Unit that he had a probable homicide. Next, he had the unpleasant job of calling the Benignos.

Louise answered and Fausak quietly asked if she and Al could come down to the station house. He had a few more questions he'd like to ask. Louise immediately began to sound panicked, and Fausak found himself getting uncomfortable. He hated moments like this. Just clearing up details, he said weakly.

To Fausak's relief, Al came on the line and said he'd be there at noon. Celeste would come along to help out on questions about jewelry.

Fausak then called Corporal Millward back and said that he would be coming down later that afternoon with some family members to identify the body.

When the Benignos arrived, Fausak took Al aside and told him that they'd found a body in Pennsylvania. The description seemed to fit his daughter, but they had to make sure. Would he go down to take a look?

His face pale and his voice shaking, Al agreed, but he wanted to have his son, Phil, come along.

Louise almost fainted when she heard about the body in Pennsylvania. "It's her, it's her," she cried. "I know it. Something awful's happened."

"Maybe it's not her," Al said. But Louise was fast becoming hysterical, and nothing Al could say helped. At one point Fausak even suggested that they call in a doctor, or, because of her heart condition, perhaps they should take Louise to the hospital.

But when Angela and Peter Rozak arrived, Louise began to calm down.

Fausak asked the Rozaks privately what Teresa was wearing the last time they saw her.

127

"A white sweater and tan-colored culottes," Angela told him.

When Phil Benigno arrived he hugged his mother and the family stood around in stunned silence while Detective Fausak quietly called Pennsylvania again and requested that a local ambulance stand by. They might have to transfer a body back to New Jersey.

The Rozaks took Louise home with them. When they had gone, Al and Phil climbed into the backseat of the car. Patrolman Visconi was in the front with Fausak as they set off on the grim two-hour trip.

From the Reading barracks Corporal Millward drove north to Pottsville Hospital. Al and Phil followed the officers numbly. No one spoke much. There was no need for words. Other Pennsylvania state troopers joined them as they waited in the corridor outside the morgue. The body was wheeled out on a gurney.

Al and Phil stared at the sheet-covered form before them. When the face was uncovered by the forensic pathologist, Phil couldn't move. He started to cry. Al took a hesitant step forward, tears also running down his cheeks. "Yes," he said hoarsely, "this is my daughter."

He bent over and kissed her forehead.

The pathologist looked over at Phil. "Is this your sister?"

Phil could barely speak. "Yes," he finally said. "That's my sister."

Fausak gently took them by the elbows, turned, and led them down the hall. It was better to get them away as quickly as possible.

When the formalities at the hospital were completed and all the papers signed and documents filled out, it was nearly 11 P.M.

They had a long drive back to Manalapan. But before they left Al called Celeste to tell the family.

Teresa was dead.

Chapter Nine

Al and Phil Benigno reached Manalapan a little after 1 A.M. They were exhausted, both from the long day and the emotional wringer that they had been through. They drove straight to the Rozaks' to be with Louise. Detectives Fausak and Visconi stayed on in Pennsylvania "gathering information."

Several things had happened during the afternoon and early evening while they were in Pennsylvania identifying Teresa's body. Fausak's call to the major crimes unit of the Monmouth County prosecutor's office had brought quick results. Lieutenant William Lucia and one of his detectives, Guy McCormick, arrived at the Manalapan police station. McCormick was Lucia's top investigator and had at one time been on the Manalapan force. He knew Fausak, and the two men got along well together.

The investigation team had been energized by Fausak's news that Teresa Taylor's body had been identified. An immediate search began for her husband. Several times during the afternoon and evening a patrol car had driven by the Valley Road house. Ken Taylor's two Staten Island dental offices had been contacted. There was no sign of him and since he was already a prime suspect, concern grew that he might in hiding or trying to escape.

Around midnight, about an hour before Fausak and the Benignos returned from Pennsylvania, Detective McCormick called Celeste White. Her parents had called earlier and the news of her sister's death had shaken her to her core. She seemed hysterical to McCormick, and he tried to calm her. He asked her if she knew where they could contact Dr. Taylor. Barely able to talk through her sobbing, she told the investigator to try his parents in Marion, Indiana. She gave him the number.

When Zach Taylor answered, McCormick apologized for calling so late, but the body of his son's wife had been found and he needed to talk to Doctor Taylor.

Zach was stunned by the news. After a moment he asked if her death had been caused by drugs. McCormick was surprised by this. It was the first time he'd heard anything about the possibility of drugs being related to her disappearance.

No, he said cautiously, he didn't know. They didn't have all the details and that was why he had to talk with Ken.

Zach said that Ken could be in Pittsburgh, visiting his daughter. He didn't have the address, but he would call and see if he could locate him.

"If you do," McCormick asked, "please have him call me as soon as possible. It's very important."

Early Sunday morning, a little after 1 A.M., Lieutenant Peter Vanderweil, a Manalapan police officer, was awakened with a message that they had received a telephone call at the station. It was Ken Taylor from Pittsburgh. Dr. Taylor had left a number where he could be reached.

A half hour later Vanderweil returned the call. He explained that he was sorry he had to inform Ken that his wife was dead. She had been killed. Her body had already been discovered and identified by her father and brother.

After a moment of silence, Ken asked what had happened. Where was she found? Did they know who killed her? Vanderweil thought it sounded like the man was crying.

"No, not at the moment," Vanderweil said. He didn't want to scare away the prime suspect. It was important, he went on, that they talk with him about his wife's last movements — starting with the time he'd dropped her off at People's Express.

Could he come back to New Jersey? Vanderweil asked.

"Yes, of course," Ken said. He would be there on the first available flight.

Vanderweil offered to meet Ken at the airport, but Ken assured him that it wouldn't be necessary. Vanderweil persisted, saying it would be no trouble; he'd be glad to do it.

The verbal dance went on for a moment, Vanderweil trying to get as immediate a connection with Taylor as possible, but Ken was strongly resisting the idea. He was at his ex-wife's home and she would accompany him to Newark. He had left a car at the Newark Airport parking lot, and his ex-wife had said she would even drive him to the Manalapan police station if necessary.

Vanderweil didn't want to sound too anxious, or to get Ken upset, so he finally agreed. They'd wait for him at the station.

132

By now it was approaching 2 A.M. and Ken said that he'd be in Manalapan by 10 A.M. that morning.

Immediately after hanging up, Lieutenant Vanderweil started dialing. One of the first people he called was his immediate superior, Captain Richard Canneto, head of the major crimes unit in the county prosecutor's office. Canneto, along with a parade of top county and township police officials, descended on the Manalapan station early Sunday morning to await Ken's arrival.

On the previous morning, Saturday, at around 10 A.M., Ken first went to his bank in Staten Island to cash some checks and deposit a few others before driving to Newark Airport in Teresa's Cutlass. Unknown to Ken, while he was flying to Pittsburgh later that afternoon, Al and Phil were on their way to identify Teresa's body.

He had called ahead and Marilyn and Rhonda met him at the airport around two-thirty. They all then drove directly to the home of Marilyn's friend Kelly, where a birthday party was being held for Kelly's daughter.

When the party ended they returned to Marilyn's new condo in Bridgeville, a suburb of Pittsburgh. Tired from the excitement of the party, Rhonda took a short nap while Ken and Marilyn discussed Teresa's disappearance.

Ken again told the story about Teresa going off hopped-up on cocaine. Marilyn would later testify that Ken seemed normal that evening, although he was obviously concerned about Teresa.

When Rhonda awoke, she put on a new dress Ken had bought her on a previous visit and they went out

133

to dinner to a restaurant nearby called Charlie's Place. It was to be their last supper together.

Later that night Ken and Marilyn were just falling off to sleep when the phone rang. It was around 1 A.M.

Ken's father was weeping as he told his son that Teresa had been found dead. Zach gave Ken the name of a detective who wanted to speak with him. Both Zach and Jean promised to come to New Jersey immediately, along with Philip.

When Ken hung up he started crying. His agony seemed to reach into Marilyn and she burst into tears along with him. Marilyn felt sick to her stomach. She had heard enough of the conversation to understand what had been said. It was all so horrible. Something that happened to other people.

But each of them was crying for different reasons — Marilyn because it was so shocking and tragic, Ken because he had a guilty secret that was rushing things toward what he knew was the inevitable conclusion. His were tears of grief mixed with fear and anxiety.

After a while Ken pulled himself together and called New Jersey to talk with Lieutenant Vanderweil. When he was finished, Marilyn telephoned her airline and booked passage for them both. Rhonda would go back to the party house and spend the next day with Kelly.

Ken and Marilyn arrived at the Pittsburgh airport in the darkness just before dawn, around 5 A.M. Ken noticed that a Pennsylvania state police officer nearby seemed to watch him the entire time they waited to board their flight to Newark.

It had been a long night for Bob Fausak, who found himself becoming ever more deeply immersed in the Taylor case — especially since viewing Teresa's battered

134

body and sharing in the anguish of Al and Phil Benigno as they identified her. He was staring out the window when he saw the Cutlass pull up. The license number 464 YEE was clearly visible. It had been part of the bulletin sent out earlier when they were trying to locate Ken, a number he wouldn't easily forget.

He watched as Ken got out of the car to talk briefly with a tall, attractive red-haired woman, kiss her on the cheek, and walk toward the station. The woman backed up, turned the car, and drove off.

Fausak walked to the station's entrance and met Ken in the reception area. Even though Dr. Taylor was already suspected of killing his wife, Fausak offered his condolences. He was sorry they had to meet again under such difficult circumstances.

Lieutenant Lucia joined them and Fausak led them into one of the station's interrogation rooms. It was a small, square room with a table and three chairs. Ken later recalled that both men were "pleasant enough," but he was immediately aware that he was a suspect and that this was not simply a search for information about "Teresa's last movements" but a dead serious, all-out interrogation.

Any remaining doubts in Ken's mind about his position were erased when Lucia started off by informing Ken that he was a major suspect. Lucia read him his Miranda rights and then he willingly signed an agreement permitting them to question him without his attorney present. When the questions began it was a little after 10 A.M.

There was no stenographer present and no tape recorder, but Lieutenant Lucia took copious notes as Ken again related his story about Teresa being despondent and wanting to be alone and his taking her to Newark Airport the previous Sunday. Teresa had been under

135

stress, Ken explained, ever since the baby's birth—especially from the tensions between her and her parents. But his and Teresa's marriage was happy. They had no major problems. For the first time, however, he told them about Teresa's drug abuse and his growing concern over its effects on both her and the baby.

The night before her disappearance, Saturday, November 10, Ken said he went to bed around midnight, not long after the Rozaks had gone home. Teresa had stayed up. He awoke in the middle of the night, around 3:30 or 4 A.M. Teresa was still downstairs, strung out on drugs. They had talked for a while, and Teresa had finally admitted that she did have a drug problem. She wanted to do something about it, but could not sleep then. She was too wired. Ken went back to bed by himself.

Teresa awoke him a little after eight. She had decided that she had to get away. She had to deal with her drug problem. He then took her to the airport.

Ken said that Teresa had wanted him to take Philip to his parents in Indiana. It would be best, she thought, for both Ken and the baby.

At this point in the interrogation they paused for a coffee break.

When they began again, Lucia asked Ken to describe his relationship with Teresa, starting from the time they met and he had hired her. Was there anyone he knew in her life who might dislike or hate Teresa enough to hurt her? Lucia asked.

No, Ken said, everyone loved Teresa. She wasn't the kind of person who made enemies. There was only one person he could think of who might hurt her, and that was her previous boyfriend, Jack Lombardi. Teresa had told him that Lombardi had once hit her, bursting her eardrum in the process.

136

Lucia wrote down Lombardi's name on his notepad, although it seemed to him that Taylor was throwing smoke in their eyes.

Then he began pressing Ken about Acapulco. Ken again related the story about being attacked and robbed in their *casita,* his ordeal in jail, and Teresa's hospitalization. He had never been charged with anything, he said. It was all a scam by the Mexican police to extort money.

Around noon Lieutenant Vanderweil and Captain Canneto appeared. They brought a search warrant for Ken's home, which he immediately signed. "I really didn't care," he later described his feelings. "At this point I didn't care about anything. My life was in ruin."

Lucia left the interrogation room and gave the search consent to Lieutenant Vanderweil, who, along with forensic expert Lieutenant Newman and an investigator from the prosecutor's office, Detective Glenn Meyer, left to search the Taylor house.

As the questioning continued, Lucia asked Ken to retrace all his moves since Teresa's disappearance. Ken detailed his actions of the previous week, including his trip to Indiana with Philip and his visit to his ex-wife in Pittsburgh.

The questioning was interrupted again for a coffee break.

Outside the interrogation room, Vanderweil grabbed Lucia by the arm. They finally had some hard evidence. They had found a diamond earring with dried blood on it in the garage. It matched the earring found on Teresa's body.

Captain Canneto and Lieutenant Vanderweil returned with Lucia to the interrogation room. Canneto showed Ken a Polaroid photo of the earring. A ruler had been laid next to it to indicate its size.

"Doctor Taylor," Canneto asked, "Do you recognize this?"

Ken saw that the photo showed the floor of his garage, but he couldn't make out the small object next to the ruler.

"A cigarette butt?" he said.

"No," Lucia responded. "It's an earring. The other was found on your wife's body."

"Can you explain how this earring got in your garage?" Lucia asked.

Ken again stared at the Polaroid. No, he couldn't. Perhaps Teresa had met someone at the airport and they'd come back to the house.

That didn't make any sense, Lucia said. A stranger wouldn't pick her up at the airport, bring her back to her house, kill her, and then take her body to Pennsylvania.

At this point Vanderweil began pushing harder, intimidating Ken, trying to get him to break down and confess.

Ken remembers that at that moment, "suddenly it was clear that all of the cops thought that I was the killer."

Lucia leaned forward and in a soft voice said, "Doc, did you kill your wife?"

Ken denied it indignantly. He loved his wife. He wouldn't do anything to hurt her.

"Take a moment," Lucia said. "Think about it; it'll be easier on all of us."

All the men except Vanderweil then left the room. They wanted to give Ken time to collect himself. He was clearly close to breaking down. He looked drawn and pale. A thin sheen of sweat had broken out on his face.

Alone in the room, Vanderweil stared at Ken. After a moment he said bluntly, "I believe you killed your wife."

Ken didn't respond, but his eyes welled up with tears.

"Maybe something happened that we don't know about, that set the whole thing off?" Vanderweil suggested.

Ken's head was down, close to the table, nodding slightly. But still he didn't speak.

It was just before three o'clock that afternoon when Lucia and Canneto returned.

The men were all staring at Ken when he suddenly looked up, his eyes swimming, his lips trembling.

"What would you do if you found your wife giving your infant son 'head'?" he blurted out.

He openly began sobbing, tears streaming down his face.

"Is that what happened?" Lucia asked.

"Did you kill her, Doc?" Vanderweil added, leaning forward.

"Yes," Ken said in a choked voice. He began to cry convulsively.

After a moment he tried to explain the events leading up to Teresa's death. When he finished, everyone was silent for a moment.

Lucia then informed Ken that his parents and son were there to see him. "I was too embarrassed to see them, too humiliated," Ken recalled. "I wished then that I'd killed myself."

Lucia persuaded Ken to see his parents and son. He pointed out that it might be a while before he saw them again.

"Our meeting was highly emotional," Ken later said.

139

"We were all crying. I was finally facing the reality of what had happened. It was all over now."

A burly, balding officer took Ken from the visitor's room to be fingerprinted, photographed, and put in a holding cell. As he was led from the room, his head down, he was sobbing, "I couldn't take it anymore. I just couldn't take it . . ."

Zach and Jean returned to the Valley Road house with Philip while Ken was booked and charged with murder. He was taken to the Monmouth County Jail and Judge Arnone set bail at $500,000, payable in cash only.

Chapter Ten

How can someone kill his wife? A woman that he loved? That is a question I have asked myself a thousand and one nights as I lay in the dark cell with only the sounds of men grunting in their sleep, or the occasional jolting sound of metal striking metal when a distant door slams shut.

Kenneth Taylor,
Prison Notebooks

Eventually Kenneth Taylor would give several conflicting descriptions about what occurred on that Sunday morning in November. His memories, while uncorroborated and no doubt self-serving, still deserve full attention—if for no other reason than to give the guilty a full hearing, and because it just might help others understand the man's motives.

After his earlier false stories didn't fly, and Ken had confessed, he then told his "true" version of what happened. His memories of those violent moments are graphic, acute, and full of anguish. Here is what Ken Taylor claimed occurred on that fateful night in the house on Valley Road.

It was sometime close after dawn when Ken said he

awoke again. It had been a restless, unsettled night. Each time he had come up out of his deep, troubled sleep he was vaguely aware that Teresa had not yet come to bed.

Drowsy from his bad night of sleep, and strangely upset, he wondered if Teresa was still high. Ken had claimed over and over again that by this time Teresa had been on a cocaine and alcohol binge for three days and he was sick with worry. The mix of drugs and alcohol was dangerous enough, but she was using codeine and pot as well. It had never been this bad before.

He rubbed his eyes and squinted at his watch: it was a little before 7:30 A.M. The first cool rays of Sunday morning sun were streaming in the window. Groggily, he rose from bed and stumbled into the bathroom to relieve himself, then went into the baby's room. Philip was not in his crib. For some reason a sense of alarm shot through him. His apprehension made no sense at all. Many times Teresa would take the baby early in the morning and change his diapers and feed him. But the empty crib nagged at him now. Something was wrong. Call it intuition, instinct, he couldn't name it. The empty crib felt wrong. Perhaps it was his lack of sleep? Or Teresa's behavior for the last three days? She had never been drugged out like this before. It was so unlike her. Yes, at parties, social get-togethers, at moments of stress or exhaustion . . . they both liked to get high. But she had never taken so much for so long.

He stopped for a second and listened. The house was quiet. No voices, no morning baby laughter, no sounds of breakfast. The silence added to his unease. He moved to the stairs, anxious now.

Ken said that it had all started three days before. Thursday night, November 8, was the beginning of the end. If he could have only seen earlier the shadows

142

that had been gathering for so long . . . but as black and forbidding as they were, he had somehow ignored them.

On Thursday nights Ken worked on the bookkeeping for his dental practice, totaling the week's receipts, preparing the taxes and payroll checks for his staff. On this Thursday night, even though she was dog-tired, Teresa decided to stay up with him.

It was a loving gesture, an expression of their need to be together. He smiled and kissed her. He was lucky to have her. She was a talented and pretty woman, he thought, with a round face, large, expressive dark eyes, and a full mouth. She was a little overweight after the birth of the baby five months before, but in a strange way it made him feel comfortable. She seemed more maternal than before Philip's birth, less prone to wear extravagant clothes and tint her hair wild colors.

They'd always had this electricity between them, a basic physical attraction, and if he felt older and more experienced than her at times, that was all to the good. The age difference didn't bother either of them. Many people thought that women in their early twenties were good for men in their mid-thirties. It had clearly worked out fine in their case.

As he collected his papers, Teresa said she wanted to work on sewing an outfit she was making for Chrissy, her cousin Angela's baby daughter. But first she wanted to snort a few lines of coke to give her a boost. Ken noticed that she added a few codeine tablets and flushed them down with several shots of bourbon.

Ken joined her with a couple of bourbons of his own, which he normally had while doing the books. He opened his files and settled down to the tedious work. In the middle of his bookkeeping chores he looked up to see Teresa wander off and do a little more coke and booze. She seemed a bit heavy into it and he almost said something, but he caught himself and turned back to his work. She was a big girl, and he knew with her stubbornness it wouldn't make any difference anyway.

By the time Ken finished the books it was early Friday morning, November 9. Ken noticed that the kitchen wall clock read 2:35 A.M. He was exhausted and ready for bed, but Teresa was flying. Ken dragged himself upstairs and fell into bed, too tired to care that Teresa stayed downstairs. He awoke to the smell of coffee. Teresa's side of the bed hadn't been slept in. When he entered the kitchen, breakfast was waiting. He kissed them both and sat down. She had already fed and diapered Philip.

"What happened last night?" Ken asked.

Teresa shrugged, her dark eyes hollow and tired. "I couldn't sleep," she said, cleaning Philip's face. "I felt good so I decided to continue working on Chrissy's outfit until I finished it."

Ken watched her cleaning up the kitchen. She looked exhausted. "When Philip naps today, why not grab one for yourself?" Ken suggested.

"Yeah, I probably will. I'm coming down now and I'm beat."

"How much more coke do you have?"

"Only a few more lines." She looked at him curiously, waiting for criticism. When it didn't come, she said, "Don't worry, I won't do any today. I'll save it for tonight."

Ken glanced up from his coffee. "What's happening tonight?"

"My brother and Kathy are coming over."

"Damn," Ken muttered softly into his coffee cup. He didn't like the idea at all. Wanting to avoid an argument, Ken gulped down the last of his coffee, kissed them both quickly, and left for the clinic.

144

The morning went smoothly, with a few new patients coming in. Fridays were his favorite days. He could work a half-day, pay his employees, and spend most of the afternoon relaxing at home.

He finished at the clinic and returned home just after two o'clock. Philip was playing in his playpen. The baby was at that pudgy, energetic stage, always laughing and searching for something new that was within his reach. He was always rolling back and forth now, threatening to roll over onto his stomach. It was a moment both he and Teresa were waiting for. The baby never seemed to be still unless he was sleeping. Holding him was like exercising with a giant ball of silly putty. He wanted to *go*. At five months of age he couldn't walk yet, of course, but he was reaching out to the world, twisting his body, pushing with his fat little arms and legs. He was a beautiful little boy, healthy and vigorous, and everytime Ken looked at him he almost burst with pride.

The afternoon with Philip went too quickly. Both Ken and Teresa were laughing out loud as they watched the little ball of pink energy wriggling in his playpen, surrounded by toys and stuffed animals that were too old for him.

Ken remembered that Teresa prepared one of her incredibly delicious Italian meals that evening. She had learned traditional Italian cooking from her mother, and like most things she undertook seriously, she excelled at it. Tonight, her ravioli and thick Italian sausages were exceptional.

It was a good day, Ken recalled, and he felt particularly happy.

Phil and Kathy arrived around nine that evening, and predictably Phil brought a half ounce of cocaine and three bottles of wine.

Phil was a lean, younger version of Teresa—the same

handsome round face, dark Italian eyes and hair. He laid out some lines of coke and opened the wine. The girls joined him, but Ken, who didn't like wine, stuck with his old reliables . . . pot and bourbon.

The group sat around and chatted, mostly about family and their jobs. Teresa and Kathy, a short, pretty blonde, talked for a while about their friends and babies.

Around midnight Ken began to tire. He excused himself and headed for bed. Tomorrow was a work day. On alternate Saturdays he worked at the clinic from 10:00 A.M. to 1:00 P.M. It allowed him to treat a few patients and handle any emergencies. It was a system that let him maximize his time with his family, freeing his Friday afternoons, and allowing him still to have most of the weekend free.

Teresa, Phil, and Kathy stayed up partying, Ken remembered. He wasn't sure of the exact amount, but the three of them had snorted nearly three grams of coke and finished all the wine, Teresa told him later. Ken also noticed that Teresa had plugged into her codeine again and was downing wine like it was water.

The next morning Teresa shook him awake. In the bright morning light, the dark circles under her eyes stood out in stark contrast to her pale skin. She looked like hell, exhausted to the point of collapse. Ken stared at her, wondering what to do . . . or say. With a shock he realized that she had not been to sleep since Wednesday night.

Perhaps sensing that he was about to say something again about her getting high, she tapped him on the butt and said lightly, "Coffee's ready and waiting, sleepyhead."

When Ken walked into the kitchen he saw that she had already fed and changed Philip. She begged off breakfast but joined him for coffee.

146

After the late-night partying, Phil and Kathy had spent the night in the guest room and were still sleeping.

A little hung-over himself from the pot and bourbon, Ken didn't know how to express his concern to Teresa. She had put on some lipstick and a bit of makeup and looked like she was almost back to normal. But Ken knew her too well. He could see she was dragging, forcing herself to function. Anything he said now would, he knew, be taken as criticism. He'd think about it and try to figure out what to say and deal with it tonight.

While Ken finished his breakfast Teresa described her day in a hoarse voice. She planned to leave Philip with her mother and spend the afternoon shopping with her girlfriend, Cindy Diaz.

Saturday was unseasonably warm for November, so after he returned home from the office, Ken puttered in his garden until late afternoon. Teresa was already home, and when he went inside for a drink or to use the toilet, he noticed that she was still into the coke.

The second time he walked in on her she looked up from her sewing, smiled briefly, and murmured something about having to "stay up" that evening. The get-together with Teresa's friend Angela, her husband Peter, and the baby Chrissy had been planned for a long time.

Ken had forgotten all about it. He cursed under his breath. All he wanted was a little time alone with his family. Christ, there never seemed to be any peace. Except for a moment here or there with the baby, or out in his garden for an hour or two, there was always something. Another social evening was the last thing he wanted—and the last thing Teresa needed. Another long night of partying. He prayed that the evening would be canceled.

147

But no such luck. Angela, Peter, and Chrissy arrived at seven-thirty, and the first thing the girls did was to try on Chrissy's new outfit. Teresa had done an outstanding job on creating the cowgirl clothes. Both Angela and Chrissy were thrilled with the little skirt, blouse, and matching vest. The whole outfit could have come directly from the window of a Fifth Avenue boutique in Manhattan.

As Ken had expected, the evening was boring. He and Peter had little in common, so they talked about nothing in particular, just the usual social chitchat. But thankfully it was also a relaxing, quiet night. Angela and Peter weren't heavily into drugs, and it was a welcome break from the partying that had been so common on other weekends. A few drinks were had, but nothing like the night before, with Phil and Kathy. Ken was relieved. Two days and nights were enough. Maybe things were getting back to normal.

Around nine o'clock Teresa followed Ken into the kitchen and clutched his arm. Her eyes were sunken inside dark circles.

"I'm exhausted, Ken. I really need to do some coke."

"For Christ's sake, Teresa. Let's just ask them to leave, and go to bed."

"No, I couldn't. It's too early. Just keep them busy for a few minutes while I do some lines in the bathroom." She reached up and kissed him lightly. "I won't be long, honey. Please?"

He didn't like it, but she was obviously at the end of her strength. "Okay, Teresa. But that's it, then we ask for an early evening and go to bed."

"Thanks, sweet." She started for the bathroom, then turned. "Do you want some?"

Ken shook his head and finished filling the ice bucket.

"Just thought I'd ask," Teresa said. "Sometimes

148

you do some lines when you're tired."

Peter and Angela did finally leave around ten-thirty. Ken helped them carry the bundles of baby stuff Teresa was giving them to their car and said goodnight.

Teresa was having another drink and sitting on the couch watching the late news when he came back in. He poured himself another drink and joined her.

When the news was finished, Ken stood up and stretched. He picked up their glasses and took them into the kitchen. "I'm exhausted, honey. Let's go to bed," he said when he returned.

"Okay, I'll just clean up a little and then do a couple of lines of coke. I won't be long. Why don't you wait up for me?"

She smiled, her dark eyes suggestive. He recognized the look but ignored it.

A volatile mix of pent-up anxiety and anger at her irresponsibility flashed through him.

"Wait for you?" he said, his voice heavy with irritation. "For Christ's sake, Teresa, if you start snorting more coke you'll be up all night again. Do you realize you haven't slept since Wednesday night?"

Teresa stared at him, her hand on her hip. It was her "ready for battle" stance.

As he looked at her pale, exhausted face, a surge of panic rushed through him. For the first time it hit him full force that maybe she was hooked. "What's going on with you, anyway?" he asked, cooling off. "Don't you know when to stop?"

"Oh, and you do?" she snapped. "Since when have you become so holier than thou?"

Controlling his anger, Ken bit off a nasty retort. She was in trouble and arguing wouldn't help.

"Okay," he said. "Have it your way, but you just can't continue snorting blow, popping codeine, and flushing it down with booze."

149

Her expression softened. "Look, Ken, nothing's wrong. I know I haven't slept. But I'm fine, just tired and a little disoriented. Go ahead to bed. I promise I'll just do a few more lines and then I'll join you."

She grinned, her large dark eyes sparkling. "Maybe I'll even wake you up, if you understand what I'm saying."

"Sure," he said, kissing her lightly. "Just try to get some sleep. Don't you have a baby shower or something tomorrow?"

"Yes, tomorrow afternoon. Don't worry, honey. I'll be fine."

Upstairs Ken checked on Philip, who was sleeping peacefully. Then he brushed his teeth and slipped on his pajamas. The late nights, alcohol, and pot were beginning to take their toll on him, too. He fell asleep within minutes of hitting the bed.

Suddenly Ken was awake. He swore he had heard a telephone. Still groggy with sleep, he sat up and glanced at the bedside clock. It was after 3 A.M. He listened for a moment, but everything was quiet. Since he had to relieve himself, he got up and walked across the hall to check on Philip, who was still fast asleep. After using the toilet he looked out over the stairway landing, searching for Teresa.

She was in the living room, on the telephone.

"Teresa," he called down from the landing, "who's on the phone?"

"Oh, Ken, come here," she said, turning her head to look up the stairs. "C'mon, you've got to hear this."

"For Christ's sake, what now?" he mumbled, too tired to care who was on the damn phone.

Teresa handed him the phone, pressing it against his ear. A woman's voice was purring descriptive obscenities. In a soft, sexy voice she described what she wanted to do to the listener.

150

Ken handed the phone back to Teresa, dumbfounded. She had dialed one of those porno "phone-sex" numbers.

Teresa listened to the last of the tape while Ken stared at her, too surprised to speak. This wasn't at all like Teresa.

What the hell was going on?

She had always been one of the most sexually active women he had ever known, but this wasn't her style. She had never made "phone-sex" calls before. At least, it had never shown up on their telephone bills. True, she had her own telephone credit card, but the calls would have been reflected on the bill anyway.

When she hung up, Ken was still staring at her. "What the hell is happening, Teresa?" he asked.

She looked up at him, her face white, ravaged with exhaustion.

"That was wild, wasn't it? Look," she said, grabbing a *Hustler* magazine on the table. "Jeff and my sister were over last week and left this magazine," she said, leafing through the pages and stopping at an ad for phone sex.

"Jeff and Celeste were reading it and I forgot I put it in the magazine rack. I was really buzzing from the coke, so when I picked it up I found these listings."

Irritated now with lack of sleep and worry, Ken snapped, "I'm not the least interested in Jeff's *Hustler*, Teresa. This isn't like you. You're so high you're going over the edge."

Teresa grinned, immune to the anger in his voice. "Oh, I am high, it feels *soooo* good," she said sexily, touching the front of his pajamas.

She smiled up at him, her full lips open. "Look, I'll call another number. You listen to the woman and I'll give you something else to think about while she talks dirty to you."

151

"You're out of your mind. I'm going to bed. How much blow did you do, anyway? As if you'd know."

"Oh, come on," she said, dialing the telephone. "Just one more."

"To tell you the truth, you scare the hell out of me, sometimes."

"Bullshit," she said, listening as the phone rang. "I don't scare anybody."

"I can see you've done more than just a couple of lines, Teresa. And I can smell the bourbon on your breath. You couldn't sleep now even if you wanted to."

"No, I couldn't sleep, and I don't want to," she said. "Here, here she is, listen," she said gleefully, holding the phone out to him.

"Christ, Teresa, I don't want to talk this out all over again now. Whether you know it or not, you're a wreck and you've got to come to bed."

"No, I'm fine. I feel great," she said, pressing the phone to her ear.

"Yeah, sure you do," he said, shaking his head.

"Okay, I can see you're flying and you're not going to come down for a while. I'm going to bed."

Depressed and more than a little irritated, Ken walked back upstairs. She had never been this bad before. They'd both had their fair share of stupid highs, but this was really over the line. Maybe it's because she hasn't slept in three days, Ken thought. Either way, whether it was because of the dope, booze, or no sleep, this couldn't continue.

He stopped at the top of the stairs and looked back down at Teresa. She was dialing another listing. He shook his head, more sad than angry now. They'd have to have it out tomorrow. It couldn't go on.

In bed he stared into the darkness, Teresa's voice and her occasional giggle drifting up to him. He took a long time falling asleep, and when he finally drifted off, his sleep was fitful, unpleasant dreams coming and going rapidly.

When he awoke again at 7:30 Sunday morning, November 11, memories of the night before flooded back. The anxiety he felt pressed in on him as he went into the baby's room and found the crib empty.

Ken got halfway down the stairs and his anxiety was obliterated by a surge of shock and disbelief. Stunned immobile, he stood on the stairs and stared into the dining room, trying to comprehend what he was seeing.

It was a scene he would never forget. Ken recalled vividly seeing Teresa leaning over the table where she had placed the baby, probably in order to change his diapers. Her skirt was raised in back, bunched up over her hips, her panties down over her buttocks. Her right hand was fondling herself from behind.

Still disbelieving, his mind unable to accept the image before him, and almost in a trance, he watched Teresa's bobbing head. Then, as if a telepathic link had suddenly made her aware of his presence, she looked back over her right shoulder.

What he had not wanted to see was now agonizingly plain. The naked baby lay quietly on the table, his swaddling clothes jumbled around him.

Teresa's hair had fallen over her cheek, straggily and unkempt. Her mouth was wet, her eyes dull. She seemed an animal surprised at some primitive ritual. But she didn't move, didn't try to hide what she was doing. Ken could swear that she was simply unaware of the enormity of her mistake.

Their eyes met and held. She was alien, worlds apart, existing in a hazy, drug-darkened universe. Neither spoke. She didn't move, her face gravestone pale, her expression uncomprehending. All this had taken only a few seconds of real time.

Then, her mad tangled hair sticking to her perspiring white skin, she shook her head gently back and forth in a quiet rejection . . . he didn't know of what, his unexpected presence or an awakening realization at what she was doing. . . .

Her movement seemed to shake Ken out of his trance; his stomach suddenly rushed up and threatened to burst from his open mouth.

Then he screamed, "What the hell is going . . . oh, my God, *nooooo* . . ." and bolted down the stairs two at a time, a hot anger racing through him. This was it. Enough . . . enough. The whole damn thing would stop now.

Ken Taylor's continuing description of what must have been a horrendous moment (if true) sounds cool and manipulative, even disingenuous. Relating this most shocking scene, he writes that his emotions as he bounds down the stairs to confront his wife sexually abusing his child were "confused and very angry, but I was not combative at this point. I was determined to make Teresa take charge of herself and seek immediate therapy."

At other moments in his description there is more a tone of plausibility.

"The woman who stared at me was not Teresa. This was some zombie, some possessed, diabolic clone of the woman who was my wife."

Even as he sprang down the stairs two at a time, roaring with anger, he could see that Teresa's face didn't register any recognition. She stared at him with

154

glazed confusion, her eyes holding on him impassively.

"That brief moment," Taylor wrote, "maybe two or three seconds as our eyes held, seemed like an eternity."

As Ken reached the bottom of the stairs Teresa suddenly broke from her spell, turned, and ran into the kitchen. Ken dashed into the dining room, picked up Philip, and secured him in his infant seat attached to the table.

Still furious, he followed her into the kitchen. It was empty; she had run on into the sewing room.

All the time he was following her, rolling over in the heat of his anger was the thought that the "party was definitely over. Teresa had gone over the edge now."

According to Ken's recollection, as he entered the doorway to the sewing room (which also contained his weights and workout equipment), he sensed a blur of movement to his left. He ducked as Teresa swung a five-pound dumbbell at his head. The blow missed his head and struck him on the shoulder. The force of that blow, combined with the quick jerking away of his head and body, threw him off balance, and he fell into the doorway. He lay on his back, his legs sticking out into the hallway, when Teresa leaped on him and began flailing at his chest and face.

A dumbbell bar—without any weights on the end— was propped against the base of the door to keep it open. Ken grabbed it and rolled to his right, knocking Teresa off him. He leaped to his feet. Teresa was up again, crouched like a wild animal. Her face had been transformed into a red, angry mask. She seemed a woman possessed, her mind ravaged by drugs and alcohol.

When she sprang at him, swinging wildly, he struck out, smashing the metal handle into her head.

"The blow snapped her head back, but she shrugged it off like a horse shooing away a fly. She was so high

155

she felt no pain. She was so high that normally painful and destructive blows seemed to have no effect.

"She charged again, swinging her bar. Then I went off. I struck her again. From that point on I functioned in a blackout of fury—fear for myself as well as for my son.

"When I came to, I was in the hallway, my wife on the floor a few feet away."

Blood was everywhere. Teresa's head and face were already unrecognizable. A wet stain was slowly spreading around her head in a scarlet halo.

Ken stared at her. Even before he knelt to feel her pulse he knew.

Teresa was dead.

The hot fury that had possessed him only seconds before was gone, washed away in a flood of confused feelings. Horror, panic, fear, even terror—all mingled in the chaotic swamp of his emotions.

"My God, she's dead, she's dead," he repeated to himself as he knelt beside her, staring. "How could this have happened?" he mumbled. He couldn't think coherently, stunned by the devastating sight before him.

She lay facedown, her arms and legs twisted at unlikely angles. Blood was everywhere. He looked away from Teresa's dead face. Blood had splattered the hall floor and the walls.

"I had never known panic before," he wrote. "Teresa was dead, my own life seemed meaningless at that moment. What could I do? Call the police? Explain what had happened? Who would believe it? Besides, it wasn't Teresa doing that to the baby . . . it was the drugs and booze. Teresa would never hurt the baby if she had been in her right mind."

"Oh, God," he moaned, shaking his head, "it was all so unnecessary. How could it have happened? How could I have lost control that way?"

156

For long moments he stared at her, undecided, not having any idea about what to do next. He realized his life was in ruins. His son's life would also be ruined.

It was the thought of Philip that snapped him from his reverie. He stood up and went into the dining room to check on his son. He stopped in the doorway and stared.

Incredibly, Philip was asleep. . . . He could hardly believe it. Philip was sleeping in his baby seat, blissfully unaware of what had just happened.

Ken stared at the sleeping child. Then his eyes took in the rest of the dining room. The vase of pastel pink, orange, yellow, and white roses that he had bought for Teresa Friday afternoon on his way home from work was on its side, the roses scattered over the table. He had bought the pastel-colored flowers as a change from the usual red roses he was continually bringing home.

The roses had still been fresh Saturday night. Now they were beginning to wither, the petals curling and turning dark around the edges.

The longer he stared at his sleeping child and the violent confusion of spilled flowers and overturned chairs in the dining room, the deeper it sank in: his life was over. Teresa was dead.

He shook his head. It had all been so sudden, so swift, so final. He couldn't think clearly, but he knew one thing—that it was all over.

"I had killed her. I hadn't divorced her, I hadn't left her . . . I killed her."

The thought of her bloody face pressed into the hallway floor just a few feet away horrified and depressed him. "There would be no happy endings. No second chances, no rebirths."

Philip. He had to get the baby away from this. He'd take him to his parents in Indiana. But first he'd have to clean up the mess. Hide Teresa. Buy time.

157

It was 9:15 A.M. when he walked back into the hallway and stood above Teresa's body.

He remembered the gray carpet padding in the spare room. He returned down the hall and grabbed a length of it, wrapped Teresa's body in it, and carried the body through the kitchen, dining room, hallway, and into the garage. He put the heavy bundle on the floor and opened the trunk of Teresa's Oldsmobile Cutlass. He remembered how excited she had been to get the car . . . and how she loved driving it. He gently placed her body into the trunk and closed the lid.

He was on automatic now, one plan energizing everything else: clean up the mess and get Philip to Indiana.

He washed the blood off the floor and wallpaper and carefully rinsed the mop and cleaning sponges. The activity must have disturbed the baby because he slowly woke up.

Ken mixed some formula, fed the baby, changed his diaper, and then dressed him in warm clothes. He packed several cans of formula and a few toys and gathered up a bundle of the baby's clothes and put the whole load in the backseat of the car. Then he strapped Philip into his carseat and secured it in the front seat of the Cutlass.

In his prison diary, he wrote: "We left the house on a journey that I believed would surely be the last few days that I would ever see him."

Chapter Eleven

Ken drove out of New Jersey in a daze, his mind and emotions numb. As he wrote later, "I was on automatic pilot. I didn't consciously think 'what if?' I'm pulled over. 'What if' I have an accident? Those concerns were for the hopeful. If I allowed my mind to think of anything except my single purpose I believe my control would have broken. I had one goal in mind, to drive to my parents' home and leave my son. Then I would return to New Jersey and end my own life."

But Teresa's image kept coming back to him. Her face, both smiling and broken, grinning happily and pressed into the bloody floor, kept creeping into his consciousness as he drove. But she had wanted their son to be with his parents if anything happened to her. She had wanted this.

In Stroudsburg, Pennsylvania, he pulled off Interstate 80 into a fast-food restaurant parking lot. Philip had begun crying. He was hungry.

Ken fed Philip in the car, cleaned him up, and then took him into the restaurant. He needed a cup of coffee to keep going.

He hadn't made any reservations for the night, but

he noticed a motel across the street. After he had eaten he took Philip into the restaurant's men's room and changed his diaper and dressed him in a fresh pair of pants. The men's room was smelly and depressing, but Philip didn't seem to mind. He was grinning and cooing as Ken clumsily changed him, completely unaware of the painful reality he was living through.

Ken decided against staying at the motel. It was too early and he wanted to make the trip as quick as possible.

A light snow began to fall as the sun set, and the driving became more difficult. Still in Pennsylvania, Ken again pulled off I-80 and stopped at a Holiday Inn.

Glancing at the baby, the desk clerk asked him how many people would be registering.

Placing Philip on the counter next to him, Ken automatically answered, "three."

The clerk began to write it down and Ken suddenly said, "No, two. I'm sorry, just two."

The man looked curiously at him. Ken smiled weakly. "Tired, it's been a long drive."

As he registered, the clerk continued to glance up at him curiously—probably because he was a single father traveling alone, Ken thought.

Ken asked if the motel provided a baby bed and one of the clerks, a woman, smiled and said, "Of course. We'll have one sent to your room right away, sir."

She grinned at Philip, who was contentedly staring at all the new and strange sights around him. "He's so cute," she said, reaching out and caressing his hair.

Ken drove the car around to the back of the motel and parked near the room. He had begun to think of the Cutlass bitterly as "the Oldsmobile hearse," and when he walked past the locked trunk with Philip in his arms, he paused abruptly, freezing for a few seconds, staring at the closed lid. He didn't let his mind linger on the corpse wrapped in its gray cocoon inside. The images were too painful.

Moments later, as he was undressing Philip, the crib arrived.

He fed him again, changed his diapers, and put him in the crib.

Once Philip had gone to sleep, Ken, who was emotionally drained himself, collapsed onto the bed. One more long day of driving and it would be over. He felt he was functioning "as a living dead man, void of feelings."

The snow fell lightly outside the curtained window and Ken almost immediately fell into a deep, troubled sleep.

He dreamed that night, vivid dreams he would remember clearly but not understand the significance of until almost a year later when he sat in the New Jersey Department of Corrections reception area in Yardsville, waiting to be transferred to Trenton State Prison.

In his dream Teresa was explaining to him how much he reminded her of the William Hurt character in the movie *Body Heat*. She had often made the same comment to him before. For some reason his personality reminded her of the sexy, romantic character played by Hurt.

As he sat in the prison at Yardsville a year later watching a video of *Body Heat*, he was reminded of the dream and began to see uncanny parallels with his own life.

The character Hurt played in the film was having an intense affair with a woman portrayed by Kathleen Turner. The woman wanted Hurt to kill her husband. In a plot twist, Turner's character had also set up her own "murder" as well—but in fact, the person killed would be another woman.

The dream that night in the Holiday Inn was full of dark images, violence, and passion, and it all came back to haunt him. Coincidence or not, Ken was struck hard by the twisted parallels that day in the Yardsville prison.

He awoke early Monday morning, November 12, ordered coffee from room service, changed Philip's diapers again, and bathed and dressed him.

In the restaurant Ken fed Philip and had a light breakfast himself. Philip quickly became the center of attention with the waitresses.

After breakfast, Ken returned to the room. He had to call his office, to buy some time and to delay discovery of what had happened at any cost until he got Philip to his parents.

He called the Grandview Avenue office. Phil Benigno was scheduled to work that day, and when he picked up, Ken told him "hurriedly and shakily that Teresa had a severe drug problem."

As Ken told Teresa's brother the story about her trip to "dry out once and for all," he sensed that Phil was skeptical, but he didn't care. "The lie bought me time to get across Pennsylvania and Ohio and maybe even half of Indiana."

On the road the morning sky before him was a dull sheet of soft snow. As the snow continued to fall, everything was tainted a morbid gray color. It was a miserable morning, giving the day's travel a surreal quality, something like a silent movie with fleeting pictures quietly swooshing past, not touching him or Philip in the comfortable cocoon of the smooth-running car.

Around noon he stopped again in a roadside restaurant to change and feed Philip. As he had a quick

162

sandwich and two cups of coffee his thoughts kept returning to Teresa's corpse in the trunk but he couldn't let his mind linger too long on the bloody images.

They continued west through Ohio, and at dusk he stopped for dinner and called his parents, giving them the same lie he had told Phil. They sounded puzzled but seemed to accept what he told them. They said they'd wait up for him. He and Philip then got back in the car for the last leg of the trip. He hoped to make his parents' home by midnight.

When he finally reached Marion he was exhausted. It was well after midnight as he handed Philip to his mother.

Jean recalled that as he gave her Philip, he said, "Son, you're in safe hands now."

Jean cuddled the child and said, "I'd better change and feed him.

"Be sure to look at his penis," Jean recalls Ken saying, "and wash his genitals carefully." The remark puzzled her at the time but she let it go. The baby's genitals looked fine to her. There wasn't even any diaper rash.

A tense moment developed when Ken's brother Tom went to get the luggage. He carried Ken's overnight bag and the baby's things in from the backseat, then returned and tried the trunk.

He turned to Ken, "Hey, you got the key, your trunk's locked."

"No," Ken said quickly, "that's all the bags. There's nothing in the trunk."

As Ken replayed the story about Teresa's drug problems and her need to get away, his parents seemed sympathetic but slightly puzzled.

163

During the conversation it became clear that Jean and Zach knew something was wrong, but they had no idea of the extent of it, no way of knowing that their daughter-in-law's body was in the trunk of the car in their driveway. That grisly knowledge was kept from them until Ken was arrested.

The next morning, after shopping for diapers and a week's formula for Philip, Ken suddenly decided that he had to leave. He had intended to stay in Marion for two or three days, but it was probably better if he got back, he told his mother.

"I hope the baby won't be too much trouble," he told his mother.

"Of course not," Jean replied. Later Jean recalled that Ken seemed "depressed, not like himself at all," during this short visit.

After Ken had called Zach at work to explain that he was going back to New Jersey and had driven off, Jean found a twenty-dollar bill in her drawer. A note attached to it said simply, "Thanks, Love, Ken."

"That was my son," Jean thought. "Always thoughtful."

While shopping for Philip's diapers that morning Ken had begun thinking about his daughter. He decided that he would drive home via Pittsburgh and stop off and see Rhonda on the way.

He arrived at Marilyn's condo late Tuesday night, a little before midnight. He had called Marilyn and she was expecting him. Ken remembers her greeting as happy; she seemed excited to see him. She made him a grilled cheese sandwich and listened sympathetically to his story about Teresa's sudden departure. Of course, she had no idea that Teresa lay dead in the trunk of

164

the Oldsmobile parked in front of her door while her ex-husband ate his midnight snack.

Ken and Marilyn slept together that night, but there was no sex, no laughter. The evening together was subdued. Marilyn did notice that Ken seemed remote and preoccupied, but she attributed it to his concern over Teresa's disappearance. Under the circumstances, sex seemed inappropriate. They both quickly fell asleep on their own sides of the bed.

Wednesday morning was difficult for Ken. He played a game with Rhonda in the living room and took her for a short walk before it was time for her afternoon kindergarten class.

Then it was time to go. He kissed Marilyn good-bye and she mentioned a birthday party that Rhonda had been invited to the following Saturday. Rhonda said she would love it if he could make it.

Ken said he would try. It was almost impossible for him to think that far into the future. He was acutely aware that Teresa's body was still in the trunk.

"As he drove east on the interstate, back toward New Jersey, his mind was a jumble of unfinished images, of incomplete thoughts. He couldn't imagine what to do next.

"What am I doing?" he asked himself. "Here I am, transporting my dead wife back and forth across several state lines. Driving her corpse all over, not knowing what to do with it. The whole thing was insane."

At this point Ken Taylor claims that he began contemplating suicide. Thoughts about his children, his family, Teresa's family, were driving him crazy. What should he do?

"Call the police? Kill myself and deprive my children even more? Oh, God. I'll be caught. I'll be in prison . . . prison is death. . . ."

He drove on, the sun passing behind him, the shadows of dusk appearing in front of him as the road snaked eastward.

The jolting, disjointed thoughts continued to tumble over in his mind. "To live, to die," he later wrote, "children, family, to go to prison, prison is death, but if I die, Philip and Rhonda will survive."

Finally, his own death seemed the only thing left that made any sense.

Somewhere in Pennsylvania he pulled into a gas station, filled the tank, and then drove to the end of the lot. He sat there in the car, trying to figure out what to do. It seemed his life was over, yet the visit to Marilyn and Rhonda seemed to fill him with hope. And then Philip. He needed a father, even one in prison.

Ken couldn't take it anymore. He had to move. He drove out of the station and down a rural back road. He saw a sign that read, "Hawk Mountain Bird Sanctuary." He followed the arrow. When he saw the entrance to the sanctuary, he suddenly decided he would live, try to survive, and turned left into the drive.

A short way down the road, barely fifty yards, he pulled to the side and switched off the ignition. Moving quickly, fearful of being seen, he opened the trunk and removed the heavy lump of gray carpet padding that contained Teresa's body.

He had no plans to hide the body . . . he just wanted to be free of it. He didn't even carry it into the woods but dropped the carpet-wrapped body a few yards off the road.

He realized that the body would probably be found soon, but his instinct was simply to "buy more time" — for what, he didn't know. He was still swinging on the emotional pendulum of whether to live or die, to try and survive, even if it meant going to jail, or end it all

166

now — commit suicide and get all the confusion and pain over with.

When he arrived home he had calmed himself enough to call his parents — and Teresa's parents as well. In his diaries he wrote, "I answered their questions, my mind shifting through the questions dully. I was responding with no conscious idea of what I was saying. I knew I was continuing the lie . . . the big lie. But I could think of nothing else to say.

"What could I say — that I had killed my wife, that I had killed your daughter in a crazy moment of blind anger?"

After the telephone conversations he had to "get out of that house, the death house," the house with the dead roses on the dining room table.

He hurriedly left the house, a fifth of Jack Daniels on the seat next to him. He drove mindlessly toward Staten Island, gulping shots of bourbon as he went. He needed to drink, to try to calm the wild, echoing thoughts running through his mind. After a while the heavy doses of bourbon knocked off the edge of his panic and quieted his runaway thoughts.

As he crossed the Outerbridge Crossing between Staten Island and New Jersey, he made a sharp right and drove toward the Black Garter Saloon, an old haunt.

"It was a place where I had spent many afternoons watching the dancers and downing shots of bourbon. I'd find respite, solace in the familiar surroundings."

The noisy bar, the drinks, and the familiar dancers did divert him. The din of the place overwhelmed the internal noise of his mind and gave him a kind of uneasy peace. He resolved that he should die.

"In prison, alive, I would be of no use to any of my loved ones — especially the children. I would be an embarrassment, a humiliation to all."

167

He pulled into the Valley Road garage and shut the door behind him. He connected the swimming pool filter hose to the exhaust pipe and snaked the other end of the hose along the side of the car and up into the back window.

He sat behind the wheel, took several long pulls on the Jack Daniels, and waited for the exhaust to fill the car. He waited and waited. Nothing happened. He couldn't smell any fumes. The car was not filling with the exhaust.

Frustrated, his conviction about dying waning, he got out and discovered that the pool hose had fallen off the exhaust pipe.

"I shut off the engine, visions of my children danced through my mind. Did my children, my family, deserve my death like this in addition to the tragedy of Teresa? I knew I wanted to join Teresa, but something prevented me from completing the act."

Ken realized that the path of Teresa's death, once the body was discovered, would lead back to him. "I knew I'd be arrested, tried, and convicted of some form of manslaughter. Screw it . . . what will be, will be."

He turned and went into the house and fell asleep.

On Thursday morning, November 15, after talking with Celeste, he called the police department to report Teresa missing. He had a hangover from the previous night's drinking, but he was still functioning. When David Visconi, the Manalapan patrolman sent out to the house to interview him about Teresa left, he began drinking again.

All Thursday afternoon he continued to drink large amounts of bourbon.

Late Thursday, Celeste called again about the possibility of Teresa having gone to Michigan with her girlfriend. The Benignos were distraught and grasping at any straw.

"What could I tell them?" he thought. "I'm crazy, or damn close to it? That Teresa's dead? That I killed her? That her body is in some backwoods of Pennsylvania? Surely, I couldn't tell them what had happened. I would simply have to ride out the storm, wait for my arrest, for the final solution."

Time and again Ken continued to go through the charade of living out his lie—talking to the Benignos, taking airport trips, showing Teresa's photo to employees at the airlines and in restaurants. One day dissolved into another, with everyone frantically trying to find Teresa, and Ken continuing the story of her sudden flight from Newark. He still had nothing more to say—nothing to tell the people buzzing around him desperately looking for answers—at least nothing he thought would make any sense.

When Detective Fausak arrived to question him on Friday, Ken thought his time had come. He thought that they had come to arrest him. Then he discovered they were still just searching, asking questions—it was all simply another step toward the inevitable finale. At that moment, facing Fausak, and during the walk through the house with Fausak's eyes darting everywhere, he "could see the curtain beginning to fall on the hideous tragedy that I had been playing out for five days now."

But time was short now. The lie was almost over. There was only another day to go. He'd have one more quick trip to see Marilyn and Rhonda the next day—one more time, he thought, for one last visit, enjoy the freedom of going to a child's birthday party, of spending the day with his "other" family. Then came the late night call from his father, the pained conversation with

Lieutenant Vanderweil, and the final trip back to Manalapan.

"Many have described my behavior during this period as sinister and calculating," Ken Taylor wrote later. "Calculating, yes, I was. Sinister? Absolutely not. I was calculating my last minutes on earth. There was no thought to the future, no consideration of being caught, arrested, or a trial. I honestly felt like I was a dying man."

Chapter Twelve

After Jean and Zach had their tearful reunion with Ken in the jail on Sunday, Detective Fausak drove them back to the Valley Road house, where they would stay for the time being. They were shaken by the sudden turn of events and the appalling fact that Ken had actually killed Teresa. But Zach had to pull himself together—his first task was to get Ken a good lawyer. He was to be arraigned the next day, Monday, November 19.

That Sunday evening, Ken was moved from the Manalapan station to an isolation cell in the more permanent Monmouth County Jail in Freehold. It was a barren, dark cell that fed his depression. His thoughts were random, vague, disruptive fantasies of "what might have been."

He stared at the green sheet of paper next to his cell door that read "Murder . . . purposely and wiling . . ."

"The words bothered me immensely," he wrote. He began to contemplate what would happen to him. "Surely I would beat a first-degree murder charge. But what about the lesser offenses? How much time would I serve? I had no idea."

As he reviewed all that had happened in the insane week just past, his thoughts again turned to Teresa, and he suddenly realized that he wanted to attend her funeral. His request that evening, which most people reacted to with disgust, was immediately turned down by the Benignos. Even the jail guards thought he was weird for asking to do such a thing.

"In fact," he wrote in his prison diary, "my initial request of my jailers to allow me to attend her funeral, or even to 'see' my wife in a private viewing if the Benignos objected, was viewed as bizarre and macabre. What the fuck did those goons know? I asked myself. I realized that I was now on my own and must face the whole crazy situation stoically."

Ken then asked for some letter writing materials.

He addressed his first letter to his family, "Mom, Dad, Philip, and Tom." He wrote:

> What I did was done out of disgust for what I saw Teresa doing and when she swung the dumbbell at my head, I lost all control. I had become increasingly disgusted with her periods of withdrawal and associated losses of money as a result of her habit. . . . I became enraged but only when she swung at me did I touch her. Please use this to help you keep Philip for me. I want you to be his parents as well as Tom. Fight to keep him for me.

Another letter went to Marilyn and Rhonda:

> My Mom and Dad know what happened. I know I can't make it in this environment. I wanted so much for us all to be together. If only I had slept a little longer I would not have seen Teresa doing fellatio on my baby. I'm so sick inside and I really believe I'll be here for a long, long time.

The Taylor Family circa 1960. Eleven-year-old Kenneth stands between his brother Tom and his sister Nancy. *(Courtesy of Zach and Jean Taylor)*

Ken Taylor as a young Naval officer. *(Courtesy of Zach and Jean Taylor)*

Ken with his mother, Jean (left) and his grandmother at the Benigno home the day before his wedding to Teresa.
(Courtesy of Zach and Jean Taylor)

Ken and Teresa Taylor as they walked down the aisle after taking their wedding vows. *(Courtesy of Zach and Jean Taylor)*

Enjoying a midday meal at Las Brisas, Mexico, Ken and Teresa on their honeymoon.
(Courtesy of Zach and Jean Taylor)

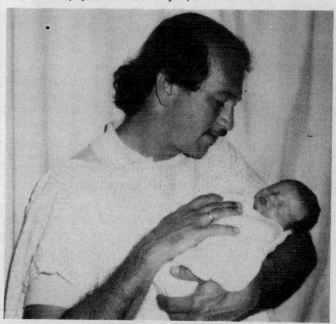

Ken Taylor, the proud father of his newborn son, Philip.
(Courtesy of Zach and Jean Taylor)

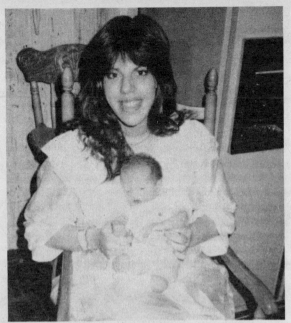

Teresa Taylor with Philip in June, 1984.
(Courtesy of Zach and Jean Taylor)

Teresa, Philip and Ken at the Taylor home in Marion, Indiana in September, 1984.
(Courtesy of Zach and Jean Taylor)

Kenneth Z. Taylor upon his arrest for the murder of Teresa.

Teresa's body as it was found near Hawk Mountain, Pennsylvania.

The Taylor home in New Jersey.

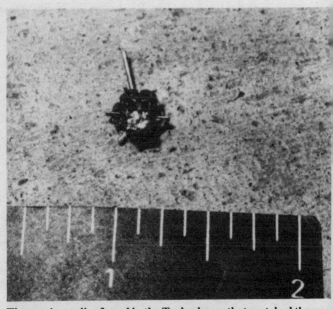

The earring police found in the Taylor home that matched the one found on Teresa's body.

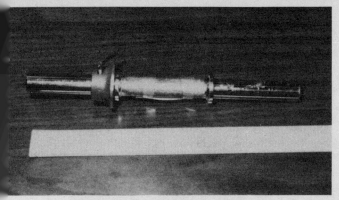

The hand weight Ken used to kill Teresa.

Zach and Jean Taylor with Philip on a visit to Ken in November, 1985.

Kenneth Z. Taylor during a prison visit with the author in June, 1991.

I truly loved you and I know that you know it. We were on our way but someone still got in our way. Maybe it was wrong from the very beginning. Please give Rhonda the best and always let her know just how much I love her. You gave me the greatest gift in the world—a child. Try to let her know how much I love you and her. All my love.

Monday morning Zach scanned the Yellow Pages and found a lawyer, Barry Shapiro, who, it happened, lived on Valley Road just three houses down from Ken and Teresa. The attorney had never met either of the Taylors, but when Zach called him he already knew of the case. It was headlined in the local newspaper, the *Asbury Park Press*. A four-column lead story blared, *"Dentist Charged With Killing His Wife and Dumping Body."*

Shapiro reluctantly agreed to represent Ken at the arraignment, but beyond that he could do nothing. He had recently been elected to the Manalapan Township Council and felt it would be a conflict of interest if he represented him during the trial.

Monday morning Ken's cell door clanged open. A heavy-set guard, his belly hanging over his thick belt, held a tray of food. Ken drank the lukewarm coffee and ate the cold toast (no butter or jelly) but ignored the solid lump of cold oatmeal.

Shortly after breakfast he was led to a room dubbed "the tank," where he joined several other prisoners waiting to be transported to various courtrooms around the state.

Ken was the only prisoner designated to go to the Manalapan courthouse. In an effort to "look presentable" he had changed from the county-issued khaki clothes prisoners wore to the same stale suit he had been arrested in.

Barry Shapiro met Ken in the visitor's room at the Manalapan police station that morning. Shapiro was about Ken's age. He was a short, intense man who without his moustache would have looked years younger.

Shapiro greeted Ken pleasantly, but then the first words from his mouth were, "First of all I want you to know that I can't represent you beyond this arraignment."

He would be happy, however, to give Ken the names of several good lawyers whom he might want to contact.

"Fine," Ken said. "But what about today?"

"Today you do nothing and say nothing. The court is swarming with reporters. Have you seen this?"

Shapiro passed a copy of that day's *Asbury Park Press* across the table.

The four-column headline and article covered most of the front page. A colored detailed map showed where he had killed Teresa and another where the body was found.

It was clear that the press was seizing on the most macabre aspects of the case—and especially on Ken's gruesome trip through four states with his wife's corpse in the trunk.

The story by reporter William Conroy quoted Monmouth County's first assistant prosecutor, Paul Chaiet, who had been assigned the case, as saying that "we believe the husband was solely responsible for her death."

In the article Chaiet wouldn't comment on motive or the circumstances leading up to the slaying, but he did say that the weapon used was "some sort of blunt instrument." Chaiet wouldn't say whether the investigation had yet turned up the weapon.

The Taylors' next-door neighbors, Lawrence and Susan D'Ambrosa, were quoted as saying that they were shocked by the news. The D'Ambrosas also said that the Taylors didn't mix much with those in the neighborhood. "He seemed more outgoing than Mrs. Taylor," Mr. D'Ambrosa said.

Mr. D'Ambrosa remembered only one time that the Taylors had him over for iced tea. And he had only one "real conversation with Mrs. Taylor, in which she said that she was having a difficult pregnancy and could not walk upstairs to see the room that had been converted into a nursery for the expected child."

"The one odd thing about the couple," Mrs. D'Ambrosa said, was that "I never saw her out at all. I remember her saying to my husband, after their baby was born, that with a baby you have to go to the doctor, and shop for food, but you never saw her. It seemed like she never came out of the house."

"They had a lot of people come and visit them, though," Mr. D'Ambrosa said. "They gave barbecues."

Ken tossed the paper aside.

"Let them print what they want," he said. "I'm sure they're going to make a circus out of this."

"They already have," Shapiro said. "The story is front-page news in the New York papers as well."

"Great," Ken said sullenly.

"When you walk into the courtroom this morning, be prepared. Flashbulbs will be popping. The media smell blood, and they really want this case."

"Will all this hype hurt my case?" Ken asked.

"No doubt about it," Shapiro said. "Look, we'll talk all this out this afternoon. I have enough information from your father to answer the press this morning. In court today it's all just a formality. You'll stand next to me. I'll plead "Not Guilty" and a trial date will be set and then you'll go back to jail."

The guard abruptly opened the door and said, "You're on, counselor."

175

Ken was led handcuffed and shackled into the courtroom and the place lit up like a first night on Broadway as a quick, blinding series of flashbulbs exploded when Ken and Shapiro walked to the front of the docket.

As Shapiro had predicted, the formal arraignment before Judge Leslie B. Tinkler was brief and functional. Around three o'clock that afternoon Ken Taylor was charged with murder and a court date was set for January. But it would only be a formality, Shapiro said. When the Superior Court reconvened next week he would request a reduction of the half-million-dollar bail and another, later trial date would be set.

Shapiro's comments to the press after the arraignment hinted at Ken's motive for the killing. He didn't actually come out and say that Ken had discovered Teresa fellating the baby, but there was enough innuendo so that the next day's headlines were even more sensational — *"Suspect's Lawyer Asserts Slain Wife Abused Infant Son."*

Shapiro was quoted in the article as saying, "I believe that the evidence will show his wife was a drug abuser and did harm to the child, and that precipitated the incident that caused her death."

The papers also quoted Zach Taylor. "Our daughter-in-law had a real drug problem. It was so bad it was threatening and affecting the baby."

In their discussion that afternoon, after hearing the details of Ken's story about the drugs, sleepless nights, and Teresa's sexually abusing the baby, Shapiro suggested that there had been sufficient "mitigating circumstances" so that first-degree murder was out of the question. Manslaughter or possibly even acquittal was more likely when the facts came out at the trial. His best defense, Shapiro said, was probably temporary insanity.

176

This seemed to make sense to Ken. "I *had* lost my mind," he said. "I believe that I was crazy during the whole thing."

As promised, Shapiro also gave Ken the name of three lawyers he might want to contact: Ron Sage, Mike Schotland and Jack Venturi.

Ken returned to his cell and later that evening called Zach and Jean. Zach promised to get hold of the attorneys for him. But in the meantime there was other bad news. The bank in New York that Ken had done business with had closed his accounts after learning of his arrest.

On Tuesday, Teresa was buried. A huge line of more than over one hundred cars followed the hearse to the cemetery. Zach and Jean Taylor decided not to attend the funeral after, they said, they had received "certain firm suggestions" that they stay away.

At the time Teresa's body was being lowered into its grave, Ken was being moved from the isolation cell to a more permanent holding cell in what was called the Grand Jury cellblock. The cellblocks were filthy and cramped. The smell of sweat, urine, male body odor, and mildew was accompanied by the slow waves of cigarette smoke that enveloped the whole cellblock in a gray cloud.

There were four cellblocks in all, fourteen men to each block, with a total of fifty-six men. The county jail system, however, held more than four hundred men at that time. This would be Ken Taylor's new home for some time. He was already getting a taste of what prison life was like—"No privacy, constant noise, one shower stall for fourteen men, institutional tasteless meals. . . Oh, yes, jail is everything one might expect—*plus*. The pressures and tension within a cellblock are so thick that they are nearly visible. It is no wonder that there is so much violence in jail. It is a living, moving volcano constantly on the edge of eruption."

Wednesday, November 21, was a full, difficult day for everyone touched by the Taylor case.

The day after Ken's arraignment on Tuesday, Celeste had telephoned the Manalapan house and talked with Zach. When she asked to see Teresa's baby, Zach agreed easily. "Of course, no problem," he said.

That evening Jeff and Celeste, Al and Louise drove over to the house on Valley Road. The two families were both subdued and carefully polite in their greetings. Every effort was made to avoid an unhealthy confrontation. In fact, Al reportedly told Zach during a private moment, "We don't hold you responsible for what your son did. He's responsible, not you."

Zach's face flushed. He didn't seem pleased.

The Benignos made a fuss over little Philip for a while and then Jean took the baby to bed upstairs. At this point the Benignos did not yet know that Ken had claimed Teresa was drugged out and fellating the baby. Nor did they know that the killing had taken place almost at their feet and her body dragged down the hallway past where they were now sitting.

An uncomfortable moment developed when the subject of Philip came up and Zach happened to mention that they were planning to return home to Indiana the coming Thursday.

Warning glances shot back and forth between the Benignos. They all realized immediately that another crisis had suddenly developed. If little Philip was going to be taken out of New Jersey, they would have no say at all in his custody or what happened to him. He would be gone—maybe for good.

The next morning the Benignos were all at their family lawyer in Staten Island. He couldn't practice in New Jersey, he told them, but he would recommend someone who could. He suggested that they get a "show cause" order to prevent the Taylors from taking the child out of state. A "show cause" order was a quick way of issuing a legal motion where immediate and irreparable harm could be claimed.

On Wednesday, while Teresa was being buried, the "show cause" order was served on Zach and Jean Taylor. The papers claimed that there was reason to believe that the parents of the defendant, now accused of the murder of the child's mother, would soon remove him from the state. The order said that there was a custody issue at stake regarding the five-month-old child, who was a resident of New Jersey, that had to be resolved first.

An emergency hearing in Family Court before Judge Julia Ashby on the order was scheduled for Tuesday, November 27.

The effect of the order was that Zach and Jean, of course, were still free to return to Indiana, but not with the baby.

The bitter and drawn-out battle for custody of five-month-old Philip had begun to move down its twisting, confusing path.

Soon after Ken had confessed to killing Teresa and was arrested, the investigation to gather hard evidence in the case began in earnest. It wasn't enough to have a confession. Hard facts backing up the prosecutor's case had to be found. First, the 1984 Cutlass Supreme that Jean and Zach had driven to Manalapan from the airport (where Marilyn had left it when she returned to Pittsburgh after dropping Ken at the police station) was impounded as evidence.

The house on Valley Road had, of course, been immediately examined by forensic technicians after Kenneth Taylor had confessed. In addition to the earring on the garage floor, the most telling clue they had found was a dumbbell bar without weights that had a brownish stain on one end. Tests showed that the stains were human blood. With so many massive injuries to Teresa's head, there would have been extensive bleeding. However, there were no signs of blood anywhere else in the house. If she had been killed there the place had been well cleaned.

To check for blood not visible to the human eye a special chemical test was requested.

Detective Fausak requested a second search warrant and telephoned the Taylors that he and some men had to come back to the house. Late Wednesday afternoon, on November 21, Detective James Fallano, a member of the New Jersey State Police crime scene investigation unit out of Princeton, along with a forensic chemist, Ted Moser from the state police laboratory at Sea Girt, went to the Taylor home to perform the test. Two other men, one from the prosecutor's office and one from state police lab, accompanied them.

Luminol is a chemical that reacts to the tiniest traces of blood. It's an effective test because nothing in this world is perfectly smooth, and no matter how well cleaned an area is, small particles will be wedged into the pores of any material.

The test had to be conducted in darkness so the investigators waited until it was dark outside and then asked Zach and Jean Taylor, who were staying in the house, to wait in their upstairs bedroom. All the shades were drawn and lights turned off.

The luminol was applied from a bottle with a spray dispenser on top. The investigators started in the laundry room, where Ken said Teresa had swung at him with a dumbbell. As one of the chemists began spraying the luminol around the room a faint greenish haze suddenly glowed on the washing machine. It was only a small spot and the glow was faint.

In the hallway outside, however, there was a startling reaction. The green phosphorescent glow bounced up from the floor.

"Got some here," the chemist said, bending over and spraying the floor behind him as he backpedaled slowly. The glowing track moved around the corner and into the living room. It had been an effective cleaning job and several times they lost the trail, the glow disappearing altogether. Then suddenly it would appear again. At moments the eerie glow was so bright it seemed to light up that part of the room. Apparently there had been a lot of blood.

The most dramatic moment came when a heavy, streaked trail of the green-glowing blood moved past the kitchen to the garage door and then into the garage itself. The bloody trail, which was eventually measured as being close to fifty-five feet, was solid but uneven. The streaked, sporadic quality of the track indicated that something had been dragged along the floor, from the back room to the garage.

To every man in the room the facts were clear. Taylor had killed his wife here, dragged the body to the garage, and put it in the trunk of his car.

Photographs using fluorescent light techniques were taken showing bloodstains on the garage floor, extended drag marks along the corridor leading from the kitchen to the garage, bloodstains on the plywood wall near the garage door.

Detective Fallano later would write in his report: "Results of this test revealed the presence of a large amount of blood throughout the first floor and garage area of the home. Blood splatterings, footprints, and what appeared to be drag marks, as well as areas where blood was apparently wiped off the floor, were all revealed by the test."

This was the first step in a complicated series of moves that the prosecutor's office would take in building its case against Kenneth Taylor—for none of them (and especially the assistant prosecutor Paul Chaiet, who would be handling the case) believed Ken's story about the fellatio and his claim of a "crime of passion." Chaiet was going all the way and shooting for a first-degree murder conviction.

Chapter Thirteen

By the following week Ken had contacted all the lawyers Shapiro had recommended. The first he talked with, Ron Sage, impressed Ken as a dapper, arrogant, high-priced hired gun who was not sufficiently enthusiastic about taking his case.

The next day he met Mike Schotland in the bullpen while he waited to appear in court for a procedural matter concerning the convening of the grand jury. He liked Schotland, who impressed him as being intelligent and clearly competent. But he did not immediately hire him during that initial meeting, for reasons he couldn't put his finger on. Perhaps he wanted to meet all three attorneys before he made his decision; he wasn't sure.

The next day, on November 28, he met Jack Venturi at the jail. At 33, Jack was the youngest of the lawyers Ken had met, and Ken hired him. He liked his aggression and his confidence. He liked the way Venturi said that there was "no way" the state could get a first-degree murder conviction.

Jack Venturi grew up in New Jersey but had graduated from New York University's School of Law. Afterward he had returned to New Jersey and clerked in Newark Superior Court for a judge who specialized in criminal cases. Then he'd done a stint with the New

Jersey Public Defender's Office and another for a prominent law firm before hanging out his own shingle.

In the previous two years he had several minor successes and had even recently won a seven-hundred-thousand-dollar liability case against the Ford Motor Company. His reputation in New Jersey law circles was growing. He was considered smart, capable, and resourceful.

Since Venturi had been practicing on his own for only two years, he didn't have an office in Monmouth County. But this didn't bother Ken. In fact, Ken thought it was a plus. Venturi wouldn't have "to kiss any political or courtroom ass" while defending him.

During their first session together Ken laid out his story again to Venturi—emphasizing Teresa's drug habit. She would go on intense binges, he said, literally racing through two or three grams of coke. For the three days prior to their fight she had not slept, and Ken believed that she was truly out of her mind. He told Venturi about their intense sexual life together, and about Teresa's own lusty habits. Being high on coke, and with that kind of sexual drive, it became plausible that she sexually abused the child. It was a story Venturi could live with.

In Venturi's notes, the lawyer recalls Ken as saying:

"Then it hit me, all of it. Her forging prescriptions, signing medical insurance checks and cashing them, using our money for cocaine and codeine. She couldn't care for our son when she was high. She used me to do it for her. 'Please Ken, I can't handle it when I'm high.'

"I shouted at her, 'What the fuck are you doing?' And she ran, and I went after her, and she came at me with the dumbbell bar, and I hit her."

It occurred to Venturi that the whole thing might

184

have been a mistake, Ken's misunderstanding of innocent playtime with the child, and he asked, "Maybe she was just kissing the baby. You're certain she was doing that? You weren't imagining it?"

"I know she was doing it," Ken answered. "I saw it. Her head was bobbing up and down."

For his part, Venturi was impressed with Ken. He seemed truthful, and telling his story caused him obvious pain. He was more grieved than angry. It didn't seem that there were the necessary ingredients for murder one in New Jersey here. No premeditation, no willful or knowing elements to the case.

Manslaughter would be the most probable charge.

Venturi explained New Jersey law regarding capital cases to Ken. Aggravated manslaughter, which involved "reckless indifference" with a "high probability" that death would result, would bring a twenty-year sentence and a sure ten years with no time off for good behavior.

Reckless manslaughter was similar, but it was defined as having the "possibility" that death would result instead of the "probability." The sentence was therefore less—ten years with a sure five.

Then there was simple manslaughter, the death of someone caused by reasonable "provocation" and occurring in the "heat of passion." Here the judge could show some discretion in sentencing. The maximum would be ten years, but with parole and good behavior he could be out in three years.

Of all the defenses available, several stood out as more likely to succeed. Venturi could probably prove "heat of passion" by showing Teresa's drug use, the general problems and stress in the marriage, Ken's witnessing the fellatio, and Teresa's attacking him with the dumbbell bar—all of it enough, obviously, to arouse the passion to justify Ken's actions.

185

Problems developed, however, when Venturi laid out two other possible defenses: "temporary insanity" and "self-defense and the defense of a third party."

Ken claimed that he had wanted a defense of temporary insanity for he had indeed "blacked out." It was Venturi, Ken said, who insisted self-defense against Teresa's attack (and his defense of his son against her sexual abuse) was the best approach.

But according to Venturi, Ken insisted that he wanted self-defense (and defense of a third party), and he pointed out that this defense presented problems. When Ken had confessed to the police that he had found Teresa performing fellatio on the baby and "gone after her," he had also said, according to the police notes, that he had taken the dumbbell bar from her and "given it to [attacked] her."

The moment he took the bar from her, Venturi explained, she was in fact disarmed and self-defense would therefore no longer apply. According to Venturi's notes, Ken replied that he was under a lot of pressure at the time. He was exhausted and emotionally distraught.

"I was disoriented when I talked with the police," he explained. 'But there were two dumbbell bars. And I was mad as hell when I yelled at her from the stairs. After she tore off through the kitchen, I chased her into the laundry room. I saw a blurred movement as she swung the bar at me and I tried to get out of the way. She got me on the shoulder. I lost my balance and fell on my back in the doorway. She jumped on me and was pounding on my chest and head. There was another bar holding the door, like a doorstop, and I reached over with my left hand and grabbed it. I rolled out from under her and got to my feet. She charged at me with her head down, like she was going to butt me or something. I hit her in the head and she came at

186

me again, dazed-like. Then I hit her again. And that's all I remember. That's the truth."

The strategy of self-defense turned out to be monumentally, disastrously wrong.

As Ken would later say, he regretted allowing Venturi to use "self-defense" during the trial. He believed, he later wrote, that a temporary insanity plea was "more realistic and appropriate" and he should have insisted on it.

"But in all fairness to Venturi," Ken also wrote, "I honestly did not care at that point in time what type of defense he selected. Who cared if I killed Teresa in self-defense or in a 'fugue' state, or if I was temporarily out of my mind? I surely didn't know what had been the reason for Teresa's death. She was dead. I had killed her. Nothing else mattered. I just wanted to get it all over with."

The following week a hearing in Monmouth County Family Court before Judge Julia Ashby on the custody of Philip produced a split decision. As in many such cases, child custody was awarded to both parties.

In her "temporary" split-custody decision, Judge Ashby ruled that Philip would stay in the Manalapan house with his grandparents for long weekends — Friday through Monday — and then be transferred to the custody of his aunt and uncle, Jeff and Celeste White, in Staten Island for Tuesday through Thursday.

It was a situation that infuriated Ken, who sat in his cell fuming. His son was the last vestige of his once sane life, the only thing that still made any sense to him, and to have Philip taken away from his parents drove him mad.

Zach and Jean were faced with additional serious problems. Zach had not worked for several weeks now, and Jean had temporarily left her job as hostess in a Marion restaurant. They had to arrange something whereby Zach could return to work and yet Philip would be taken care of. It was decided that Tom would drive out to New Jersey at Christmas. When Zach returned to Indiana, Tom would stay on and help Jean take care of the baby.

A week after he hired Jack Venturi, Ken wrote a letter to Teresa's friend Cindy Diaz. It was a strange letter, full of self-justification, guilt, and elaborate attempts to "explain" himself and to elicit help in his effort to keep Philip from the Benignos. It was a letter that surprised Cindy and her husband, for while they had gotten along with Ken, Teresa had been their true friend and they had been shocked and deeply hurt by her death.

"I've wanted to write to you, but my grief and sorrow have prevented me from communicating. I chose [to write to] you because Teresa and I thought very highly of you and felt that you knew us and how we felt about each other. Teresa and I had a great relationship. We truly loved each other. We loved our son more than life. This is a tragedy beyond anything I've ever known.

"I am not at liberty to discuss what happened or what caused the whole situation. I can say that Teresa had family problems which in my mind led to her excessive drug habits. I can't be specific, although I wish I could clear up many of the questions concerning our relationship. Unfortunately this cannot be discussed until my trial.

"Another matter that several people keep throwing out is our honeymoon. What happened is exactly as Teresa and I explained it to everyone. I have an investigator who will prove this as it seems her family wants to try to use this against me. I've lost my wife and my life will never be the same. Teresa and I were blessed with joy and happiness and closeness that most people just don't find in this world. The judge, jury, prosecutor, and my lawyer will settle the case, and in that I put my trust. But another issue is at hand which is a total miscarriage of justice.

"I'm not asking for help but understanding and the Truth. Celeste is trying to take my boy. Her caring for my son is beyond my wildest imagination. Teresa told me and all her friends how much she objected to her mother and Celeste caring for Philip and how poorly they cared for him with improper feeding, sleeping, etc. You both know Teresa was opposed to this. As you surely recall *Teresa* asked my parents to come from Indiana the week she gave birth because she didn't want her family hanging around getting in the way and screwing up the works. My parents love my son like their own, they truly love him and can give him the best of care. Yet in court Celeste and Louise acted like their relationship with Teresa was the best possible, and we all know how unjust and untrue that is.

"If not for me, please try to understand for Teresa and my son. You will not have to do anything except answer to this fact that Teresa did not want Celeste and/or Louise caring for our son. Now that Celeste is going to have a child I can just imagine the horror show of her trying to take care of two babies. And YOU KNOW which one of the 2 babies would get her attention as well as I do. I'm distraught. I've lost my wife and

189

now these people are trying to take my son.

"Once again the facts will be brought out at the trial, all of the facts, so please keep a clear head about that, but do try to consider my request in behalf of Teresa, myself, and Philip for his custody until my trial is over. . . .

"If I have rambled on, I can't help it. God bless you. Merry Christmas.

"P.S. I hope I have read you correctly and can trust you in this matter. Your confidence here will be most appreciated."

Ken's motives in writing the letter left Cindy and her husband stunned. His complaints about losing "his" wife was a bit like the murderer going before the judge after killing his parents and pleading for mercy because he was an orphan. It seemed he was trying to manipulate their minds, to create a scenario and convince them of its truth. They realized that Teresa had fights with Louise, and that she had often bad-mouthed Celeste. But that kind of stuff happened in every family. It was normal family heat. It couldn't, at least in their minds, be translated into the basis for legal action in a custody case. Ken, they finally decided, was blowing smoke, trying to arrange things for the coming court battle, and they would have none of it.

Chapter Fourteen

Ken Taylor's bitterness and resentment toward the man who would prosecute his case, Paul Chaiet, began almost immediately and knew few limits. Even years later in his prison diary he wrote that from the first moment Chaiet was "like a shark in breeding season. He smelled blood, victory, headlines. His ambition knew no bounds, [he was] an opportunist making the most for himself out of other people's tragedies. Chaiet approached the case as if Ted Bundy or some other mass murderer was the defendant."

In fact, Chaiet took his job seriously and he genuinely believed Kenneth Taylor was a murderous beast.

Paul Chaiet, the first assistant prosecutor for Monmouth County, was a muscular, square man with a thick head of dark hair and a lantern jaw. He looked tough, just as you would expect of a man who was once an outstanding linesman in football at Albright College in Pennsylvania. But he was also smart and ambitious. For six years prior to the Taylor case he had been the first assistant in the prosecutor's office, which he had joined in 1973, where he handled major felonies—including homicides.

Since Kenneth Taylor had already admitted killing

Teresa, Chaiet's job was easier in one way—but extremely difficult in another. The easy part was that unlike most murder cases, he didn't have to prove the killing; his problem was in establishing the circumstances under which the killing took place.

To get a first-degree murder conviction, which is what he wanted, he had to prove that Taylor had knowingly and purposefully murdered his wife. In short, he had to establish motive. And in this case there didn't seem to be any. There were none of the usual reasons when one spouse kills the other—no insurance money, no inheritance, no other woman waiting in the wings—just the peculiar claims of the killer: that his wife had been fellating the baby and that in a fit of rage he had struck her down.

To get a first-degree murder conviction, then, the motive would have to focus on the man himself, which meant that Chaiet had to begin delving into the man's background. He had to find out everything that he could about Ken Taylor. He had to at least make it seem plausible to the jury that Taylor was a brutal man, a man capable of killing someone out of anger and meanness.

On the other hand, to defend himself, Taylor had to convince the jury that he wasn't simply a brutal, wife-abusing monster—that he had a plausible reason for killing his wife.

Would it make sense to the jury that he bludgeoned his wife to death in a fit of rage after seeing his child sexually abused? Or does this defense of "a crime of passion" become merely an excuse for brutality? From Taylor's viewpoint it was a hell of a good story, even a unique one. But for Chaiet it was a real problem. Admittedly it was a bizarre case, and Taylor's justification was equally unique. Chaiet had never encountered this kind of excuse for murder. If the jury believed Taylor's story it could generate a lot of sympathy, maybe even get him off with simple manslaughter.

Chaiet knew he was faced with a monumental task. He had to prove that the killer's version of what had happened that morning was not true, that Ken Taylor had knowingly and purposefully murdered Teresa Taylor. And he set about doing it with energy and unwavering resolve.

The first thing he did was to begin to look into the man's background. When he was finished, he would know Kenneth Z. Taylor as well as any man could.

Being a logical man, Chaiet decided to start looking into Ken Taylor's background by questioning his second wife.

But Marilyn Bergman didn't want to talk to investigators. When Lucia contacted her, he was referred immediately to Carl Gainor, her Pittsburgh attorney.

Gainor advised Lucia and Chaiet that his client wanted to be kept out of the whole ungodly mess. The attorney explained to Chaiet that Marilyn knew nothing about the killing itself. She hadn't even known that the body was in the car.

Chaiet was in a bind. He couldn't subpoena her because she wasn't a resident of New Jersey. But he did have other cards up his sleeve. He quietly let Gainor know that under a federal statute, the Uniform Act to Secure the Attendance of Witnesses, he could bring her in front of the grand jury.

After Gainor had explained the situation to Marilyn she agreed to see the investigators. When she finally did talk, her testimony covered more than thirty pages.

On November 27, Fausak and Lucia flew to Pittsburgh to meet her. The interview took place in Gainor's office.

193

At this point the investigators had no idea of any other incidents of violence in Ken Taylor's background — aside from the suspicions about Acapulco. But when Lucia logically asked whether Ken had ever been physically abusive with her, she abruptly said, "Yes." It shocked both men, who had to keep themselves from leaping forward in their seats.

Lucia kept his face expressionless. "And when did this happen?"

"Waterford. In Connecticut, when he was in the Navy. I reported it to the police."

Fausak politely excused himself and immediately went to call McCormick. While Fausak was speaking with McCormick, who would pursue the Connecticut angle, Marilyn continued to describe the night Ken had tried to chloroform her. It was a stunning lead that they hadn't expected.

As the interview progressed, Lucia also learned to his surprise that Ken had yet another wife.

"Do you know what his previous wife's name was?" Lucia asked calmly.

"I believe it was Katherine Taylor."

"Do you know her maiden name?"

"Oh, I think it was Mitchell. Yeah, Kay Mitchell."

"Do you have any information regarding their relationship, or any problems they might have had?"

"Not really. It was just something where he indicated that he had previously been madly in love with some girl. She left him and he felt like he'd never love anybody again like he loved that girl, and he was dating Kay and some other girls. Kay was the first one that was interested in getting married, so he decided when he was twenty-one it was about time, what else would he do anyway? And he got married and he said from the beginning that it wasn't right. According to him they would split up, go back, split up, go back, and at

194

one point she got pregnant and later admitted that she did it on purpose to hold the marriage together, and they agreed to stay together until the baby was born."

"During this time that you had been dating, or that you were married, up to this point, did you have any marital problems?" Lucia asked.

"Yes."

"Could you tell us what they were?"

"When we were married? Well, I just had a feeling that he was screwing around, you know."

Marilyn described how she once got a case of the crabs. "I spoke to a nurse . . . and said, 'Is it possible to get crabs working in a dental clinic?' and she said, well, yes, touching these people, you know, you could get them . . . but there was still some questions in my mind."

"You say that after the chloroform Ken was examined at the Navy hospital in the psychiatric ward. Do you know the name of the doctor or doctors that treated him?"

"There was a Doctor Wheeler . . . I can't remember his first name. And another doctor, Bill Pettit."

"Did you have any opportunity to have any discussion with them concerning their findings?"

"I went to see Ken and Doctor Wheeler said, 'Do you really want to see him?' I said yes, and he said—I don't know if this is in the right sequence or not—he said, 'Why would you want to see him? All he's interested in is doing you in.'

"That scared me. I thought it was kind of strange that a doctor was talking like that. He also said to me, 'There's plenty of fish in the sea. You're an attractive woman. What do you need with a guy like this?'

"Then I went home. I didn't see Ken. I was upset."

Marilyn started crying then. It was the second time. The first had been when she related the details of Ken's and her trip to New York to see her dying father, followed by the chloroform attack.

When Marilyn had calmed down, Lucia quietly asked if they could continue talking about Dr. Wheeler.

"Okay. He called me on the phone and said that I had better call the police in regard to this matter because he had to release Ken from the hospital and he felt that he was a homicidal maniac. If he got out, all he'd want to do is finish off the job. I said to him, 'How come you have to release him if that's the way you feel?' But it seemed that he wanted me to report it to the police. There was something about it that the Navy couldn't do. So I called any number of captains or whatever and asked how could this possibly be? How could he say this and then say he was going to let him out? I wanted Ken to be taken care of. I figured he was really sick. And yet at the same time I was afraid that he was going to be let out. So I called the Navy chaplain and we sat down and soul-searched about what to do.

"Consequently it was reported to the police. I called the police and told them."

"You said that there was also another doctor involved. Doctor Pettit. What did he tell you?"

"Doctor Pettit said that, as much as I can remember, it was an isolated incident . . . it was drug-related . . . and that his diagnosis of Ken was gross lack of adjustment to adult life. He told me that Ken had never dealt with a problem in his life. He gave me an example of constantly putting things in a closet until one day you cannot get any more in and the whole door opens and everything that has ever bothered you comes out. And that Ken was under a lot of pressure because he was driving back and forth to New York to help me see my father and not too much attention was being given to caring about him. He was being left alone.

I'm trying to think of what else. Low self-esteem, which he put into a hole. He explained that a lot of things were found at the time this incident took place."

"As a result of this incident, did you learn anything about Ken's drug abuse, number one, or about his relationships he was having with women?"

"Yes. Ken said he had taken three black beauties that night and was hearing voices, and it came out in therapy that he had been using a lot of drugs. I think they said speed, uppers, downers, whatever, and they found pornography in the wall of the house, like behind the plasterboards."

"Who found it?"

"The detectives. They searched the house."

"What kind of pornography? Did it involve children?"

"The detectives told that it was just the regular homosexual and heterosexual stuff. One them asked if I wanted to see it. I said, 'No.' It was, I think, in the garbage that there was a picture found of him, like a Polaroid, naked from the neck down and also a letter applying to a sex club in New York. [In the letter he said that] he didn't want his name used because he was a dentist, and he didn't want to be involved in any homosexual activity."

"Did you ever witness Ken using or abusing drugs?"

"The only thing I ever saw him do was smoke marijuana."

"On how regular a basis?

"Just occasionally."

"You never saw him take any type of pills or take or use another drug, cocaine or anything else?"

"No."

"You said Ken stayed at the hospital for psychiatric evaluation and then moved into bachelor quarters on

197

the base?"

"Right. He went for group therapy and alcohol abuse courses. The Navy provided us with family counseling. We'd meet for lunch, you know, and dinner. Stuff like that. We even went, I think, for dancing lessons. It was all in an effort to get things back to normal. He went to AA sessions. I went to some with him because it was important to understand alcohol abuse. The Navy doesn't deal in drugs, they didn't do drug rehabilitation, they said."

"Did you get back together?"

"What happened is I was still going down to see my father and when things were calming down, I had asked him to go in and feed the cats, or stay in the house on weekends while I was in New York, and it just kind of went from there."

"You said that you and Ken lived in Staten Island for about a year and a half after his discharge. What caused you to separate?"

"Well, I was having difficulty adjusting sexually because of what happened in Connecticut, which the doctors told us would happen. But we weren't making too much progress. At that point in time, I believe he was carrying on with the receptionist in his office."

"Is that Teresa, the same Teresa that is the victim of this particular homicide?"

"Yes, Teresa was his receptionist at the time."

"After your divorce, did he keep up his alimony and support payments?"

"Well, he did fairly well until he got married. There would be weeks when I didn't get anything. I'd think, Oh, God, how am I going to pay these bills, but then he'd come up with checks, large-amount checks to cover back periods. I would say that basically I've gotten all the child support but I haven't gotten any ali-

198

mony."

"What was your relationship with Ken after you moved to Pittsburgh?"

"It was still friendly. He still expressed wishes that he had always expressed to be back with myself and Rhonda."

"Did he indicate to you that Teresa was abusing drugs, abusing their child, or anything like that?"

"Well, I think it was last year. I remember because it was shortly before I was considering selling the house that he was telling me that she was pregnant and he told me that she had been taking drugs. She was taking codeine, writing out prescriptions on his pads, forging his name, that she was signing his checks and taking money. I figured he must be telling the truth because he said she went into premature labor and I thought to myself that if you're taking drugs, that could do it. But I'm no doctor. I just told him, 'You should really tell her doctor, because what about the baby?' "

"Did he ever indicate to you that she ever abused the child?"

"He had just said on different occasions when he was coming over and didn't come that there were extenuating circumstances like, 'You don't know what it's like at home. I'm concerned for the safety of the child.' He was never really specific about it. He just said she doesn't seem to be able to cope."

"In Pittsburgh, on Tuesday, November 13, were you visited by Ken Taylor?"

"Was that the thirteenth? Two whole weeks in between already. Yes, he came to the house then."

"Did you see his car?"

"Yeah, it was parked out in front of my house."

"Did he ever indicate to you in any way that he had any involvement in Teresa's death or disappearance?"

"No."

199

In a written part of her deposition, Marilyn described the tensions that existed in all three of their lives—hers, Ken's, and Teresa's. "Ken said she couldn't understand why I had a house and she didn't . . . Well, in the first year he bought her a house, car, etc., and was upset that I didn't let Rhonda go to his house. Our divorce agreement was that he see her in my house. Visits were less frequent, usually after work, and he paid me by signing insurance checks over to me. He was upset with me. Visits were to be on Sundays and apparently his wife wouldn't let him come.

"Around April last year, Ken started telling me that Teresa was on drugs and stealing money from insurance companies. She went into premature labor at six months of pregnancy. So I assumed the drug business was true. He said he wanted to leave her but couldn't until the baby was born and well started in life. He said he was keeping proof of the drug abuse and thefts so he could get custody of the child. After the child was born he wrote a letter expressing sincere regret for any problems he'd caused people in his life.

"It seemed the shoe was on the other foot and Ken had really learned about life, responsibility, caring . . . Here he was in a situation similar to the one he put me in when he was doing drugs. There were sometimes that he said he was concerned for the safety of his child because his wife just couldn't cope. He said he wanted to leave, get custody of his child, and be with his 'family' (Rhonda and myself).

"He visited us in Pennsylvania and at that time he told me that she had taken off because she was using cocaine and was going to straighten herself out.

"You ask if I've changed my opinion of Ken?

"I've known an extremely gentle man who left me with a note in a tea canister.

"I've seen a man who delights in growing flowers,

feeds all stray animals, and can play for hours with a child try to take my life.

"I've heard him say mean things and return with roses.

"I've heard him express regret for any pain he's caused anyone with a hint that he may not be able to go on living.

"I've seen this man cry profusely at a sad movie — just months ago.

"Now I've heard this man's father saying that his son's wife was doing oral sex to her son, Ken went after her, and she tried to kill him with a barbell. He then hit her.

"Have I changed my opinions—?

"I have no opinions, I'm not a doctor. I'm devastated. I just don't know what to think about anything anymore."

The grand jury convened on December 14. Ken's copy of the grand jury deliberations (as well as his copies of the court transcripts) are marked profusely with comments — some bitter and angry, others tinged with wry or sarcastic humor. Ken's attention to the moment-to-moment drama as his once normal life slipped away showed a keen intelligence that was feeding on the proceedings with an almost avid hunger — no matter how many times he professed to feel isolated and emotionally drained.

Several state expert witnesses, including the coroner and Lieutenant Lucia, were called. The medical testimony left no doubt in the jury's mind about the brutality of the attack on Teresa Taylor, nor did the technical language hide the extent of her injuries.

"Massive head, face, and cranial-cerebral injuries due to blunt force trauma," the medical report said. "Fractures, compound and comminuted, base and vault of skull, bilateral, with focal extrusion of brain. Acute diffuse subarachnoid hemorrhage, bilateral, severe, cerebral hemispheres, basilar and subtentorial."

Ken Taylor had smashed the foot-long steel bar with its protruding clamp into her face and head time and time again. One blow was to her right forehead, another around her left ear. Other blows had been delivered to the back of her head. Some of the blows were so powerful that Teresa's skull was shattered into three parts and brain matter was showing.

But the most convincing testimony came from Lieutenant Lucia, for he had been involved in the investigation since the beginning.

Chaiet led Lucia through the events from the time Ken reported Teresa missing until Ken finally confessed. The most difficult moment for Chaiet came when one juror asked, "Wasn't there some indication that Teresa Taylor had a drug problem?"

Chaiet wanted to avoid that issue as much as possible. He surely didn't want to give it any credence. Lucia answered the juror, "Well, that's what Doctor Taylor claimed."

Chaiet broke in, "He told us she was using drugs."

"He said she was a drug addict?" the juror persisted.

"I don't know about addict," Chaiet answered. "She had some problems with drugs. We have an ongoing investigation and we have, I guess, established that she did use drugs on occasion. To what extent she used drugs we're not sure.

"Isn't that correct?" Chaiet asked Lucia.

"That's correct."

By the time the jury adjourned, it was clear that Chaiet had succeeded in keeping the focus off Teresa.

The grand jury reconvened the following Friday. Again forensic evidence was touched on, including the results of the luminol test and the apparent extra effort the accused had made to clean up a considerable amount of blood.

Then Zach Taylor was called. After some brief preliminary questions, Chaiet began by confronting Ken's allegation of Teresa's drug abuse.

"How often did you visit them (his son and Teresa) in New Jersey or Staten Island?"

"The next time we saw them after the wedding was when the baby was born . . . We were here for ten days."

"Prior to her death did you again see them?"

"Teresa and Kenny and the baby, they visited us Labor Day weekend. They were there for two days."

"During your visit to the house in Manalapan, did you observe any drug use by Teresa or by your son at that time?"

"No, sir."

"Were you personally aware of any drug use at any time by Teresa Taylor? Through your own observation."

"Not personally, not through observation. If you mean actual taking of drugs or—"

His tone abrupt, Chaiet interrupted, "Taking drugs, seeing her under the influence of a drug?"

"On the Labor Day visit, we noticed something was different. But my wife and I, I am saying we, we didn't know what the problem was."

"When you say noticed something different, what do you mean, noticed something different?"

"She seemed to be just, I don't know how to explain it, really kind of a different person . . . She had headaches and spent a lot of time in bed."

"Did you ask your son about that at the time?"

"No, not that I recall. No, I don't think so."

Then, with calculation, Chaiet introduced the subject of Acapulco. He didn't know for sure whether there was any gold in the Acapulco story. All he had was the suspicions of the in-laws. But if he introduced it now and anything developed later, his groundwork would already have been laid. If it turned out that Ken's story about Acapulco was untrue his credibility would be undermined.

"Now," Chaiet said quietly, "were you aware of a problem that Teresa and Doctor Taylor ran into on their honeymoon in July 1983?"

"Somewhat, yes."

Chaiet, impatient now, said, "When you say 'somewhat,' tell me what you know about what happened in Acapulco, Mexico."

"Kenny said that their room was broken into and that he was knocked out, he was dazed, and he started to come to, and then he was knocked out.

"When he awoke there was glass, I think he said glass, on the floor from a broken lamp. He saw his wife, I don't recall whether he said that she was on the floor or still on the bed or what, but his first thought was that she was dead. She had been beaten and cut and he called the front desk, I guess, I am not sure whether he called the front desk or the police, or whatever.

"When they came, they took them both to the hospital, as I understand, and Kenny was released and he was arrested by the Mexican police."

"Her injuries, would it be fair to say, in his relating the story to you, were more severe than his?"

"Yes."

"The information that you related to us just now, is this your recollection of what you were told by your son, your best recollection?"

"I would say yes. But I have a difficult time because Mr. Benigno said things to me on the phone. All of his conversation is on the phone."

"Did you talk to your son about the fact that he was held by Mexican authorities and what happened? What did he tell you about that?"

"He just told me that he was arrested. And that he was put in jail and apparently in Mexico they don't feed the prisoners. He wanted some food and one of the guards said, 'I'll get you food for fifty dollars.' He got a cup of coffee and a roll.

"I don't know exactly when they released him. But he got out by paying a five-hundred-dollar fine to a Mexican policeman that just stuck it in his pocket, so to speak."

Chaiet broke in abruptly, challenging, "Is that the story your son told you?"

"Yes," Zach answered, a little taken aback by the aggressiveness of Chaiet's question.

"What did Teresa tell you about the assault?" Chaiet asked. "Did she tell you she knew who did it? Did she give a description of the people who did it?"

"Teresa said she didn't recall anything. She saw no one, absolutely no one. First she was on the bed asleep and then she was in the hospital, maybe even unconscious in the hospital."

Near the end of Chaiet's questioning, he asked Zach what Ken had said to him when they met soon after his arrest at the Manalapan police station on Sunday, November 18.

"When we went into the room where he was, I believe Mr. Lucia was with us, and he, I really don't recall what he told us except . . ." Zach paused, obviously troubled by the painful memory of those moments. Then he went on, "I honestly can't say what he told us. I am trying to think here whether the police told us what he told them."

"I'm asking you what your son told you," Chaiet cut in brusquely. Then, more softly, "I want you to use your best recollection. I realize this is difficult for you and you're under oath. But it would seem you should be able to remember a conversation with your son in an incident where he is telling you about the death of his wife."

"Okay," Zach answered, taking a deep breath. "I believe he said that he woke up on Sunday morning and started down the steps and he looked down and saw his wife performing oral sex on the baby. And he yelled at her. She got up and ran. He ran after her. And she swung at him with a, what I would call a dumbbell, which is a piece of workout equipment . . .

"That's as far as he could talk."

When it had all ended, Chaiet felt good. The only point he really had to make to the jury was whether there was "probable cause" to believe that a murder had occurred. And Lucia's testimony had clearly established that.

Chaiet had decided not to seek the death penalty in this case. In capital crimes he preferred life sentences with no chance of parole. When you were trying to convince a jury to convict a man of murder one, Chaiet believed, the issue of capital punishment could become a distraction. And even though New Jersey had not executed anyone since the United States Supreme Court had legalized the death penalty, the threat of lethal injection was always waiting in the wings.

Besides, under New Jersey law conviction of murder one called for a mandatory thirty-year sentence, which in Taylor's case was practically the same thing as a life sentence. If he could convict Taylor, the man wouldn't even be eligible for parole until he was sixty-six, in the year 2015.

Perhaps, he thought, by allowing the Acapulco issue to be brought in he had raised an irrelevancy. But no harm done. He had noticed the jurors stiffen and sit up noticeably when there was even a hint of previous violence mentioned. If there was anything solid to be found in the Acapulco incident, he would introduce it, as well as Taylor's Connecticut escapade, in the trial — which is where the real battle would begin.

The grand jury returned its indictment of murder against Ken Taylor on Friday, January 4, 1985.

Chapter Fifteen

While Detectives Fausak and Lucia were questioning Marilyn Bergman, the Monmouth County Prosecutor's Investigations Unit was continuing to probe
into Ken and Teresa's life together. Guy McCormick
took detailed statements from Ken's parents, the Rozaks, the Benignos, and Jeff and Celeste White. They
also found a new witness—Sheri Delile.

McCormick started off the interview with the
standard questions about her relationship with the
Taylors.

She had, she said, been good friends with Teresa
for twelve years. They had lost touch for a while
when she started going with Ken Taylor, but after the
honeymoon in Acapulco she visited Teresa in the hospital and the relationship picked up again.

"When was the last time you saw Teresa Taylor?"
McCormick asked.

"Monday, November fifth. I went to the office for a
dental visit. I told them not to make an appointment
for the following Monday because I was going to visit
my sister in Michigan and would be gone four or
five days . . ."

"After the office visit, when you told Ken and Teresa of your trip, did you see or speak to Teresa?"

"No."

"After returning from Michigan, did you speak to Ken Taylor?"

"Yes, Friday morning. I called and woke him up around 9 A.M., just before I went to work. I was worried and called, and asked if he'd heard from Teresa. He said no. During our conversation I asked if maybe she had recalled Acapulco and her attack and he said, 'I don't know, why do you ask?' He said everyone thought she was with me. So did he. He just didn't seem worried on the phone. I haven't spoken to him since."

"How often did you visit or stay the night with the Taylors?"

"Six to eight times during the past three months."

Then McCormick began focusing in on the heart of what he was after. "Did you ever see Ken Taylor assault Teresa or see any indications that she had been assaulted?" he asked.

"None whatsoever."

"To your knowledge, did Teresa ever use or abuse any type of narcotic drugs?"

"She used to take diet pills all the time and was on pills from the doctor during her pregnancy. She was also on codeine because of her teeth."

"The times that you stayed overnight at Teresa and Ken's house, was there any type of drug used socially?"

"Just once. There was cocaine there when we arrived. My boyfriend and I brought some marijuana with us. Ken and he smoked it, but Teresa wasn't offered any because she didn't use it. Ken had cocaine and we were watching *Star Search* and I asked Teresa

209

to ask Ken if he had any cocaine to buy. She did. And later there was cocaine on the table. Ken didn't give it to us. It was just on the table. My boyfriend gave Ken fifty dollars. All of us, including Teresa, did the coke."

"While at Ken and Teresa's house, how many times did you all use cocaine?"

"One time. It was either the second or third visit."

"What led you to believe that Ken Taylor had cocaine or could get cocaine?"

"Because he was a dentist. A doctor."

"On your other visits to the Taylor residence, or to the offices on Staten Island, did you observe Teresa or Ken using any type of drugs?"

"No, just drinks. Teresa drank light, not a lot. That night we all got drunk, the night when the cocaine was on the table."

"In your twelve-year association with Teresa, have you ever seen her under the influence of alcohol or drugs?"

"We would drink socially when we went to clubs prior to her marriage. I never saw her use any drugs—just the ones for diets, because she was worried about her weight."

"Did Teresa ever indicate to you any problems with Ken and their marriage?"

"None. She had mentioned to me that with the baby, the house, and the business, they had a lot of financial pressures."

"Did Teresa ever indicate to you any of her more intimate problems?"

"Just one time. The past month or so my boyfriend mentioned that we were having sexual problems. Teresa mentioned that she had the same thing, and Ken just smiled. The remark was to the effect that I didn't want to have sex as often—or not at all."

"Are you aware of the incident in Acapulco?"

"Yes. I didn't recognize her in the hospital in Staten Island—she was so badly beaten and bruised. The first time my boyfriend and I went over to her house, she brought out pictures from Acapulco and spoke at length about the incident. She said they had gone out for dinner, got boisterous at the table; and Ken advised he felt that Teresa possibly had insulted one of the waiters and that's why someone got even with them . . . Teresa said that she recalled a pair of bare feet but nothing else [about the attack]."

It was hard for many of the investigators to give any credibility to Ken's claims about Teresa's drug abuse; most thought it was just a cover story to justify the murder. But Chaiet couldn't afford to leave any angle unexamined, so early on he ordered a drug screen on the body. The medical examiner gave the job to a toxicology lab led by Dr. Frederick Rieders, a nationally recognized expert. He would be searching for traces of codeine and cocaine.

When Rieders' report arrived on Chaiet's desk it indicated that 121 nanograms per milliliter of codeine had been found in the victim's body. He found no cocaine. But there were traces of bensoylecgonine, which was a byproduct of cocaine.

Later Chaiet telephoned Rieders. He wanted to hear in detail what the man would be likely to say on the stand. Rieders assured Chaiet that the amount of codeine he'd found in the body was within the normal range for a therapeutic dosage (.04 parts per million) and nothing more.

Chaiet asked him if his findings would indicate

whether or not the victim was "drug-crazed by cocaine" at the time of death.

No, Rieders replied, the amount of benzoylecgonine was small and wasn't consistent with heavy or abusive use. But since cocaine began breaking down in the body almost at once, it was difficult to determine whether it had been taken the day of death or even several days before.

Chaiet was pleased by the doctor's clear assurances. His testimony would help put to rest Taylor's claims about Teresa's drug abuse.

Most of the information on Teresa's drugs use came from Taylor, and his testimony was obviously tainted. The question that Chaiet had to ask himself was: Why would Taylor lie about his wife's taking drugs? The most obvious answer was that it supported his contention Teresa was drugged out of her mind on-the morning of the killing; second, if her mind was addled with drugs, it made his argument that she was fellating the baby slightly more plausible; third, if the previous two points were true, his defense of a crime of passion became more credible. It was a devious and very smart construction—but one typical of pathological liars.

One of his investigators, Barbara Coleman, had already interviewed the doctor who had delivered Philip six months earlier. In his deposition the doctor had said that there was no indication Teresa "had been or was on drugs of any sort when Philip was born."

And only a small amount of support for Taylor's claims about Teresa's drug habits was coming in from the testimony of friends. It appeared that her use was, according to these friends, mostly recreational.

Another problem Chaiet had to confront was that

if, as Taylor testified, Teresa's brother Phil was one of her drug suppliers,* it could be argued that it was highly unlikely that he would condemn himself by admitting under oath that he sold drugs to his sister. Hard evidence would have to be found. But Taylor's accusations against Phil Benigno stood or fell on whether Teresa herself was heavily into drugs. If Taylor was found to be lying about Teresa, then his accusations against Phil Benigno would collapse as well. Chaiet was concerned, however, that some evidence of Phil's and Teresa's drug habits—beyond the "recreational use" he already knew about—might surface.

Chaiet didn't believe any of Taylor's story. Taylor was no doubt making all this up to fortify his argument that his crime was one of passion and not first-degree murder. Since there was no factual "evidence" against Phil Benigno as a dealer, or for Teresa's heavy drug use, a presumption of innocence had to be made.

But still, just to be safe, Chaiet asked his investigators to look into any evidence of Phil and Teresa's drug use. He couldn't be sure that Taylor's defense wouldn't come up with a witness that would testify to Teresa's using cocaine—and he didn't like surprises in the middle of a trial.

Fausak and McCormick visited all the pharmacies along Route 9 as they drove to Staten Island from the New Jersey Turnpike. They canvased all the pharmacies in the Manalapan and Freehold areas and turned up codeine prescriptions for Teresa Taylor. They also uncovered five others for Phil Benigno.

*This information regarding Ken Taylor's statements about Phil Benigno is taken directly from Taylor's sworn testimony, recorded in court documents used in his trial.

213

Most were for Tylenol III, which contains considerable amounts of codeine.

Chaiet also had a financial check made on Ken. Although his annual income was well over $100,000, his credit wasn't the best. In fact, while checking out Ken's Navy background McCormick had contacted Naval Investigative Services and spoken with Special Agent Mike Smith who, after some investigation, informed him that Kenneth Taylor still owed almost $26,000 dollars to the Navy Federal Credit Union.

Ken would later comment sarcastically that most of the money he made was going up Teresa's nose.

When the call came from Fausak about Connecticut, McCormick immediately contacted the Waterford police department and requested further information on the case.

McCormick talked with Detective Sergeant Joseph San Juan, who remembered the case well. Later, in his report, McCormick wrote:

> "The undersigned contacted the Waterford, Connecticut, PD in order to ascertain whether or not Kenneth Taylor had any contact with that agency.
>
> "Det. Sgt. Joseph San Juan said he believed that Kenneth Z. Taylor was a lieutenant stationed at the Groton Naval Base and that on April 16, 1979, Kenneth Z. Taylor tried to kill his wife, who at that time was Marilyn Bergman.
>
> "According to Sgt. San Juan, Miss Bergman was in bed when Kenneth Taylor stuck a chloroform-soaked sponge in her face and nearly

smothered her with it. Sgt. San Juan advised that Taylor was arrested and charged with attempted homicide, but the case was later dismissed because Marilyn Bergman made an impassioned plea before the court to have the charges dropped.

"San Juan further advised that during the course of their investigation the police found all sorts of sexual-related correspondence. The correspondence was to various smear-type magazines, and nude photographs of Kenneth Taylor were also discovered. These nude photos were of Taylor's genital area and had been apparently taken by Taylor himself while utilizing a mirror.

"This writer was advised by Sgt. San Juan that since the charges against Taylor were dismissed he is not permitted to send this writer any of his reports concerning the investigation.

"He did supply this writer with a name of a female who was believed to be Kenneth Taylor's wife prior to his marriage to Marilyn Bergman. She is Katherine Mitchell, with an Indianapolis, Ind., residence. An attempt to contact her was made at the number given, but there was no answer."

Chaiet had a mixed reaction to this stunning report. The digging into Taylor's life was bringing up some golden information. Taylor apparently had a history of violence—which didn't surprise Chaiet at all. But he was angered by the news that Connecticut officials wouldn't send him the Taylor file. He called the Connecticut State's Attorney's office and was informed that there was nothing they could do about it. Connecticut law *requires* that once charges are dropped in a criminal case the file is erased — gone. Chaiet listened in frustration as the assistant state's attorney told him that Connecticut had very clear erasure laws, General Statutes, Paragraphs 54-142(a), and that was the end of it.

Chaiet was an officer of the court, and his respect for the law was high, but he was cursing to himself as he replaced the phone in its cradle.

McCormick and Fausak doggedly made their rounds, covering every possibility, working every angle that could give them any insight into the lives of Teresa and Kenneth Taylor.

Fausak talked with neighbors on Valley Road and in the Manalapan neighborhood.

Only one woman remembered screams coming one night from the direction of the Taylor home. Another couple also heard screams but couldn't pinpoint where it was coming from nor were they even sure of the date — but they thought it might have been around the time of the killing. They did recall that when they looked out the window they didn't see anything suspicious. No one reported the screams to the police.

The landlords of the two-family house on Staten Island where Ken had rented his apartment, George and Catherine Schron, recalled hearing loud arguments. Mrs. Schron also recalled that she heard the Taylors "arguing very loudly on one occasion before their marriage" and that Teresa had left in a taxi. "Other than that," Guy McCormick wrote in his report, "the Schrons had no other knowledge of any problems and they had no knowledge of either one being involved in drugs." The landlord's son, however, recalled hearing "something or someone" being smashed against a wall. Ken had, he said, later apologized for the commotion.

One other trip McCormick made to talk with the nurse, Lynn Rogers, who was working in Staten Island Hospital while Teresa was there following her beating in Acapulco, brought an interesting bit of confirming information. Another piece to the puzzle, McCormick thought.

In her deposition, Nurse Rogers said she recalled hearing a commotion in room 28, Teresa's room, the day she was being discharged to go home. Nurse Rogers was in room 29 when she heard the "banging sounds."

"She went into the room and saw Teresa Taylor lying on her back across her bed. Teresa was wearing her nightgown and she was crying. Teresa's husband was standing over her. Kenneth Taylor advised Nurse Rogers that Teresa had slipped and fallen."

McCormick asked Lynn Rogers if she remembered seeing anything in Kenneth Taylor's hands at that moment. She wasn't sure, but "he may have had some of his wife's clothing in his hands."

"Nurse Rogers then went to the head nurse and advised her that she did not think that Teresa Taylor should go home with her husband. Nurse Rogers was asked by the writer if she had ever witnessed Kenneth Taylor ever threatening, pushing, or hitting Teresa Taylor, and she related that she had not.

"She further related," McCormick's report said, "that she had observed items that were previously on the nightstand in the hospital room as being on the floor during this incident on the day of Teresa Taylor's discharge."

Another taste of Kenneth Taylor's personality, Mc-

Cormick thought. Not enough to chew on, but they were slowly bringing together the ingredients to serve up a full meal to the courts.

Employees at the dental offices all thought Teresa was a "good" mother. Some described Ken as a loving father. Most couldn't shed much light on the Taylors' private lives or give any information pertinent to the murder investigation.

By now Chaiet was getting a more complete picture of the events in the tattered lives of Teresa and Ken Taylor leading up to her death. His case was slowly coming together. The fact that Taylor had tried to kill his former wife in Connecticut would help him build a case of "willful" murder. But, frustratingly, he still couldn't dislodge the information from the Connecticut authorities.

He had repeatedly called the assistant state's attorney in Connecticut trying to pry the files loose, but with no luck. One break did occur, though, when he was given permission to have his investigators interview the two officers who had been on the case.

On February 15, Fausak and McCormick met with the two officers in Waterford—Sergeants Joseph San Juan and Joseph Faldman. The most revealing information came when the two officers mentioned talking with Lieutenant Commander Ronald Wheeler.

In their report they noted that "Doctor Wheeler had said that Kenneth Taylor had told him [Wheeler] that he had planned to hill his wife . . ."

Two days after Ken had tried to chloroform Marilyn, on April 19, he was interviewed by the two officers in the submarine base hospital. They reported that Kenneth Taylor had told them that he had thought of killing his wife that night.

"In the past he had thought of it [killing her]," the officers said Ken told them, "but he never attempted to carry it out. He decided to use chloroform. He wasn't sure if it would hill her but if it did not kill her, it would render her unconscious and then he could suffocate her . . .

"After the struggle ended . . . he put the sponge in a Ziploc bag and told his wife to call the police. He called the Lawrence and Memorial Hospital to advise that he was under the influence of drugs and needed help. The hospital advised that . . . he contact the base hospital. Kenneth Taylor also advised the investigating officers that before he attempted to kill his wife he had taken three black-colored capsules [or speed]."

After a search warrant had been obtained, the two Waterford officers discovered in the Taylor home a list of reasons why Ken wanted to kill his wife—written in his own hand on a memo pad. The memo was dated April 17—the same day that he tried to chloroform Marilyn.

The list included:

1. Lack of affection.
2. Lack of respect from his wife.
3. Verbal abuse.
4. Sexual abstinence.
5. Belief that Marilyn was bisexual.
6. His wife had chosen to keep her maiden name after marriage.
7. Her curse that if she bore a boy child, she hoped he would be gay rather than a macho jock.

* * *

A little more than a week after his talk with the Waterford officers, McCormick received Ken's file from the Naval Investigative Service. The NIS investigation had concentrated on the possibility of drug use on the Navy base, and NIS had questioned him (and fellow Navy personnel) about drugs. The investigation did help to develop a more thorough insight into Ken Taylor's abuse of drugs over the years.

"*History.* This 30-year-old married Navy dentist with two years, ten months' continuous active duty presently stationed aboard the *USS FULTON* was admitted to the Navy Submarine Medical Center, Groton, Connecticut, on April 17, 1979, after evaluation in the emergency room . . .

"Dr. Taylor indicated that on the day of admission while at work he drank twelve cups of coffee. In addition, that evening, he drank eight more cups of coffee and took three 'Black Beauties' (each tablet contained 10 mg of amphetamine and 10 mg of dextroamphetamine). He indicated that he had also smoked one or two joints of marijuana [that day].

"As the evening progressed, he noted feelings of a 'driving sensation,' feelings like wanting to 'stand in a corner,' and a feeling that his head was expanding. Over the next several hours he noted progressive restlessness, irritability, tenseness, palpitations, and anxiety. He went to his spare bedroom to study for his board examinations.

"During that time, he noted progressive intrusive homicidal ideation toward his wife and experienced hearing a voice from within himself

220

telling him to kill her. After a period of one and a half hours of struggling with these impulses, he indicated that he soaked a towel with chloroform, went to where his wife was sleeping, and held the towel to her face. When she reacted to the towel there was a brief struggle and he indicated that he suddenly became more fully aware of what was happening and what he had done. He and his wife prayed together.

"Afterward, they began seeking means for him to get her to the hospital. He denied previous plans to kill his wife. He denied plans for behavior or the disposal of her body should he have killed her.

"He indicated that he took two 'Black Beauties' on Saturday, three 'Black Beauties' on Sunday, and the additional three 'Black Beauties' on the night prior to the alleged incident. He indicated that approximately three weeks prior to that, he had taken two 'Black Beauties' one day, followed by three on the next day, and on the third day three additional 'Black Beauties.' It was on that day during an argument with his wife that he struck the refrigerator, breaking a metacarpal bone in his right hand. He indicated that this was an option to hitting his wife.

"He denies regular amphetamine use, though indicating that he had taken them infrequently to study for major dental school exams. He admitted to Valium use, 1-2 tablets a day for approximately one year while in dental school. He had experimented with LSD on two occasions and for a period of time in dental school had taken 50-mg Seconals about twice a month.

"In addition, he had taken cocaine on two oc-

221

casions in 1976. He admitted to the regular use of marijuana as a way of releasing anxiety and tension. He admitted the use of coffee, 10-12 cups a day, on a regular basis, and smoking 2-3 packs of cigarettes on a daily basis.

"He gave his alcohol history as: first drink, age 17; first drunk at age 18. He indicated in 1975 he had a car accident while under the influence of alcohol. He admits to drinking about twice a week, 2-3 drinks, and becomes drunk about once a month. He indicated that he required the equivalent of about one pint of whiskey to become drunk.

"Dr. Taylor admitted to progressive marital discord over the previous two months. He indicated that he had experienced feelings of lack of respect and lack of affection from his wife. He indicated that he has marked difficulty in expressing his feelings and a marked fear of having verbal arguments with people, especially his wife.

"*Past History* revealed he is the oldest of three children from an intact lower-middle-class family. He admitted to severe nail biting at 8-9 years of age during a time his younger brother became the center of his father's attention. He did well in grade school but had difficulties in seventh grade, when he broke his foot. He graduated from high school and was vice president of his senior class. He lettered in basketball, football, and baseball. He graduated from college and attended dental school by working part-time and attending dental school part-time.

"He married initially during his junior year in college and was divorced after a year of separation in October, 1974. He married his present wife [in] December, 1974.

"He described his father as a 52-year-old industrial engineer who is a quiet man, a hard worker, and proud. He indicated that he got along well with him but that his father's level of interest in him seemed proportional to his athletic achievements. He described his mother as a 52-year-old housewife who is 'overly concerned about making everyone happy.' He indicated that she 'dominates in subtle ways' and tends to be very interfering with his life.

"*Mental Status Examination.* At the time of admission he was described as 'quite calm, collected, oriented.' Initially, the patient was started on 5 mg of Stelazine a day and Artane, 2 mg four times a day, with the diagnosis of acute psychotic reaction secondary to drug abuse.

"He was initially under the care of Dr. Ronald Wheeler, LCDR MC USNR. On 20 April 1979, Dr. William F. Pettit, CDR MC USN, assumed primary care of the patient after the patient's request for a change of physician.

"Over a period of six days' hospitalization, the patient became more aware of his difficulty in dealing with his emotions in an appropriate and effective manner. He indicated increased realization that he tended to hold things in and had difficulty finding adaptive outlets for the expression of his feelings. He appeared actively motivated for treatment and read a book on feelings within 24 hours after receiving it. He appeared motivated for individual and group therapy and showed marked insight into his difficulties.

"He is not felt to be drug dependent. There

223

is no evidence of psychosis or clinical depression. He denied suicidal and homicidal ideation."

The NIS closed its file on Lt. Kenneth Taylor with the comment:

"The charge of attempted murder against subject was dismissed in superior court, New London, CT, when subject's spouse declined to testify against her husband.

"NIS files contain no additional information pertinent to this investigation."

In addition to the NIS report and Doctor Wheeler's initial diagnosis, Dr. Pettit conducted a standard MMPI, the Minnesota Multiphasic Personality Inventory, which indicatea a patient's personality adjustment range. "The MMPI profile suggests no evidence of neurosis, psychosis, or character disorder," Dr. Pettit concluded.

A Medical Board, which was composed of Wheeler and Pettit, was convened and filed its report on May 14, 1979.

Both men signed the Board's findings, Wheeler probably under pressure from his Navy superiors, for his opinions on Lieutenant Taylor had apparently not changed significantly. In the Board's final report after his examination of Ken, Dr. Pettit wrote:

"My general impression is that this man has chronic difficulty in dealing directly with his emotions and tends to allow things to build to where he experiences chronic tension and anxiety. A great deal of his difficulty in expressing his feelings directly is secondary to his tremendous need for acceptance and fear of rejection.

"In addition, my impression is that the alleged incident was the result of a combination of factors which had built to explosive proportions.

1. Growing discontent with his marital relationship, accompanied by feelings of 'total emptiness, hopelessness, and helplessness' with regard to his marriage.
2. A growing feeling of lack of respect and appreciation from his wife.
3. Fear of loss of his parents' respect and their relationship if his marital relationship failed.
4. Chronic anxiety related to his inability to express emotions and frustrations in an effective, appropriate manner.
5. More recent feelings of abandonment related to his wife's absence due to her father's sickness.
6. Toxic effects of nearly 3,000 mg of caffeine in combination with four days of sympathomimetic tablets culminating in transient homicidal impulses.

"During the two weeks' period of time since his discharge from the hospital, the following has been noted:

1. The patient has actively participated in group and individual therapy.
2. No evidence of alcohol addiction. Even so, Doctor Taylor, upon my recommendation, will begin attending a 36-hour course on alcohol

education on 15 May 1979. He and his wife at this time plan to attend the course together.

3. He and his wife have sought out couples' therapy from a civilian therapist and will begin this in the near future.
4. Over a 14-day period he has taken approximately 14 tablets of Stelazine for anxiety and tension. He has denied recurrence of homicidal ideation. His mood and mental status are normal and appropriate to his present life situation.

It is the opinion of the Medical Board that the diagnoses are:

1. Acute toxic drug reaction (amphetamines, caffeine, and marijuana) with transient homicidal impulses.
2. Situational adjustment reaction of adult life with severe marital maladjustment.

"It is the recommendation of the Medical Board that LT. TAYLOR be placed on six months' limited duty, during which time he should attend group therapy one or two times per week and individual therapy as deemed indicated. Short-term use of anti-anxiety agents to be utilized as seen fit. He is also encouraged to markedly reduce his use of caffeine. In addition, he has been encouraged to gradually initiate a physical exercise program to heighten feelings of self-esteem and for the relief of tension.

"LT. TAYLOR has been informed of the findings of the Board and does not desire to submit a statement in rebuttal."

Chaiet was pleased by the NIS report. It was clear that there was a conflict of opinion between the doctors Wheeler and Pettit. But that in itself did not undermine the facts. In his talks in Waterford, McCormick had uncovered the angry disagreement between the two men. Apparently Wheeler still believed Ken Taylor was a dangerous homicidal maniac and that Dr. Pettit believed otherwise. In addition, Pettit was regular Navy and he, Wheeler, was Navy Reserve.

Even if Chaiet couldn't use the Connecticut investigation, he could call Marilyn Bergman and the two Waterford officers to the stand and introduce the Navy findings as well.

If Taylor's defense plea was temporary insanity, then his lawyer would obviously call other psychiatrists and it would finally come down to expert against expert. But any way you looked at it, Ken Taylor was now on record as having a history of violence.

Chapter Sixteen

Early in the afternoon of Friday, December 7, 1984, Guy McCormick received a telephone call from Captain Jimmie Potts of the Manalapan Police Department. It was one of those unexpected breaks that can mean so much to an investigation.

A telephone call to the station that morning around 11:44 A.M. had been routed to Captain Potts while McCormick and Fausak were out interviewing people in the Manalapan area.

In his report, dated December 19, 1984, McCormick noted that "an unidentified female caller who only provided her first name as being 'Sorayda' had contacted the Manalapan police because she had not read anything in the newspaper concerning a disposition on the Teresa Taylor homicide.' The woman claimed to have 'personal knowledge of the events that occurred in Acapulco, Mexico, in which Teresa Taylor was badly beaten and hospitalized.' "

The caller claimed that she had "become acquainted with the Taylors and that while in Mexico, they had a drink together to toast their honeymoon.

"[Several days later] she observed Kenneth Taylor in the lobby of the hotel in a disheveled state. The caller claimed that she had spoken with Kenneth Taylor, who told her that he had been in jail as a result of a fight and that his wife was in the hospital. She further related that she inquired as to what they did to her and Kenneth Taylor replied, 'Not them, me, we had a fight.' "

The news was stunning. Here was a witness who could testify that Taylor had, in fact, beaten his wife on their honeymoon. The only problem was that she wouldn't give her full name. She wouldn't come forward to testify until she had talked it over with her husband.

Fortunately, the investigators didn't have to rely on their memories or on sketchy notes taken hastily while on the phone—as often happens. This time the Manalapan station's telephone-connected tape machine recorded the conversation.

"I was calling about that man, you know, who killed his wife," the woman said. "Kenneth Taylor. We were on vacation in Acapulco when they were there. The newspaper didn't say . . ."

"I'm sorry," Potts interrupted, "I can barely hear you."

". . . that, you know, he beat her up."

Captain Potts was already involved in the investigation of Teresa Taylor's murder and realized immediately that this was an important break—if it turned out to be true, and not just a crank caller. The woman sounded nervous, and Potts tended to think she was genuine. He was careful in his responses. Calls like this could end up abruptly, with a nervous witness suddenly hanging up.

"Yes," he said quietly.

"We were at the hotel," the woman went on. "There was a big scandal about him."

"Yes?" Potts said again, not wanting to press, trying to draw her out.

"And I really wanted to know what is happening to

229

him. I mean, he killed his wife."

"Okay," Potts said evenly. "The case is still developing. Could I have your name please?"

"No. I don't want to leave my name. I have a family."

"I understand," Potts said quietly. "But you understand, too, that your information could very possibly help us."

"Well, I just . . . you know, I was wondering if he could get away with this? You know, it bothers me."

"I don't know what you mean, 'get away' with it."

"Well, is there going to be, you know, any punishment for what he did to her?"

"Are you talking about the Acapulco thing, or the . . . ?"

"I am talking about the girl, Teresa."

"I know, but is it Acapulco or the murder?"

"The murder. The thing in Acapulco . . . you know, I stayed there with my kids and my husband. All I know is that the girl at the front desk told me that Teresa didn't want to prosecute. She was hurting and he had told people at the hotel that there were four men who broke into the room, or two men. Then we found out the truth that he did it, that you know, he beat her all up on her honeymoon."

"You were staying at the hotel at the same time?"

"Yes."

"And what month is this?" Potts asked.

"This is July, 1983. The second week in July."

"Yes."

"We rode to the hotel from the airport with them in the van. We were the only others, my four kids, my husband, and I. And then we invited them to our room, you know, for a drink, because it was their honeymoon. We drank a toast to their wedding."

"Yes," Potts said, his voice carefully controlled. He

was anxiously waiting to hear about the beating but couldn't push.

"We didn't see them after that. Then, when we were leaving, he was in the lobby with the policemen and he called my name. I looked up at him and I saw his growth of beard. I asked him what happened. He said he had been in jail for four days. He said, 'We had a fight.' And, you know, I just thought that he had a fight with people in Mexico, in a bar or something. But then he started saying, 'My wife, she's in the hospital,' and I said, 'What did they do to her?' He said, 'No, not them, me. We had a fight and I beat her.' "

There it was, Potts thought.

"I was wondering if you knew this," the woman said.

"Okay, let me speak to you a second here. What you are telling me is very, very important. It could mean all the difference in the trial. Can't you please let me talk to you person to person, so you could give me a statement on this? It's extremely important."

"I'm afraid," she said after a moment.

"There's no need to be afraid. He's still in jail."

"He's in jail?"

"Yes, he's not out."

"But I'm afraid, though. He could be running around loose."

"He's not going to run loose. There is no need to be afraid."

"No?"

"I'm positive," Potts said reassuringly. "I'm married myself, and I would tell the same thing to my wife."

"You know, if something happened and he got free . . ."

"He won't hurt you, believe me. Right now all he's interested in is getting out of this thing. But you know, every little bit is going to help. What you're telling me would certainly help."

231

"Let me think about it. I want to talk it over with my husband."

"All right," Potts said. "I'm not trying to force you into it, of course. And you know that—ah, look, it could be a thing where the prosecutor could take your statement and he might not have to use you on the stand. This information could be background and it would certainly help in the trial."

"What do you mean?"

"Well, you know, I don't know for sure what's going to happen. I don't have a crystal ball. But let's suppose they say, 'Well, gee, this is an isolated incident, right?' "

"It's what?"

"An isolated incident when he hit her, you know, with a blunt instrument. Well, now we can show there is a pattern and your statement where he said, 'I did it,' that could be important. Really, you ought to bring that forth."

"I really want to."

"Okay," Potts said. "I don't want your last name. What's your first name?"

"Oh, I don't want to say it . . . I think I'm really afraid. It's just terrible . . . awful."

"I know. That's why you ought to give a statement. All I'm asking is your first name."

"I wonder about the young girl's parents. They didn't mention anything about her mother. Is the mother alive?"

"Is the mother alive? Yes, she's alive. Yes."

"Oh, they must be going crazy. Because the newspaper said that the little boy, their little child, was given to his parents."

"Well, that's a matter for the courts," Potts said carefully.

"I know, but I would think . . ."

"Sure, I know what you mean."

"It's so terrible. I have a daughter, twenty-three."

"So you know what this mother is going through?"

"Yes, it's terrible, horrible. Maybe he needs help, but he shouldn't be allowed to get away with this."

"Well, we don't want him to get away with it. Whether it's help he needs or whatever, I don't want him to get away with it either."

"I'll call back in a couple of days," the woman suddenly said.

"Let me have your first name so I'll know who I'm speaking to."

"I'd rather not. What is your name?"

"Potts. Captain Potts, with two t's."

"You know how I feel. I'm just afraid."

"I assure you, there's no reason to be afraid. Even if he got out on bail, he'll only want to save his hide. He's not that dumb, you know, that he'd try to harm somebody."

"Let me call you back."

"All right," Potts said. He'd tried his best and the woman simply was too frightened to loosen up. "When would you call me?" he asked.

"By next week, I promise. Tuesday or Wednesday."

"And you won't give me your first name?"

After a moment the woman said, "Sorayda."

"Sorayda? What is that?"

"It's a Spanish name."

"Ah, Spanish, it's very pretty."

"Thank you."

"Okay, Sorayda, my first name is Jimmie. I hope to hear from you . . ."

"I'll call you back . . ."

"Okay, please do. Thanks for the trouble to call me now. I really appreciate it. I'll wait for your call on Tuesday, maybe even Monday if you can."

Jimmie Potts never heard from the woman

233

again, but Kenneth Taylor would—when he stood trial.

In his diary Ken records learning about Sorayda's call to the Manalapan police when Venturi visited him in mid-January. When Venturi entered the visitors' room his expression seemed to say it all.

"What now, Jack?" Ken said. "They want the death penalty?"

Do you know a Sorayda Peraino?" Venturi asked as he sat down.

"Peraino? Sorayda?" Ken asked, puzzled, his memory rummaging over the years. Then it hit him. "Christ, Jack, I think that was the woman Teresa and I met at Las Brisas. Why? What could she possibly have to do with this?"

According to Ken's diary, Venturi stared at him for a moment. (Venturi, by the way, remembers this scene quite differently. In fact, he maintained that Ken avoided identifying the name "Sorayda" for some time.)

"She says that she saw your picture in the New York papers," Venturi said, "then read the story about Teresa's death and called the police. She says that you told her that you and Teresa had a fight on your honeymoon!"

"What?" Ken said, stunned. "That crazy bitch. When did I tell her this? And *why* would I have told her something like that? Think about it. Even if I had beaten Teresa, would I then go around telling people about it? Be serious, man. Forget it."

"I'd like to forget it, Ken, but Chaiet is jumping on it with both feet."

"Hold on. What possible connection . . ."

Ken stopped, his face dark. "When I was released from jail. I remember . . . I was escorted to the front desk by a couple of cops. As I was checking out I saw that dingy broad. She asked me what happened . . . or something like that. I told her we had been mugged. I don't remember what else I said. I know she seemed surprised. One of the cops spoke to her and she asked something in Spanish. The cop answered her and she ran off like her pants were on fire."

"Well," Venturi said thoughtfully. "That's it. The cop might have told her you beat Teresa."

"But it doesn't make any sense. The cops were on the take for extortion, that's all it was about."

"Not any more, Ken. Peraino is claiming that you told her you and Teresa had a fight, and Chaiet obviously wants to use it."

Both men were silent for a moment. Then, according to Ken's diary, Venturi said, "Well, they can't use it against you, anyway. There's a Rule 55 that prevents evidence of other crimes being used against a defendant."

At the time Venturi had no idea how wrong he could be. The pretrial skirmishing was just picking up momentum.

During the same month of January, 1985, several other significant events occurred.

Following up on the Acapulco lead, Detective Reyes Quinones, an investigator in the county major crimes unit, contacted Dr. Estaban Ortiz Pavon, the young physician at Las Brisas who had been so helpful to the Taylors and the Benignos.

In Quinones' report on their conversation, he describes Doctor Ortiz's memories of the incident:

"Mr. Taylor had stated they had been attacked—but once questioned by hotel security and local police, Mr. Taylor admitted that he was the

235

perpetrator and Mr. Taylor allegedly signed a release form releasing the hotel from any liabilities. Dr. Ortiz Pavon further stated that Mrs. Taylor for reasons unknown would not press charges against her husband. The doctor feels that she would not press charges because she did not want to see her new husband go to jail."

Near the end of his report Quinones says that Dr. Ortiz was willing to send a copy of his medical report, and try to get a copy of the police reports—but he doubted that there were still any official records, since Teresa Taylor had not signed a complaint.

Reflections of Connecticut. Quinones wasn't about to give up so easily. He contacted Las Brisas Security directly and spoke with Mihuel Lugo. Quinones was more than intrigued by the man's memories, for Lugo had been on duty that night.

"Lugo stated that . . . he responded with ten other officers to the Taylor quarters . . . Mr. Taylor was apprehended and transported to a local police station where, after approximately 12 hours of interrogation, he 'unofficially' admitted that he was the perpetrator that had assaulted his wife."

Quinones goes on in his report:

"This investigator requested to know if a formal police report was prepared on the aggravated assault and I was informed that once Mrs. Taylor came to her senses, she refused, stating that they were on their honeymoon; she loved her husband and did not want to see him go to jail."

Then, after some minor league haggling, Quinones

236

managed to get hold of Gabriel Santoyo, the director of Las Brisas Security, who said that he would be happy to send all of the hotel's investigative reports to the prosecutor's office if Quinones asked for the information in a formal, written request to the hotel's general manager.

Quinones was only too happy to agree. He sent the letter off immediately.

The pretrial investigation during the first three months of 1985 was a heated race to collect information about the Taylors before trial. A massive amount of material had already been collected from witnesses, relatives, and friends. Chaiet now had tenuous leads to two other violent episodes in Ken Taylor's life—the ones in Connecticut and Acapulco. By now he had the Waterford police officers' depositions, the Navy investigative and medical reports on the chloroforming of Marilyn Bergman, and provocative hints that Taylor had also beaten Teresa on their honeymoon. In fact, Quinones' preliminary reports of his Mexico contacts were encouraging, but they were mostly suggestive, not solid enough yet. He needed more.

Chaiet also had another intriguing bit of news at this time. It was a letter that the Benignos had received from Las Brisas—something that he would have to share with the defense as part of his discovery material—and that Ken, when he read it, would brush off as the hotel simply defending itself. The letter supported the Benignos' contention that it had been Ken Taylor who had beaten Teresa, and not some fictitious strangers.

Louise Benigno had written to Doctor Ortiz at Las Brisas soon after the honeymoon asking for more information on Teresa's beating. She had received a return letter, dated September 13, 1983, from the executive assistant manager of the hotel.

The Las Brisas letter read:

"The answers to the questions in your letter are as follows: The approximate time Mr. Taylor telephoned regarding the incident was 9:30 P.M., at which time he used the expression 'attack, attack' . . .

"The assistant nanager and the security man, together with the bell captain, went to the room immediately and found it in a terrible state, with broken bottles, bloodstains on the walls, and your daughter lying on the floor on the side of the bed nearest the telephone. It appears she had been trying to reach the phone, but didn't make it. According to our records, your daughter was taken to the hospital between 20 and 30 minutes after the initial call.

"Unfortunately, your daughter was in no condition, in fact she was unconscious, to make a telephone call to you that night. Whether she tried prior to the incident we do not know.

"As you may know, Las Brisas is not open to the public, strangers cannot get into the hotel without the knowledge of our Security Department. In addition to this, there was a security man on duty in the area of your daughter's room and he would have seen anyone entering or leaving the *casita* and would have stopped them if they were not guests of the hotel. We are convinced that the injuries your daughter sustained were caused by someone in that room and not by someone outside it.

"I am sorry to have to be so frank, but all indications lead the police to believe that Mr. Taylor was responsible.

"I understand from Dr. Ortiz that he will be sending you the medical report from the hospital. The police report is basically the same as I have set out above. The only addition I can make is that Mr. Taylor was released because your daughter did not, or could not, sign a complaint."

It was another tantalizing piece of the puzzle. But for Paul Chaiet, the most frustrating—even maddening—piece of evidence was the mysterious phone call from the woman Sorayda. She could supply the hard evidence about Acapulco, the eyewitness account that he needed.

Robert Fausak was assigned the task of trying to track down the mysterious caller. Fausak first tried to get a list of reservations of the people who were staying at Las Brisas during the Taylors' honeymoon. It was a dead end. The hotel explained that luxury resorts couldn't stay in business very long if they handed out their guests' names. Privacy was part of their service.

Next he tried to check any reservation slips for the Westin hotel chain (which owned Las Brisas) that had been made around the honeymoon time period in New Jersey, New York, and Pennsylvania, on the assumption that the news reports "Sorayda" had seen were local. He eventually received almost two dozen reservation slips from the Westin people—but the name Sorayda was not among them.

Chapter Seventeen

As Jack Venturi received the discovery material from Chaiet (which legally he had to share with the defense), he was faced with an ever-growing list of difficult questions.

One of the few positive moments for the defense came, oddly, from a stack of documents that the prosecutor had worked hard to get. Chaiet, after almost a month of pressuring the Connecticut State Attorney's office, was finally able to pry loose the Waterford police files from the Connecticut authorities. The documents arrived in the Monmouth County prosecutor's office on April 15. When Chaiet received the police documents about Ken's attack on Marilyn, they also contained a letter from the superintendent of Fairfield Hills Hospital. Fairfield Hills was the state psychiatric center that had evaluated Ken (at the request of Ken's attorney at the time) independently of the Navy's psychiatric staff soon after the chloroforming incident.

For Chaiet it was an unpleasant surprise—great material for the defense, lousy for the prosecution. The Fairfield Hills psychological study, in part, said:

"Examination revealed a depressed and anxious-appearing white male who was clearly cooperative and in every respect attempted to be helpful during the interview. It was my impression that during the examination he was altogether truthful with me.

"Other than the aforesaid depression and anxiety, Lt. Taylor showed no gross psychopathology other than responses and history which made it clear he suffered to a substantial degree from a passive, submissive, dependent personality (which is not a major psychiatric disorder, even though it accounts for a person's lifestyle). In addition to the above, Lt. Taylor gave a history of both alcohol and amphetamine abuse.

"The lieutenant conveyed to me that on the night of the crime he was not only depressed and extremely resentful of his wife but had been abusing amphetamines and claimed that that night he heard a voice telling him to kill. According to his story, he did attempt to chloroform his wife. She pleaded with him, he interrupted his activity, subsequent to which they both prayed. Through a chain of misadventures he ultimately wound up in a base sick bay, where a psychiatrist, who examined him briefly, purportedly made a statement to the wife that he might repeat his assaultive behavior and allegedly recommended that a complaint be made to the police. On the other hand, subsequent to this examination, the lieutenant was seen and treated by a more senior psychiatrist on the base and in fact remains in treatment at the time of this examination. Further, that not only has the 'injured' wife returned to live with the accused, but also they embarked on a course of marital ther-

241

apy at the recommendation of the base psychiatrist.

"It became apparent through the interview that the lieutenant has an extremely long history of being unable to deal with women and has never been able to properly handle feelings of fear and rage. His rage at the real or fancied humiliation from his wife was dealt with by helpless rage and ultimately this abortive assaultive act. It should be stated that on one occasion in a rage he struck a wall with his hand rather than strike his wife, which to me indicates some degree of control. Further, that though under the influence of controlled substances at the time of the act, he was able to regain control of his behavior and abort his attempt.

"I should also state that in view of the treatment in which he has already embarked and the new insights and personality changes which have begun that the possibility of his repeating assaultive behavior is virtually nonexistent and that in this instance on the one hand incarceration would not help and on the other hand further psychiatric treatment on an ambulatory basis would restore this young doctor to his intended role as someone beneficial to society."

Chaiet read the letter carefully. One comment almost leaped off the page—the bit about the "virtually nonexistent" possibility of Taylor repeating the violence. Tell that to Teresa Taylor and her parents, Chaiet thought.

Venturi, however, was pleased with the letter, because along with the NIS's report and Commander Pettit's psychological evaluation, it established that while Ken might have psychological problems, they fell within "normal" parameters and undercut the prosecutor's inclination to describe Ken as a sex-crazed and brutal maniac.

In addition to the material sent to Venturi about Connecticut, and the continuing growth of information about Acapulco, there were many little things Chaiet was uncovering in his pretrial investigation that troubled him. For example, Venturi was surprised—and disturbed—when Chaiet passed on information uncovered by McCormick that showed a number of telephone calls had been made on the night of the killing to different "sex phone" numbers.

When Venturi showed Ken the telephone logs, and the list of places the calls were made to, he didn't seem surprised. Ken explained that Teresa had been making calls to "sex phone" outfits all night. She was high on coke, he said, and wanted to go down on him while he listened to the woman "talking dirty" on the phone.

He went along with it, Ken said, even though he was exhausted and wanted only to sleep.

Ken told this additional twist on his story factually, sincerely, without hesitating a moment. It all sounded so "true," but then, Venturi had heard many lies that sounded like the truth.

When Venturi brought up the medical examiner's findings about Vaseline being smeared all over Teresa's anus and vagina, as if there had been anal sex going on, Ken still wasn't shaken or even surprised.

"She had her hand between her buttocks," Ken said. "Her culottes were down, not to the floor or to her knees, but half down and off her ass. It flashed on me the second that I noticed her hand between her buttocks and I saw what was going on on the table . . ."

243

Things were not looking good to Venturi. Too many partial truths falling together like a jigsaw puzzle . . . and they weren't falling in the defense's direction.

Venturi's task was clear. He had to counter the psychological profile Chaiet was obviously building up against Ken. Everything would hinge on the credibility of Ken's story. It had to all hang together and be believable. If the jury didn't believe Ken's version of things, then finished the defense was finished. One way to counter Chaiet's profile and help establish Ken's credibility was with expert testimony. It was early in January when Venturi began to develop the idea. Hire experts to examine him. Build up their own psychological profile of Ken Taylor.

Dr. Robert L. Sadoff, a renowned psychiatrist who had been an expert witness in the infamous murder case involving Jeffrey MacDonald, the Green Beret doctor who was convicted of murdering his wife and children, was called in by Venturi.

A preliminary, lengthy psychological examination of Ken Taylor was made on January 25 by Dr. Cook (an associate of Sadoff's)—preliminary, that is, to the use of the drug sodium amytal.

Dr. Sadoff was a recognized expert in the use of sodium amytal and had even been hired by the State of New Jersey on a number of occasions. Of course, Venturi knew that sodium amytal, often referred to as "truth serum," was not admissable in New Jersey courts to establish guilt or innocence. But still, it would carry weight as they tried to establish the state of Ken Taylor's mind and add credibility to his story—that is, if the drug evaluation turned out favorably.

There were several problems with using sodium amytal, however. One was that, like polygraph tests, there were no standardized parameters for measuring results. Creating the proper questions, in the proper context, and interpreting the answers were all left up to the "practitioner" conducting the interview. In the case of polygraphs, that could mean simply any technician familiar with the equipment. At least with Sadoff, Venturi had a psychiatrist, a medical doctor who had administered the drug and assessed the results many times before.

Dr. Sadoff told Venturi that he normally used the drug to help patients retrieve lost memories. He found it especially helpful in criminal cases where there was amnesia surrounding specific events.

But there remained another essential problem with sodium amytal. As with polygraph tests, certain people could "void" the test. In fact, Dr. Sadoff warned Venturi, "It should be noted that people can lie under the influence of sodium amytal and they can also fantasize and give answers that are not reflective of objective truth. Mostly the person may believe that what he is saying is true, but it may not be verified by the facts of the case."

On March 6, Ken was taken to the Jersey Shore Medical Center, in Neptune, New Jersey, which was only a few miles from the jail. For over an hour and a half he answered questions put to him by Dr. Sadoff. In addition to Dr. Sadoff, there were a nurse and a police officer in the examining room, and Jack Venturi, who sat off to the side where Ken couldn't see him.

Dr. Sadoff began the session casually, establishing a relaxed atmosphere.

Ken was lying on his back, dressed in a short-sleeved shirt and slacks. His head was slightly elevated by two pillows. A video camera was at the foot of the bed, focused on the upper half of Ken's body. An IV was attached to his right wrist. Dr. Sadoff stood just off camera to Ken's right.

"What I'm going to do now," Sadoff said, "is give you just a little bit of an injection at this point, as a test dose, to see if you have any reaction. I assume that you will not, because you told me that you are not allergic to medication . . .

"You may tend to inject words that you don't mean and have slips of the tongue, but that's all right. We'll all be aware that it's the effect of the medication and not you."

"Okay," Ken said.

"I'm going to have you relive the experience of the death of your wife and also have you relive other experiences. And by reliving, I mean to have you actually be there, rather than telling me about it in narrative. I want you to see what's going on, look around you . . .

"That way you'll actually experience what happened. What'll happen is, you may have some emotional reaction to it and that's all right. You might shout or scream, you might cry, you might do a lot of things. Again, that is all right. Okay, I'm slowly injecting it. Are you feeling any numbness yet on your tongue?"

"No, not yet."

While waiting for the drug to take full effect, Sadoff asked Ken about his family.

"Tell me something about your mother," Dr. Sadoff suggested.

". . . A very good person. I don't know. She's a religious person, but she's very strong in the family. She tends to try to keep the family together. She's very good with children. That's another reason I wanted her to have my son."

"How was she with you, growing up?"

"Very patient. Very understanding, loving, caring."

"Were you her favorite?"

"I would say so."

At this point Ken was quick with his answers. There seemed little obvious reaction to the drug yet—or even much befuddlement about general information. When asked, he easily supplied places, names, numbers, and even analysis of his feelings.

"How old were you when you had your first sexual experience?" Sadoff asked.

Ken's expression didn't change. He had first had sex when he was about sixteen or seventeen, and the experience had been "fine."

"Have you had any negative sexual experience, or have they all been pretty positive?"

"Positive," Ken replied evenly, "knowing what we know now, and considering everything, the problems I had with Teresa."

"Know what we know about what?" Sadoff asked.

"Maybe, maybe she was a bit oversexual, but I didn't see that as a problem."

"By 'oversexual,' you mean what?"

Ken was now beginning to slur his answers slightly. Words came slower. His face had taken on a more relaxed demeanor.

"Oh, she, let's see, well, the bit with the telephone calls."

"That was her idea?"

"Yes."

"How did you feel about it?"

"I didn't object. I didn't like it, though."

Ken was not yet reacting as Dr. Sadoff had expected. Even though he was searching for words and was slurring more often, he clearly wasn't "reliving"

247

the events. He was talking in a cool, calm voice. His emotional scale was, to anyone watching, relaxed but obviously not involved.

Dr. Sadoff asked Ken questions about events highlighting his and Teresa's life together — including Teresa's drug problems, the baby becoming drugged from Teresa's milk, what happened in Connecticut with Marilyn and in Acapulco with Teresa. Through it all, Ken delivered his story in a calm, relaxed voice. Occasionally he would lift his right arm behind his head to make himself more comfortable, threatening to entangle the IV taped to his forearm. From the side, off camera, the nurse's hands would gently return Ken's arm to his sides and straighten the IV lines.

As the interview went on, his words came harder, the slurring growing stronger. He frequently licked his dry lips.

"How's my pulse?" Ken asked at one point, indicating clearly how alert he still was.

"Normal," Dr. Sadoff said. "It's seventy, seventy-five."

Some small variations began to appear in Ken's story as he related details about his chloroforming Marilyn and about what had happened in Acapulco.

By the fifth or sixth year of their marriage, Ken explained, "Marilyn had become completely frigid and considered me a pig. A male pig. I had had sexual relationships, affairs, if you will, with numerous girls in the Navy. That night I took the chloroform, put it on a sponge [note — not a towel, as he had said earlier] and put it to her face, tried to render her unconscious and rape her."

["Rape" *was* something new and was, of course, in direct contradiction to his own written list of reasons why he wanted to kill her and his earlier admissions to the Waterford police that didn't mention rape.]

248

Ken's expression didn't alter much even as he described the hallucinations, the voices that told him to rape her. Quietly, his voice a pleasant baritone, he said, "I reached a point where I was mad. I was acting like a child."

As the interview progressed, he seemed to begin to lose his train of thought. He was yawning frequently. At moments, genuine emotion began to show. You could tell he didn't like Ronald Wheeler when he described his confrontation with the Navy psychiatrist. "The first thing he said to me was, 'I'm going to shrink your head.'"

By the time Dr. Sadoff opened the subject of Teresa's death, Ken was clearly less in control. At moments he even seemed to be working to control repressed feelings.

In his slow, now almost sleepy baritone, Ken described the night of Teresa's death and how he had gone to sleep only to wake up and find Teresa still not in bed. He woke at about two-thirty in the morning to urinate and asked her what she was doing up. She said that she was still high but would be coming to bed soon.

"At three-thirty I woke (again) and she was still up. At three-thirty we began these, what I call 'sex calls' on the telephone. She wanted me to talk to a woman and have the woman talk to me while my wife performed sexual acts on me."

"What kind of sexual acts?" Dr. Sadoff asked.

"Not intercourse. Oral sex. Petting and one time, anal sex."

Listening intently, Venturi realized that this was also new. Ken hadn't told him about performing anal sex that night. That would account for the large amounts of vaseline on Teresa's genitals and anus. But there

249

had been no evidence of sperm mentioned in the medical examiner's reports.

"On you?" Sadoff asked.

"Yes, while the woman was talking to me. This lasted approximately three hours. I think you have a telephone bill that will . . . list the amount of time.

". . . Okay, of these telephone calls. She used her credit card. She asked me to do the calling. She was embarrassed, for whatever reason, I don't know. She used [sic] a telephone call with her credit card. So I did. Two people would not accept the fact that it was her card. I said, 'Fine, we'll call someone else.' Thereafter I went to bed. Four-thirty. At seven to seven-thirty, I'm guessing more seven-thirty, I woke. My wife was not upstairs. I looked in my son's room. He was not there. He was not asleep. I thought, she's downstairs changing her [sic] diaper. So I went downstairs and this is when I couldn't believe my eyes."

"I want you to be there," Sadoff said, guiding him, trying to get him to experience the emotions of the moment.

"I am," Ken replied, but he still seemed simply tired rather than emotionally involved.

"Can you be there?" Sadoff pressed gently.

"I am."

"What do you see?"

"I am. I'm at the stairways. I believe there's eighteen stairs."

Ken was having much more trouble speaking clearly now. At moments it almost seemed he would fall asleep.

"Orange carpet, white whales . . . right whales . . . rails. I walked two-thirds of the way down the stairs and she didn't see me. Now she's got good ears. She

250

hears sounds all night and wakes me. I say, 'Teresa, that's just the house settling in or expanding. There's nothing to it.'

"What happened here . . ." Ken said dreamily, almost questioning himself.

Then his voice quiet, soft, he went on. "Oh, this is the night my wife was killed. I got halfway down the stairs and I said to myself, 'I believe my wife is doing fellatio on my son.' I got to the bottom of the stairs and I was convinced. I said, 'What the fuck are you doing?' She looked at me very glassy-eyed, very . . . her eyes were red . . . very glassy-eyed, drug-crazed. She had probably done a gram of cocaine that night . . . a gram of cocaine.

"She had her culottes pulled down. And now I did not know this at the time, but I have since been informed at the autopsy that she had smeared Vaseline all over her buttocks, her anus and perineum. Now she was fellating my son on the table and trying to put her fingers into her anus or rectum, anus or vagina . . . I don't know . . ."

Ken paused and sighed and took a deep breath. He seemed to be falling asleep. Then he began again. "She looked at me, as I said, and ran, scurried, her skirts and pantyhose were down. I've been questioned on that. Okay, how fast can a woman run with her panties down? She scurried across the hall, approximately twelve to fifteen feet across the room into the hall, and then into the laundry room. I pick my son up off the mat, because I knew he would fall over, and put him in the baby bed.

"I followed my wife to the laundry room and she tried to kill me . . . she tried to kill me. She swung a set of dumbbells at my head. I've since been informed that they are twenty-five to thirty pounds, which is not

251

surprising. She was five-seven . . . uhh . . . two, three, but she was strong."

Ken yawned again and his eyelids fluttered. He was clearly feeling the influence of the sodium amytal, but it didn't appear to have much effect on his emotions.

"I didn't know if she would try to render me unconscious, knock me out . . . which is the same thing . . . or run in and hit my son. So I fought. I went down . . . somewhat. I grabbed the barbell that was waiting by the door to hold the door open as a doorstop. I picked up the doorbell [sic] and I hit her in the head. She fell to the floor . . . I fell to the floor. It was like I hit the wall and then just slid down. Moments . . . probably twenty to thirty moments later . . . I came out of what I call a robot or trancelike stance . . . a trancelike stance. After that I had become a robot. I checked my wife's vital signs and she had none. She looked like she was in bad shape. Apparently, she was in bad shape. Apparently, I hit her more than once. Apparently, the autopsy report says nine . . . uhh . . . skull fractures."

"Try to be there," Sadoff said quietly, trying to get him to let loose emotionally. "You *hit* her with the barbell?"

"Yes . . ."

"How many times do you remember hitting her?"

"Twice . . . and she fell. I hit her once and I hit her on the way down . . . and she fell."

"Do you remember hitting her more than once?"

"No, sir."

"Is that the first time you remember twice? Usually you say once."

"The second time was when she was falling . . . grabbing at my leg as if to punch me, claw me or trap . . . tackle . . . me."

252

"Have you ever told anybody you hit her twice?"

"No, sir . . . I think I told my lawyer."

"Because he told me you hit her once. Can you remember hitting her a third time?"

"No, sir."

"Fourth time?"

"No, sir."

"You think you did . . . or do you think you could have given her nine skull fractures by hitting her twice?"

"No. I believe I hit her more."

"Why don't you remember?"

His eyelids heavy, and clearly fighting to stay alert, Ken slowly reached his right hand up to scratch his ear. The nurse gently moved his arm away and again straightened the IV tubes.

"What happened that you don't remember?" Sadoff continued.

As exhausted as Ken appeared, he still was thinking rationally, analytically — even argumentatively.

"Well," Ken said, "it's not that I don't remember. It's just that nine cumulated fractures could come from three blows."

"Why couldn't it come from two blows?" Sadoff asked.

"It could. I'm just saying the odds are better that they could come from three."

"Or could they come from nine blows? Do you think you hit her nine times?"

"They were all in the same area . . ." Ken said, appearing to mull over the question.

"All in the same area?" Sadoff asked. "So a couple of good swings might have given her nine fractures. You didn't have to hit her more than twice, did you?"

Ken sighed and paused, seeming to drift off. "I . . . I don't know," he finally said.

"Well, you remembered everything else up to that point in great detail."

"I know she was breathing."

"She was what?"

"Breathing . . ."

"She was breathing, and you know you hit her. You remember hitting her twice?"

Ken yawned again and paused, almost as if he forgot that he had been asked a question.

"Why do you think if you hit her a third time or fourth time that you wouldn't remember?"

Ken seemed to arouse himself. "That I wouldn't?" he asked.

"Yes."

"You mean with this medicine in me?"

"Now, yeah. Even now, if you'd hit her a third time, suppose she's lying on the ground . . . you take that barbell and you keep smashing her and smashing her. Wouldn't you remember?"

"I don't believe so . . . I have dissected skulls and I know where the bones come into each other. And I know that a fracture here . . ." Ken slowly raised his hand and pointed at the side of his head. Then he continued, ". . . is most likely going to fracture two or more bones."

"So you could have hit her only twice?"

"That's very possible."

"Okay. Then you went into some kind of trance?"

"Yes, I remember slumping against a door."

"What was on your mind when you hit her?" Sadoff asked, still trying to get Ken more involved in the memory. "What were you thinking? What was going on?"

254

"I was thinking, I've saved my life and my son's life. I didn't know she was dead until I came out of the trance."

"Did you intend to kill her?"

"No."

"What was your intent?"

"My effect . . . my intent . . . was to defend myself."

"Against what?"

"Against the attack that she was doing to me with the swinging of the doorbells [sic] on my head."

"How did you save your son's life?"

"I knocked her in the head and removed the doorbells [sic]."

"What makes you think she would have harmed your son?"

"She was already harming my son."

"How?"

"By performing fellatio on him."

"That's harmful to him. How did you feel . . ."

"It's not harmful physically, but I can just imagine the child's complex later in life when he goes to his mother for fellatio."

"How did you feel when you saw her fellating your son?"

"Berserk . . ."

"Berserk? Why should that make you so berserk?"

"Because I knew she was high. A few hours before we had these phone sex . . . while she was doing that to me and having me and the woman on the other end I just thought . . . This is enough, this really is enough."

"When you told me how you saw her doing this to

255

your son, you didn't sound as though you were berserk. You were just describing it very calmly to me. But in fact you got very upset?"

"Yes."

"Why aren't you upset now talking about it?"

"I am, but I think I'm sodium amytaled out . . ."

"When you talk about it without the sodium amytal, do you get more emotional?"

"Yes, I usually get emotional and tear."

"You're crying a little bit now. You were somewhat emotional."

"I cried a lot with Dr. Cook."

"Did you? Why?"

A flicker of a smile crossed Ken's lips. "Boy, you have a way with questions. He [Dr. Cook] mentioned my daughter. My daughter and I were very close. The fact that I can't communicate with her . . . can't call her . . . I can't write to her. I can't see her. Can't hold her. I can't play with her."

"You seem to have more feeling about her than you do about your son . . ."

"No, that's not true."

"Do you know of any other mother who has ever fellated her son?"

"Yeah . . ." Ken answered, his words slurring badly now.

"Who?"

"A sleazy couple . . . in Ohio."

"People you knew?"

"Yeah."

"Anybody in your family?"

"No."

"Did what you saw between your wife and your son bring back any memories about you and your mother?"

256

"Yeah . . . because she had done it to me that night."

"Not your wife. I'm talking about your mother."

Pausing, and seeming to pull his lumbering thoughts together, Ken finally said, "My mother? No."

"This is your son's mother doing it to him. Did you have any feelings at all about your mother at that time?"

"No, none whatsoever."

"The harm that your wife did to your son by fellating him was one thing. Did you think she was going to harm him physically as well?"

"Not until she ran into the laundry room and picked up the barbells and tried to kill me."

"Did you think she might do something to him?"

"I thought that if she rendered me unconscious, she would kill him."

"Why? Why would she do that?"

"Teresa was very strung out. We're talking months of cocaine and codeine."

"Okay, how do you account for that trancelike state that you said you had?"

"I think I was not believing . . . but believing . . . not being able to believed that my wife was dead. That she had been so good to my son . . . except for the fellatio. And my wife had been so good to me."

"When did you come out of that trance?"

"Three hours."

"Three hours?"

"Not even. Two hours."

"Two hours. When you came out of it what did you do?"

"First? The very first thing I did was walk to see if my son was in the infant seat, and he had fallen

257

asleep. Then I hurried back to my wife and she had no pulse."

"She had no pulse? What were you feeling at the time?"

"Well, I know I had hit my wife in the head, uh, twice, and I believed she was dead."

"What did you do?"

"What did I do? I wrapped her in a carpeting pad that's used for carpeting. I brought her to the car and put her in the trunk of the Oldsmobile. I decided to take my son to Indiana and then come back and either one of two things—turn myself in, report what had happened, or kill myself."

Ken was almost nodding off to sleep by this time, but Sadoff kept probing. When he asked, "Why did you drive around for so long with Teresa's body in the car?" Ken didn't seem to grasp the question. Then, pulling his thoughts together, his eyes still closed, he answered in his calm, analytical way:

"So long . . . because it was cold and the body gases were not starting to smell a lot . . ."

"Why did you choose that place to leave her body?"

"Why? First of all I was beginning to panic. Secondly, it was a very nice place . . . an animal sanctuary."

"Why didn't you bury her?"

"I didn't want to leave her."

"Why not?"

"I loved her. What happened was just a freak. We were so happy together. I had been married three times. I knew what hell was in marriages. I knew what problems were. We just didn't have those. We were best friends at first. We were totally supportive of each other and very loyal."

"So you kept her as long as you could?"

"Right."

"Why didn't you bring her back to New Jersey?"

"I felt my life was over. My life was ruined. I killed the woman I loved."

"Why didn't you kill yourself?"

"I tried . . . I took a bottle of Jack Daniels into the car and garage . . . I began thinking of my children, my parents, my family. They don't deserve this. They've lost Teresa. Losing me is not going to help. I'll take my chances. I'll go to jail."

Sadoff paused for a moment, then asked, "Anything you want to tell me or ask me that I didn't ask you?"

Ken thought this over for a few seconds. "I wanted to know . . . and I think Jack mentioned this to me . . . that there was a psychosexual problem or possibility with me."

"With you?"

"Yeah."

"With respect to what?"

"Well, I don't know. I didn't know how to understand that. I'm not a homosexual. I've never raped anyone. I attempted to rape my second wife. I have not been with children. I've been with two women. I've never been with a man."

"Two women at the same time?"

"Yes. But I don't know what that means . . . psychosexual possibility in relation to me?"

"I'm not sure we can answer that right now."

"Well, okay, let's face it. I had the Acapulco thing. I had this thing, I had the chloroform."

"The Acapulco thing you said was people who broke in."

Ken's eyes opened suddenly. "That's right."

"So, if that's true, there's no psychosexual problem, is there?"

"Right."

"Okay," Sadoff said. "I think that's enough. Are you tired? You think you'll be all right?"

"I could sleep . . ."

Now that it was over, Venturi had a mixed reaction to the sodium amytal session. On the one hand, much of Ken's basic story had been supported under the drug's influence. There were minor discrepancies, sure, but depending on Sadoff's report, the tape did help establish Ken's state of mind at the time of the killing and immediately after it.

But in another way, the tape didn't really matter, simply because sodium amytal couldn't be used to establish innocence in New Jersey courts. Venturi could get around that by avoiding using the name of the drug and have Sadoff testify as an expert witness only on Ken's "state of mind."

Venturi had to hope that Sadoff would find Ken's story credible and that his report would reflect that. It would be hard for a New Jersey judge to deny Sadoff's expertise in describing Ken's state of mind. He had recently been an expert witness before a New Jersey state commission that was determining whether to change the standard M'Naghten insanity test ("knowing right from wrong") used in state courts. It was Sadoff's testimony that had influenced the state legislature to leave the law on the M'Naghten standard intact.

What was most disturbing, however, was the unemotional way Ken related even the most tragic and dramatic parts of the story. Even under drugs he gave the impression of distance, of lacking involvement in the most emotional moments — an unemotional "iceman,"

260

as some of the witnesses' depositions had described him.

To any objective observer, Ken never did achieve Sadoff's goal of "actually being there rather than telling about it in narrative." He surely didn't, as Sadoff had hoped, "actually experience what happened . . . have some emotional reaction to it . . . shout or scream . . . or cry."

Ken, however, was delighted with the tape when the videos was played back for him later. Under the influence of the renowned "truth serum," his story had basically been supported.

Soon after the sodium amytal session (and Ken's viewing of it), Venturi received a letter from Ken. It was a defensive letter full of self-justification, almost as if the description of him as "cold" and "unfeeling" was finally begin to bother him. Or perhaps he simply realized that it would be a destructive description of him before a jury and he had to set down a defense.

"Jack," *Ken wrote,* "After the interview on Wed 3/6/85 I understand some things about my case and my personality. Until the last two years I was not 'cold' as you and others are describing me. There are several reasons for this. First of which is I have had a very tumultuous and tough adult life. I've had a lot of pain, hurt and disappointment. I've seen a hell of a lot and I've lived a hell of a lot. I've been through some times that could change the toughest of individuals. I'm a strong person but I've been through so much hell that I've become hardened. I can handle pressure and I always have. I have always been the clutch performer but over the years all these clutch performances have

261

worn the edge and flattened my personality.

"I can handle pressure just as always but I've become the 'iceman.' I love my family and children like nothing else and more than ever. In all of the athletic events and teams I've participated with, I've always and consistently been the clutch performer and I've always provided. In the Navy my captain depended on me to carry the load for the clinic. There were times when he said I save his ass by carrying the load and keeping up 'production' while our staff was cut into half and we still got the work done.

"In Brooklyn I worked sixty hours a week, managed ten girls, four dentists, the 'books' for the office, and trained the dentists as well as did at least one half of the entire patient load. It was hell but I did it. (Dental school did a number on me also—I'd rather discuss that issue than write about it.) In fact, I'd rather discuss the whole thing so I'm going to stop writing. I've seen and done so much that I know why I've hardened."

As if the letter itself was not enough self-explanation and justification, Ken sent along an accompanying memo that was printed in large, almost angry block letters.

COLD?

I. As a hospital orderly—
   1. Three all-night "death" watches (two of these people died while I was "watching" them).
   2. Walked into room to take vital signs and found patient had died when I began to take pulse.

3. I had to take four *babies* to the morgue wrapped up and put them in the freezer waiting autopsy (four separate occasions).
4. Assisting a surgeon in surgery—
He did not tell me what he was doing. He told me to hold the boy's (sixteen yrs.) leg. He picked up an instrument and amputated the boy's leg from the thigh. I was left holding the leg. He laughed!
5. I had to care for a quadriplegic (twenty-nine-year-old man), turn him, clean him, hold urine bottles for him.

II. I've had women come to me—in the Navy (officers' wives, enlisted wives, dental assistants, patients, etc., etc.)—and do everything from asking me to take them to actually walking into my room and taking off their clothes. I have had a commanding officer of a submarine ask me to take his wife while he was out to sea. I have been bombarded by women in so many ways I became cold. I couldn't believe the number of wives and others, girlfriends, etc., who came on to me. I really didn't like it. (They came to my house!)

If I appear to be cold, maybe I am. But there is a reason for everything.

I had a lot of sleazy-type girlfriends. Druggies, go-go girls, and even two hookers. They would pick me out. Six different times go-go dancers *asked me* to take them out after their jobs was finished that night.

I told Dr. Cook about a hitchhiker who practically raped me. She was gorgeous. This just doesn't happen to people.

Two airlines stewardesses (separate incidents) *picked me up* on flights (not including Marilyn Bergman). Each one gave me a note—one to meet her in Indianapolis and *one* to go the back of the plane with her.

Jack, if I appear cold, there are good reasons.

III. The two broken marriages took a lot out of me. Losing Rhonda was devastating. That little girl loves me. I can't think about her without tears coming to my eyes.

IV. Drug abuse—No explanation needed.

V. Teresa—

Ken's bold block letters suddenly changed to a thready script. His pen was no longer digging hard into the paper but racing across the page.

She was the epitome of what I wanted. She was by no means the most attractive woman I had. She was chubby. Teresa was so good to me and love [sic] me so totally. We were best friends. We were best lovers. She was the one woman I could have lived a lifetime with. Teresa and I could say anything to each other and do anything together.

After all the bullshit with women, I finally found the one woman I loved as a person. We were partners. We were friends, lovers, spouses, business partners, parents, homemakers, etc., etc. Jack, I've lost her. The one woman, the one person, my best friend, is gone. She's dead. You wonder why I'm cold?! I could have spent my entire life with her and been forever happy.

Yes, I'm cold. I've lost my wife, my profession, my daughter, and now people are trying to take away my son. I have memories and nightmares that would put most people in a straitjacket, but I continue to function. Yes, I'm cold, but I love my familyand children. I want to have a simple life caring for my family and giving them the best I can. I want my freedom and need it. Now that I'm certain about what happened, I know-for sure I'm okay.

P.S. I could go on and on about the experiences and situations in my life that have hardened my exterior, but I think you get the message.

Venturi filed the letter and memo. It was a mystery why Ken Taylor felt it necessary to make such an impassioned plea for understanding. As revealing as the letter and memo were about the man, there was nothing Venturi could use in them to help build the defense's case.

Chapter Eighteen

The Waterford police had interviewed Ken's first wife only by telephone during their investigation of Marilyn's being attacked. McCormick wanted to speak to Katherine Mitchell directly, to get an official deposition, but it would be more difficult than he had imagined. First, when he called he discovered that her phone had been disconnected, so McCormick then contacted the Indianapolis police, who put him in touch with the principal of the school where Kay Mitchell was working as a teacher. The principal turned out to be very protective of his staff, explaining that Kay didn't really want to become involved in her ex-husband's troubles. Only after McCormick explained that this was a capital crime, a murder investigation, and that she could be subpoenaed, was it arranged that they could meet her—along with her attorney at the Indianapolis police station.

In late April, 1985, Detectives Fausak and McCormick flew to Indianapolis.

With her strong body and dark hair, Kay Mitchell was not unattractive, but she did nothing to accentuate her virtues. She wore no makeup or jewelry and sat quietly with her ankles crossed and her hands clasped in her lap. Her overall impression was "proper." It was hard to imagine her married to the womanizing, alcohol-binging, and drug-taking young Ken Taylor.

After some preliminary questions about identification and about when she had last seen or heard from Ken Taylor, McCormick asked her to explain the circumstances surrounding her divorce from Taylor.

"During my marriage to Kenneth Taylor, he began to become involved in drugs and was seeing other women. Near the end of our marriage, he met a gal, I believe her name was Marilyn Bergman, whom he went out with, and when I was nine months pregnant, we separated and were divorced later that year."

"Could you please elaborate about Mr. Taylor's being involved with drugs?"

"During our marriage, Kenneth Taylor and I went to several parties during college, and there was pot being passed around and we would smoke. Then, as the years of our marriage grew on, and I began to work and become the breadwinner, and the people I associated with were quite different than the people he was with, he wanted to continue this kind of experience. I was really not very interested. At that time I could begin to see that we were starting to go apart and had differences. Near the end of the marriage, approximately six months before we had separated, he had stored in the spare bedroom closet of our apartment three large garbage bags of pot or hashish, or whatever it was. I went into a fit of rage and they were removed immediately. Then later on, another month or two, when I was home from work ill and he did not expect me to be there, he came in with several large quart-sized plastic bags full of pills, and again I went into a rage . . ."

"You mentioned you were the breadwinner?"

"I was a teacher."

"Were you supporting the two of you?"

"Yes, I was."

"Was there any indication that he was going to leave you?"

"Ken and I were having differences. But there were no plans for us to separate. I came home one day and he had packed his bags and moved out."

"Has there been any contact with Kenneth Z. Taylor since the birth of your daughter?"

"I have not seen Kenneth since he left that one day in early June, 1974 . . . He filed for divorce later on that summer or that fall . . . He was ordered to pay twenty-five dollars a week in child support. He did pay very inconsistently for the first two or three years. The child support would come to me in strange amounts, like thirty-two dollars, forty-nine cents, or one hundred twenty-two dollars and two pennies . . . Somewhere along the second or third year I hadn't received any child support for some time. I attempted to contact Ken while he was in the Navy and did speak with him very briefly on the phone for maybe a minute or two, concerning payment of the support. I have filed for contempt of court on several different occasions."

"Did Mr. Taylor display any indications that he was upset or unhappy with your pregnancy?"

"Early in the pregnancy, before I had gone to the doctor to find out for sure, Ken indicated at that time a lot of delight. He told many of his friends that I was pregnant, seemed to be very happy and pleased with the idea we were having a child. Throughout the remainder of the months, he really did not show any affection toward me one way or the other.

"He didn't, you know," she went on, "show any extra

268

consideration because of the pregnancy, but also I can't say that he neglected me during that time, either."

"Do you recall any particular occasion where there may have been a physical altercation between you and Mr. Taylor?"

"Only after we separated. I was speaking to his parents one evening on the phone. They wanted to speak to their son and I informed them that he had moved out . . . I gave them the telephone number of a friend . . .

"Later on they did call and say that he was coming over and to expect him shortly. When Ken came into the apartment he was very angry, the most anger I'd ever seen him display. He picked up a basketball and threw it at a rocking chair and broke the back of the chair."

McCormick and Fausak glanced at each other. Normal temper tantrum, or shades of coming events?

"At this point, is there anything else that you would like to add?"

"No," Katherine said, relieved that the whole thing was over.

In tying up the leads he had uncovered during the pretrial investigation, McCormick had subpoenaed the Taylors' telephone records. He wanted to check more closely into the "sex phone" calls made during the early hours leading up to Teresa's death. In searching for patterns in the sex calls, he also asked for the telephone records for several months prior to November 11.

Bingo. Three calls to a whorehouse in Manhattan the night of the killing. Then he found that the same whorehouse had been called the night Teresa had given birth to Philip. The discovery would make it practically impossible for Ken Taylor to claim that Teresa made all the calls. There was no way that a jury would believe she was so oversexed that she would call a whorehouse from her hospital room only hours after giving birth.

Fausak had tried every angle he could think of to locate "Sorayda" and still the woman eluded him. Every time the subject of Acapulco came up, Chaiet would look at him and ask how he was coming on Sorayda.

Fausak had reviewed the Westin Hotel reservation slips until his eyes were crossing, and still no Sorayda. He went back to the recording of Sorayda's conversation with Officer Potts. This time he noticed that the woman had said she had gone to Las Brisas with her husband and children.

Jesus, maybe he was looking for the wrong thing on the reservation slips . . . He went back to the pile of paper, but this time looking for families traveling together.

There *was* something—"Mr. and Mrs. L. Peraino & Family." They had reserved two rooms, 510 and 511. There was also the name of a Long Island travel agency on the slip. His instincts were vibrating that this was the right one, but to be sure, he called the agency and talked with the manager.

It was he—the couple had registered as "Louis and Sorayda Peraino."

At first she was reluctant to give a deposition, but

after continued coaxing by McCormick, Fausak, and then Chaiet, she finally agreed to talk.

She was what many would call a handsome woman, with long black hair and a still astonishingly young body for a woman in her late thirties who had given birth to eight children. She sat nervously, holding her husband's hand and speaking quickly to the detectives.

She described how they had met the Taylors and their brief social evening together.

Then McCormick asked her, "When did you next encounter either Kenneth or Teresa Taylor?"

"On the last day of our week's stay, I saw Ken Taylor. It was in the lobby of the hotel. He was standing on line with two Mexicans. I believe they were Mexican policemen. That's what Ken Taylor said. Ken had seen me in the lobby and called my name. He told me he had to get his money, to get bail to get out of jail, and asked me would I lend him some money if he didn't have enough."

"What did Ken Taylor tell you regarding his situation?"

"He told me, 'We had a fight.' I thought he meant in town, and I asked, 'Where's Teresa?' He said, 'She's in the hospital.' I still thought they had a fight with someone in town. And I asked what hospital was Teresa in, and he began to tell me that he and Teresa had fought. lie told me that they wouldn't let him see Teresa, that he had knocked her teeth out and they wouldn't let him fix her teeth, that he was a dentist.

"He went on to say that she had bit him on the foot, and 'I hit her,' that they had been drinking and had a fight. After I walked away upset, I spoke with a Mexican lady who worked for the hotel, and she told me that it was terrible what happened to his wife, that he had called and said that four Mexicans had broken

271

into the room, and he did admit to the police that he was the one that beat his wife up. The lady said it was terrible what he had done to her on the honeymoon."

"Do you recall Kenneth Taylor saying anything while at your suite when they came over for the honeymoon drink?"

"He was very quiet, but while Teresa was saying something about his being a dentist and them being married, and speaking about clothes she had purchased, he replie, 'Now that she's my wife, I'll straighten her out.' "

She was going to be one hell of a witness—obviously wealthy and attractive, yet warm, emotional, and full of compassion for Teresa and the Benigno family. Her nervousness and reluctance to be a witness only added to her credibility.

The day after Venturi gave a copy of Sorayda's statement to Ken, he received back a memo in which Ken consistently misspelled the woman's name, even though it had been written clearly a number of times in the police report.

SORYADA

"Upon arriving at the hotel with my escort of 5 policemen, I noticed Soryada in the lobby near the reception desk. When she saw me, she exclaimed, 'What happened to you, Ken?'

"I was in bad shape. I was filthy, dirty, and very shaken from no food, clothing change, or shower for 4 nights. I had not shaved, and in short, I looked like a bum from sleeping on the floor of the jail, as there were no beds or mats to lie on.

"I told her I had to pay the police $500 to let me go see Teresa. The police (one on either side of me) stood behind me slightly. The other 3 police were scattered about the lobby: one talking to the man at the reception desk and the other two talking to hotel employees (2 maids).

"I told her Teresa had been beaten badly and that I had been hit on the head, cut on the arms, hands, and also cut on the foot. I told her the police had told me Teresa had broken teeth from her beating and that I wanted to be able to at least repair the damage to her teeth and try to make her comfortable.

"I told her the police had taken me to jail to cover up for the hotel security deficiency. I told her the police had not charged me with anything as I had not done anything, just that they wanted to lay the blame on me instead of damage their reputation with their tourist trade.

"At that point, Mr. Nilo Lopez, who was at the reception desk, came to me and took me to an office where all of our belongings were located. From there I could see that two police who were standing near me were talking to Soryada. (She spoke Spanish and therefore these 2 'police' explained to her in Spanish their version of the story.)

"Upon viewing our belongings, I noticed that we were missing the tricolored gold bracelet, a gold cigarette lighter, and my Cross pen that had been stolen by the police captain, Gutierrez Mendoza. After meeting Teresa in her hotel [sic]

273

room, I discovered she was missing 2 pair of earrings and her diamond engagement ring.

"There was an insurance claim made with USAA insurance in San Antonio, Texas. Because the items were not individually insured, we were paid a lump sum of $500 allowed for stolen jewelry. (I believe it was $500. I valued the total loss at $2500, as I recall.)

"Soryada was in an excited state trying to check out of the hotel and appeared to be upset. She spoke fluent Spanish and did seem to like both Teresa and I. I feel certain that she misunderstood me and got the 'official version' from the police."

Venturi had hired Jeff Prusan, a private investigator, primarily to check into Teresa's drug use, and he now decided to send the PI to talk with Sorayda. But Sorayda, already nervous from the police visit and the possibility of having to testify at an open trial, wouldn't see him.

It was not a good day for Jack Venturi. Connecticut had always been hanging over their heads—and now there was Sorayda Peraino and Acapulco.

On May 8 Jack Venturi notified Chaiet that "Dr. Kenneth Taylor intends to claim self-defense of self-protection and protection of another."

This puzzled Chaiet. He had expected a plea of temporary insanity, or even one of the several categories of manslaughter "in the heat of passion," which would have been more logical. But this defense really didn't change much—both he and Venturi still had to contend with the key element—Ken Taylor's "state of

274

mind" at the time of the killing. That was why Ken's history of violence was so important. And that was why the prosecutor wanted the previous assaults admitted, and the defense was going to work like hell to keep both Connecticut and Acapulco out.

And then there were Rule 55 and Rule 8—legal precedents that would determine what evidence would be allowed. In fact, the trial might very well hinge on how Judge Ferran would rule on those two issues.

During the first week of May, Ken broke his ankle while playing basketball in the rec yard of the Monmouth County Jail. He was moved from the controlled chaos in the grand jury cellblock to the medical wing, where a cast was put on his foot. This move to the medical wing would result in Ken Taylor's first escape attempt.

Three weeks had passed since Chaiet had received the Las Brisas security reports on the Taylor assault. There was little new in the material, but the few things that caught his attention were significant. The fact that Ken did not appear injured (a "tiny cut," according to one statement) while Teresa had been savaged to the point where she had defecated on herself didn't make any sense. If burglars had broken in, the normal thing would have been to attack the victim who could be dangerous and fight back—the man, not a sleeping woman. And another thing that bothered Chaiet was that the bed Teresa was supposed to be sleeping in was "still made up," according to one report.

There was no doubt in his mind: what happened in

Acapulco had to be pursued, otherwise he probably couldn't use it in the trial. On March 11, the same week of Ken's sodium amytal interview, Chaiet sent McCormick, Fausak, and Reyes Quinones, as translator, to Acapulco.

They stayed-in the same room as the Taylors—*casita* 249. Chaiet wanted a complete description of the hotel's physical setup and the security arrangements.

Fausak walked around the area, photographed the grounds, drew a diagram of the *casita* and grounds, and checked on the spacing of guards and patrols.

Quinones immediately tried to telephone Alvaro Gutierrez Mendoza, the Commandante of the Acapulco police. Quinones had tried to telephone the man from New Jersey and failed. He had no better luck here in Acapulco. It was clear Gutierrez was avoiding them.

It was also clear that many of the hotel employees were nervous about talking with them. The investigators got the distinct impression that they didn't want to say the wrong thing—and get either the hotel or themselves in trouble.

Quinones and McCormick did, however, talk with Gabriel Santoyo, the director of security at the hotel.

Santoyo's story was basically what the investigators already knew. The security at the hotel was extensive—three twenty-two-man shifts each day, and in addition, five mobile patrols and a guard on foot walking the perimeter chain-link fence.

In McCormick's report he noted that Santoyo was asked if there had been any other incidents involving intruders at the hotel near the period when the Taylors were staying there.

"He [Santoyo] advised that since he has been with the security forces at Las Brisas—for the

276

past five years — there have only been two incidents of such assaults, one in May 1984, the other in June. In both incidents, the perpetrators were apprehended. Santoyo advised that in 1983 [Teresa Taylor had been assaulted there on July 14, 1983] there were 192 reported thefts at the hotel. It is believed that most of these thefts are committed by certain employees, but unless they are caught in the actual crime, the union they belong to protects them from being fired."

(Venturi would later be pleased with this news. Two assaults during a two-month period in 1984 supported the fact that such things can and do happen at the resort, regardless of its security arrangements.)

McCormick and Quinones also interviewed Miguel Lugo, a security captain who had been on duty that night. When he arrived at *casita* 249, Lugo described seeing Taylor talking with Jose Romero, an assistant manager who had been on duty that night. Romero had been one of the first hotel employees at the scene. Taylor had told Romero that they had been assaulted by "one individual wearing blue pants."

In his report, McCormick noted that Lugo had told them he was very suspicious when he arrived "because everyone, including Taylor, believed Mrs. Taylor was dead and that Taylor was not upset."

After checking Mrs. Taylor and finding a slight heartbeat, Lugo went to Mr. Taylor and Romero, who were still standing on the balcony, and asked Romero to translate to Taylor that his wife was still alive and that an ambulance had been summoned.

"Taylor just sat there emotionless and remained emotionless even after Mrs. Taylor started to moan and call out for help. Lugo went to her and attempted

277

to comfort her. After doing so, Lugo had Romero ask Taylor for a better description of the assailant. Taylor responded that 'he was like you,' indicating that [the man] was about the same size as Lugo. Lugo had Taylor stand and related that he could not understand how an individual the size of Taylor could have been assaulted by anyone as small as himself.

"Lugo examined Taylor and observed fingernail scratches on the inside of both of Taylor's forearms. He also noticed a small, very slight reddish mark on Taylor's forehead but did not observe any other injuries on him . . .

"The doctor arrived and attended to Mrs. Taylor, who was taken to the hospital. When she was being taken out, she began to moan in pain and ask for help. Taylor made no attempt to comfort her."

When Ken Taylor had called for help that night, the assistant manager, Jose Romero, who was fluent in English, had answered the switchboard and heard Taylor call out, "attack, attack!"

Romero had jumped into a Jeep, and along with another assistant manager and a security guard, raced to *casita* 249.

"Mr. Romero stated that as soon as he got into the room, he smelled blood and excrement. He observed Taylor lying on the floor of the room by the bathroom. Taylor was clothed in a short-sleeved shirt and yellow swimming shorts. He appeared in a daze. The shower stall door was open and the water running. His legs appeared wet.

"Romero then turned to the corner of the room, where he saw Teresa Taylor on the floor covered with blood, wearing a pink baby-doll type nightgown. The

278

floor under her was covered with blood. There was a broken green glass water bottle on the floor, as well as broken glass on the bed. Romero advised that the sheets to the bed had been turned down, but the bed did not appear as though anyone had been in it."

Another employee that Quinones and McCormick succeeded in questioning was Doctor Ortiz Pavon, the physician that had first attended Teresa Taylor.

"Dr. Ortiz advised that Mrs. Taylor appeared dead. She was covered with blood. There was blood all over the walls, as well as on the floor where she was located. Mrs. Taylor's pulse was weak. She was given immediate attention for her eye and a deep gash on her throat. Teresa Taylor had been beaten so badly that she had defecated on herself.

"He advised that he did notice an odor of alcohol on Mrs. Taylor's breath, but he failed to notice the same on Taylor because he was only with him a short time . . .

"While he was in the room treating Mrs. Taylor, Taylor was placed in a chair on the balcony by security people who were speaking to him. He said that Taylor acted very calm and cool during the incident . . ."

A few days after the assault, Dr. Ortiz visited Mrs. Taylor in the hospital. "He said that Taylor was with her and that when the doctor [Ortiz] asked her what had happened, Taylor appeared to become frightened. Mrs. Taylor said that she preferred not to discuss it. When Mrs. Taylor's father arrived at the hospital, Taylor again became frightened—that he was nervous and shaking and repeatedly asked the doctor when his wife would be able to travel."

279

* * *

After trying several more times, McCormick and Quinones finally succeeded in meeting the elusive Commandante Gutierrez. He was, according to Taylor, one of the main figures in the extortion and bribery. The two men realized that they had to move carefully and not even get near the subject of bribery.

When McCormick asked why, if Taylor had been such an obvious and logical suspect in his wife's beating, official charges hadn't been brought against him, Gutierrez explained that they (the Mexican police) had to be sensitive to the economic realities involved. Doctor Taylor was an American, and if the affair had progressed too far it might have created bad publicity and tourism might have been affected. Besides, a complaint had to be signed, and Mrs. Taylor refused to do that. No charges were brought, and therefore there were no police records.

Gutierrez, a short man with black, darting eyes, was unpleasant. He shrugged a lot during the interview, smiled with his mouth but not his eyes, and didn't hesitate to tell the two American investigators that when he visited Mrs. Taylor in the hospital she was so grateful for his concern and help that she had given him her beautiful watch, which he promptly gave to his own wife.

Another Mexican police officer, Armando Vallarino, was more pleasant to talk with—and more helpful. Vallarino was fluent in English and had interrogated Taylor that night.

During the long hours of questioning, Taylor had repeatedly said that two terrorists dressed in black had assaulted them. At one point, Vallarino claimed, he had said, "You're lying . . . don't make a fool out of me," and had slapped Taylor hard across the face.

A little while later, Vallarino told the two Americans, Taylor confessed that he had had a fight with his wife. Such a confession after being hit in the face obviously wouldn't stand up in an American court, but still, Vallarino's testimony should be helpful.

Sworn depositions were obtained from everyone with even the most tenuous connections to the events that night—except Gutierrez, who was still being careful and playing his devious games. Vallarino, Doctor Ortiz, and Romero all agreed to come to the States and testify at the trial.

It was clear to everyone working for the prosecution that the case against Ken Taylor was coming to a head.

When Venturi received Sadoff's report a few days after the sodium amytal interview, he was enormously relieved. He had had enough bad news for a while and he read it over anxiously. Fortunately, Sadoff had found Ken

> ". . . without psychosis. He is not mentally ill. He does not require psychiatric treatment. He is mentally competent to proceed legally in that he knows the nature and consequences of his current legal situation and can work with counsel in preparing his defense."

From the defense's point of view, it even got better. The report went on:

> "With respect to his state of mind at the time of the death of his wife, it is my opinion that

Dr. Taylor was in such a state of mind that he believed that his wife was having fellatio with their son, and that she posed a significant threat of harm to the son since she had been under the influence of drugs and alcohol, and that he found her 'crazed with drugs.' Furthermore, his state of mind was affected by her attack upon him, knocking him down with one of the barbells kept in the laundry room. He believed both his life and the life of his son were in danger at the hands of his wife. He reacted instinctively by picking up the nearest object in order to stop his wife from harming him and harming his son, too. He hit her with the object and his recollection even under sodium amytal is that he hit her only twice with the door weight.

"There is no indication that Dr. Taylor was M'Naghten insane at the time of this occurrence, and there is no indication that he was hallucinating or distorting his perception. He is consistent in his reports about her attack on him and on the baby. In my opinion, he acted to protect himself and his son from serious bodily harm or death at the hands of his wife, who was under the influence of drugs and acting irrationally."

There it was: the supporting opinion Venturi needed to put Sadoff on the stand. First, Ken was not M'Naghten insane.

In addition, several key points regarding Ken's state of mind literally leaped off the page.

1. "His state of mind was affected by her (Teresa's) attack on him . . ."

2. "He believed both his life and the life of his son were in danger . . ."
3. "He reacted instinctively . . ."

That last point was important. During the trial he wanted to use Ken "reacting instinctively" in a confused state of mind when he saw Teresa sexually abusing the baby. If he succeeded, then he would be able to establish provocation.

Now he could put Sadoff on the stand with confidence. He would be a hell of an expert witness.

As soon as Ken read Sadoff's report he was ecstatic. He immediately shot off a letter to Venturi:

"Jack,
After reviewing initial discovery, digesting the report concerning the sodium amytal interview, and knowing what's true and what is not true, I have drawn certain conclusions. There are several false statements being made, especially by my in-laws, which we will not be able to prove as false. The way I see it, it's their word against mine.

"1. I didn't have them fill prescriptions and give them to me. Any prescriptions written for them were for *them*.
2. Teresa abused my prescription writing privilege. I did write numerous prescriptions for her.
3. I did not use drugs in my office during working hours. I did use cocaine after work on several occasions before I left to go home.
4. Acapulco is a total frame by the Mexican police and Las Brisas hotel security to cover their

asses against a lawsuit. Jack, I tell you I did not do it. Any and all statements to the contrary are false and fabricated to protect the hotel against liability.

5. Agar & Sutton [Ken's dental partners in Brooklyn]—I told you from the beginning that I did steal from them and I told you why I did it.

6. The sodium amytal depicts the incident at my home with Teresa. Anything to the contrary either comes from (a) false witnesses, and (b) pressure and/or disorientation when I made my statement to the police concerning the manner in which Teresa was struck.

7. Disposition of Teresa's body and all actions and/or statements concerning the incident that I made are all efforts on my behalf to stall the eventual and inevitable discovery, so I could make my 'goodbyes' to Marilyn and Rhonda as well as ascertain my son's health and safety in the custody of my family.

"Anything else in the additional discovery will be what it is and I'll give you an honest evaluation of the material."

Ken was clearly enthusiastic about Dr. Sadoff's report. He saw it not only as an exoneration of his story, but as a powerful weapon for the defense during the trial itself.

In his letter to Venturi, he wrote:

"If the [New Jersey] State Senate puts so much confidence in Dr. Sadoff's opinion, then the local county assistant prosecutor, judge, and jury should have confidence in his statements concerning me. I think the jury should be very much

284

impressed with his credentials and credibility."

Venturi also saw Sadoff's report as vital. In fact, it carried such weight in his mind that he decided to use it and go to the court in a second attempt to get a bail reduction.

The first time he had tried to get a reduction in bail—from $500,000 to $100,000—was in early February. His original argument at the February 1 hearing was simple: Kenneth Taylor had no criminal convictions, paid child support for all three of his children ($50 weekly for his daughter by his first marriage, and $200 weekly for his second daughter), and was a success in his academic, military and professional careers. He had voluntarily gone in to the police and confessed the crime. There was very little chance that he would fail to appear for trial.

But Chaiet immediately filed a strong opposition, his point of view equally straightforward: Kenneth Taylor had had three bad marriages marked by violence or irresponsibility, and he was a bad financial risk who still owed the Naval Credit Union more than $25,000.

Venturi countered that the debt had been incurred for Teresa's benefit: "Following the incident that occurred in Acapulco while he and Teresa were on their honeymoon, Teresa was unstable [rarely even leaving the house]. Dr. Taylor felt it would be much safer if they moved away from the Brooklyn, New York area. Dr. Taylor therefore borrowed from the Naval Credit Union to open his own offices and capitalize his business, and he and his wife moved to New Jersey."

The first hearing had been held before Superior Court Judge John Arnone, who promptly denied the request for bail reduction. Judge Arnone said that although Taylor might not be convicted of murder, there had been serious allegations made by former wives, too serious to justify reduction of bail.

On May 10, a few weeks before the trial was to begin, and armed with Dr. Sadoff's report, Venturi again tried to get Ken's bail reduced. This hearing was held before Superior Court Judge Michael D. Farren, the same judge who would preside over Ken Taylor's trial. This time Venturi put into his motion the results of Sadoff's report on Ken's state of mind during the killing. Venturi argued in his motion that his client's story was corroborated not only by the results of the sodium amytal interview, but by the toxicological tests done after Teresa Taylor's autopsy, which revealed the presence of alcohol, cocaine, and codeine in her blood four days after her death.

As for the charges of financial irresponsibility regarding child-support payments to his daughter by his first marriage (raised by Chaiet during the first motion to reduce bail), Venturi argued that he had canceled checks to prove that Taylor had indeed paid child support of $250 a month.

"For all of the foregoing reasons," Venturi wrote, "it is respectfully requested that Notice of Motion for Reduction of Bail be granted."

In his turn, Chaiet argued that regardless of Dr. Sadoff's expert opinion, the rejection of bail reduction during the first hearing was reasonable and should stand. "It would seem foolhardy," Chaiet said, "to allow the defendant an opportunity to flee the jurisdiction."

In denying the bail reduction motion, Judge Farren responded strongly against Venturi's request. Since sodium amytal revelations are inadmissible in a trial, there was no reason to accept them in a motion for bail reduction. Ken was not a reliable individual, Farren implied, citing his lies about Teresa's disappearance and his having changed his story so many times.

Judge Farren then went even further. The next day, May 11, 1985, he was quoted in the *Asbury Park Press* as stating that "The proofs are strong enough for a conviction."

When Ken read the headliness, he exploded. "HOW DARE HE DO THAT *BEFORE* MY TRIAL EVEN STARTS. He knew he would be the presiding judge in the case and that the jury would be selected from the area that reads the *Asbury Park Press*."

Indeed, the judge's comments so close to trial and jury selection would become the grounds for a number of mistrial motions by Jack Venturi.

On Ken's copy of Chaiet's opposition to the bail reduction certification, Ken scribbled a single word in bold letters — *"Asshole!"*

At one point during the preparations of his case, Venturi had asked Ken what he thought about various witnesses who were coming forward and giving depositions to Chaiet. Each of them, people Ken had known and even lived with, like the Benignos, would be called by the prosecution, and Venturi would have to cross-examine them.

Ken then volunteered a few choice comments on each of them. His observations were laced with dislike and bitterness.

According to Ken's heated descriptions, Celeste was a "very stupid woman. Very easily confused. Very confusing in her explanations. Can be very easily manipulated to sound like she's confused . . . She is also a pathologic liar."

Jeff, Celeste's husband, was "calm but not intelligent. Jeff can 'lie' very well but should be easy to manipulate and confuse."

Teresa's brother, Phil Benigno, was described by Ken as a "no-good thug."

Louise Benigno would not be a difficult or dangerous witness — except to create sympathy for Teresa. "She says," Ken wrote, "that she made me a sandwich after I came back from Indiana. She doesn't say that she insisted on making me the sandwich."

Al Benigno would be the most dangerous witness in the family. "Al could be the toughest, as he is the most intelligent."

It wasn't lost on Venturi that Ken's advice to him most frequently mentioned how easy it would be to manipulate someone, and in several cases how he described what good or pathological liars these people could be. Lying and manipulation seemed to be something he relied on heavily in his analysis. It was ironic that so many people had commented on how they thought Ken Taylor had exactly the same traits.

After hearing the case that Chaiet was building against him in the bail reduction hearings, Ken began to "sense real trouble." Another ominous sign had come when Venturi told him that as part of the pretrial investigation, Chaiet was pursuing Acapulco — in fact, he had sent three men down there to gather information.

Ken's anger at this point was almost universal. Even Marilyn had turned her back on him. He had telephoned her the first week he was in jail and they had talked for a half hour. She had been nervous but had sounded sympathetic and had cried a lot during their talk. But when he called her back, her number had been changed. He had written her and Rhonda dozens of letters over the previous few months. None of them had been opened—and he had never received a letter in return.

There was no one except his immediate family—the children, Tom, and his mother and father—who was free of his wrath. But Paul Chaiet was digging a particularly deep hole in the darker chambers of Ken's emotions. When Ken wrote in his diary that he was now beginning to "sense real trouble," he finished his thought with—"But I sensed also that Chaiet was an immoral [pig of a man], a man who cared nothing for justice; rather he savored only victory over me at any cost."

Just before they went to trial, Venturi received another letter from Ken. But this letter was different. Gone were his anger, his bitter renunciations and furious denials; now he simply reiterated his undying love for Teresa and his innocence of Acapulco.

"Jack," *he wrote*,

"Before we go to trial I want to let you know something about me that we will have to deal with. I did not beat my precious wife on our honeymoon. I did not at any time or any place sell cocaine. I loved Teresa more than I love living. She meant the world to me, and now my world is gone. Anything else you want to think about me, and God knows you have enough, okay—but just know what I state above is true.

I'm guilty of certain accusations; I'm not pure and you know it. But believe me, I loved Teresa. I'll do anything to protect my children, and I did not sell cocaine.

"I realize this will be a very difficult case. God bless you for your skills, effort and concern."

For the first time in all his letters to Venturi, he signed the letter, "Dr. Kenneth Z. Taylor."

Venturi filed it and went back to work preparing his case. They would start selecting a jury the next day.

Chapter Nineteen

Superior Court Judge Michael D. Farren had been active in New Jersey Republican politics and was considered shrewd and capable. He and Paul Chaiet were acquainted before the Taylor trial, for Farren had been an assistant in the county prosecutor's office when the younger man had started there several years before. When Thomas Kean was elected, the first Republican to be governor of New Jersey in some time, he appointed Farren to the Superior Court.

As for Chaiet as prosecutor, the Taylor trial was Farren's first big trial as a judge.

Just prior to the trial, during the May 10 hearing, Venturi would move to keep both Connecticut and Acapulco out of the trial. He would rely on Rule 55 in New Jersey's "Rules of Evidence." Rule 55 maintained that similar crimes on previous occasions were inadmissible if the prosecution was only attempting to show a defendant's inclination to commit such crimes.

Chaiet, however, brought forward a counter rule on evidence—Rule 48, which provided that Rule 55 could be set aside to prove motive or intent. For Chaiet, "intent" (still harking back to "state of mind") was the key, and he argued that in Acapulco, the assault showed "malicious intent." As for the Connecticut incident, Ken

291

Taylor had "complained of marital pressures" and even written out his "intent" before attempting to murder his wife. He was not arguing, Chaiet said, that either previous assault proved Taylor's inclination to assault Teresa Taylor, but they did "prove motive and intent and refute the defendant's claim of self-defense."

On May 15, Farren delivered his decision—and shocked both Venturi and Chaiet by rejecting both the prosecution's and the defense's arguments. Referring to Rule 55, Farren decided material on Connecticut would not be allowed.

Then, in one of the first of several odd or even perverse rulings, Farren said he wasn't going to decide on the final admissibility of Acapulco until the issue was raised during the trial. But his inclination was to allow it, pending further proof of the incident. His final decision would be based on "clear and convincing evidence" that Kenneth Taylor had indeed beaten his wife in Acapulco.

Again, both Venturi and Chalet were surprised. Farren's reasoning was almost bizarre. Clearly, while there was incontestable evidence that Ken had chloroformed Marilyn (then was even Ken's own admission of guilt), there was considerably less evidence regarding Acapulco. Mexican police officials were not the most reliable prosecution witnesses, especially since one (Vallarino) had even admitted to slapping the defendant; and the hotel's security and management testimony could be questioned as being tainted with self-interest. The only witness, Sorayda Peraino, would provide "hearsay" testimony, with no corroboration from my other people who had been standing in the vicinity.

If Farren finally allowed Acapulco after rejecting Connecticut, Venturi would have a much stronger case for a mistrial. For Chaiet, it meant that he had to quickly pull his Acapulco case together. If Farren finally allowed it, he would have to prove that Ken beat Teresa while they were on their honeymoon. To do this, he would have to rely most heavily on Sorayda Peraino.

The May 16 headlines in the *Freehold Press* read: "Beating of Wife on Trip Ruled Admissible in Murder Trial."

Jury selection was set for May 28.

Selecting the jury from more than two hundred people took more than two days. Venturi was sensitive to how much press coverage the case had received, and he questioned everyone closely on what they had read or heard about the case. He challenged all who seemed biased, and even eliminated those who said they had had bad experiences with dentists.

Chaiet wanted men who were middle-class in their values and who would draw their own conclusions about what they would do if attacked by a five-foot-three-inch woman.

Sixteen jurors were finally selected to hear the case. Of these, twelve would be chosen by lot at the end of the trial to deliver a verdict.

Judge Farren had ordered tight security for the trial. The sheriff's department searched everyone who entered the courtroom, with handheld metal detectors. The prisoner, riding in a gray bus and surrounded by armed guards, was escorted by a "lead" and a "trial" vehicle, each containing more armed guards. On the roof, snipers armed with assault rifles covered the courthouse parking lot. Plainclothes detectives and sheriff's deputies filled the hallway and the courtroom itself.

All of the extra security just added fuel to the already blazing fire of Taylor's anger that he was being "tried as if he were a serial killer or a mass-murderer — a Ted Bundy or a Charlie Manson."

On Thursday morning, May 30, 1985, Paul Chaiet rose slowly from his chair to give his opening statement. Normally Chaiet was a low-keyed man, measuring his words carefully and then delivering them in a deep, well-modulated voice that carried considerable authority. But this morning he seemed an indignant Baptist preacher full of fire and brimstone.

Facing the twelve men and four women in the jury box, Chaiet started off dramatically: "I will call upon you for a murder conviction for this defendant because that's what he committed when he smashed the head of Teresa Taylor into pieces on November 11, 1984."

The burly prosecutor went on, pacing up and down the courtroom like a bulldog, gesticulating passionately. He stood near the defendant, jabbing his finger at him, only inches from Taylor's face.

Sitting at the defendant's table next to Venturi, Ken Taylor was furious.

"I was seething with rage," *he wrote in his diary,* "as I listened to this crude, maniacal prosecutor rant and rave, spewing malice and hatred for me, urging the jurors to see me as some calculating, sinister man who for no reason bludgeoned his wife to death . . . as if loudness and theatrical gesturing would prove his case."

Kenneth Taylor "cracked open" his wife's skull, Chaiet said loudly, and then carefully cleaned up the

294

blood, packed her body into the trunk of their car, and drove across four state lines to Indiana. The defendant then lied about his crime, lied to his family, lied to her family, and lied that she was addicted to sex and drugs. The defendant dumped his wife's corpse into a Pennsylvania ditch and then went to a topless bar to watch the dancers perform.

Ken sat listening mesmerized, horrified, by Chaiet's dramatic presentation. "It was the worst, the very worst connotation of events being presented as unquestionable facts by the STATE'S PROSECUTOR!! Surely the jury was seduced by this madman's rantings . . . As Chaiet continued to debase me before the jury, I felt true hatred and I knew that at that very moment I could have easily killed HIM, Paul Chaiet."

Then, almost as a rational afterthought, Ken wrote, "And I suspect that Chaiet wanted me to show that base emotion to the jury—but I managed to remain calm and aloof from my true feelings."

Toxicological studies would show, Chaiet went on, that there was only a small amount of cocaine in Teresa's body, so she couldn't have been drug-crazed. Ken's story about his wife sexually abusing their five-month-old child was simply a "sordid tale" to cover up his brutal murder.

"He then told a perverted tale," Chaiet boomed, shaking his finger into Taylor's face, "and it's just that—a perverted tale by a sinister and calculating mind."

Several times during Chaiet's impassioned speech Venturi had risen to object. Each time Farren brushed him off, silencing him.

Venturi rose and walked toward the jury box. He

thanked the jury for taking time from their busy daily lives to sit on a jury. "The charge here," he began in earnest, "is murder. That is the most serious charge that can ever be brought against anyone . . . and it is horrible, as the prosecutor put it, but that doesn't make the state's burden [of proof] any less. We are not talking about probabilities here . . . about our feelings, our likes or dislikes for somebody in this case. We are talking about proof beyond a shadow of a doubt.

"I heard the prosecutor open and say a lot of things concerning what happened before and after this terrible tragedy, but I didn't hear him [talk] about how or why this happened . . . and what proof there was."

Then, perhaps recalling Chaiet's success, Venturi became slightly more dramatic in his presentation: "I anticipate in this case what I call the kitchen-sink prosecution of Dr. Taylor, and that is that the state will try to introduce into evidence anything it can, including the kitchen sink, in order to arouse your passion, your sympathy, your prejudice, and inflame you against Doctor Taylor."

Chaiet objected loudly, and Farren immediately sustained his objection. "Mr. Venturi," he warned, "please confine your remarks to what you contend is the position of your client."

"That *is* our position, Your Honor."

"I understand that is your position. The prosecutor objects to the position. I sustain the objection. Proceed."

"Dr. Taylor is not a totally innocent man," Venturi began again. "He is guilty of obstructing justice. He is guilty of giving false information to the police. But he is not on trial for those charges. There are no winners here," he said quietly. "You see, ladies and gentlemen, this is not a murder. This is a family tragedy."

296

Venturi then recounted Kenneth Taylor's background and family life and gave a brief description of his two previous marriages.

His marriage to Teresa Taylor "was not trouble free . . . but there was a loving, caring relationship between the two of them, and one of the problems during the marriage was Teresa's abuse of cocaine and codeine. And also alcohol.

"That night," Venturi went on, "the night of the incident, Teresa was unfortunately using all three of those substances."

Venturi continued to recap Ken's story about the sex phone calls, seeing Teresa fellating the baby, their fight with the barbells, and his subsequent going into a blackout or "trancelike state."

As for Ken's lies about what had happened to Teresa, and his bizarre trip to Indiana with his wife's corpse in the trunk, Venturi had a justification.

"Dr. Taylor did a terrible wrong in making up that story about going away. He did a terrible wrong in not reporting that to the police right away, but he wanted to be sure his baby was safe . . . He did not want to tell that 'perverted tale' referred to by the prosecutor. He didn't want anyone to know . . ."

Only after being questioned by the police had Taylor admitted that there was a reason for the fight. Then he had confessed, "sobbing uncontrollably" as he related what had really happened.

"At the end of this case, ladies and gentlemen . . . there is only one issue for you to decide: not whether Dr. Taylor did right or wrong in connection with other actions or other statements, but whether the state has proven him guilty of murder . . . or manslaughter beyond a reasonable doubt, or whether Dr. Taylor is not guilty [because] he was acting in imminent danger of serious bodily harm to himself and his baby."

When Venturi had finished his opening statement, court was adjourned until Monday, June 3, when testimony would start.

Ken was led from the court furious and shaken from "Chaiet's malicious opening remarks, Farren's accommodating manner, and Venturi's inability to defuse the runaway prosecution."

Ken's reaction to Chaiet's opening was predictable. He'd hated it. But his animosity toward both Farren and Chaiet (which was returned in kind by both men) was intense. "I did not meet Chaiet or Farren," he wrote in his prison diary, "until the first day of jury selection for my trial. The vibes we shared—at least the vibes I experienced—were awesome. I felt intense anger directed at me from these men. And I felt an intense loathing for them in return. We did not like each other."

Ken's descriptions of the two men in his diary are graphic evidence of his dislike. "Chaiet was a brutish, crude-looking man: stockily built, broad, and very hyperactive. Farren was a large man with small, weasel eyes, a cherubic face, and possessed a haughty demeanor. Neither man would establish eye contact with me . . . What were they afraid of? I found them both loathsome. I despised them even before the trial started. I sensed that they were both cowardly . . . they were my enemies. They embodied the word 'enemy' in the purest sense—foe, antagonist, adversary, archenemy, nemesis . . ."

Ken ended his description of the two men with a single word: *"Bastards!"*

His consolations at the start of his trial were meager,

even to the point that he was becoming obsessed with who looked better. Venturi had been concerned that Ken look "professional" and nonthreatening, and so Ken dressed carefully. "My appearance in a three-piece navy blue pinstripe suit, white shirt, dark blue tie, and highly polished black Italian shoes outshone the scuffling prosecutor. I took a mild degree of pleasure in knowing that I was better dressed than my nemesis in this contest. I was taller, slimmer, and better dressed than Chaiet. Chaiet's stocky, swarthy appearance was piggish, even in his court costume—a cheap polyester suit."

The trial was getting off to a heated start. Everyone could sense the dislike between the defense and the prosecution—and between the judge and the defense counsel. Emotions were already running high.

On May 29, even before the actual trial began, the *Freehold-Press* headlines had blared: *Judge Won't Step Down from Trial.*

The local press was having a field day with the growing animosity between Chaiet and Venturi on the one hand, and Farren and the defense lawyer on the other.

"A Superior Court judge yesterday denied a motion by the lawyer for Staten Island dentist Kenneth Taylor that the judge disqualify himself . . ."

"Lawyer Jack Venturi indicated that Superior Court Judge Michael D. Farren . . . was biased against Taylor."

Back in Monmouth County Jail the morning after the trial opened, Ken Taylor was being walked to the converted school bus with its steel mesh windows—

painted gray and therefore called the "Gray Goose" by both guards and inmates—for his ride to the courthouse for day two of his trial.

As Ken boarded the Gray Goose, Officer Hopkins ("Hoppy" to the inmates) grinned at Ken and said, "Hey, Doc, Chaiet really tore your case open yesterday, didn't he?"

"You think so, Hoppy?" Ken replied. It wasn't the kind of comment he wanted to hear, even if, as seemed likely, Hoppy was just making a bad joke. It rubbed too close to his own fears.

Chapter Twenty

The trial of Kenneth Taylor technically began on May 28 with jury selection, but for Chaiet and Venturi, who would be confronting each other day after day for several weeks, the real trial would begin with the give-and-take of testimony being presented.

For contending attorneys this is often the psychic equivalent of Christians entering the Colosseum. One lawyer, Harold Klawan, described it as "concentrating the mind wonderfully to know that someone you are going to meet in a courtroom tomorrow is preparing with care a case that has no other purpose than to make you look the fool before judge and jury."

In the judge's chambers, before testimony began, the first of many heated discussions took place between Judge Farren, Chaiet, and Venturi. Chaiet objected to Venturi's move to introduce Dr. Sadoff's testimony. Chaiet complained that he hadn't seen the video of the interview and therefore could not adequately cross-examine Sadoff, and, in fact, he had already talked with a psychiatrist who said he couldn't testify either without seeing the tape.

Venturi argued that it wasn't really necessary to view the taped interview itself. Dr. Sadoff had "examined, interviewed and tested the defendant, and these [his written reports] were his findings without any reference to sodium amytal."

Farren disagreed, and siding with Chaiet, gave Venturi two days to supply the tape; if he chose not to supply it, then Sadoff could not testify.

Venturi became progressively angry as he saw which way the wind was blowing, so when Chaiet brought up the idea of introducing colored graphics from the medical examination of Teresa's body and the autopsy findings, Venturi vigorously objected. Such graphic photos, or even drawings, would be highly prejudicial, Venturi insisted. He wanted Dr. Bindie, the Pottsville pathologist who had conducted the autopsy, to be restricted in his testimony to what he had written in his report. "Under rules of discovery," Venturi argued, "an expert is only permitted to testify within the confines of his report." Further, in all fairness, he had been supplied with these graphics only a few hours before, when he had entered the courthouse.

Farren made short work of Venturi's objections. "It may be of assistance to the jury," Farren said, ". . . I'll permit it. The objection is overruled."

Twice knocked down, Venturi had other problems to air. He was told that over the weekend the local press had contained articles about the Connecticut incident that he, Judge Farren, had already ruled was inadmissible. "I would ask that the jury be individually polled to determine whether or not they recall any of that information . . . and whether or not members of this jury have been tainted by those news articles."

Chaiet immediately pointed out that the judge had instructed the jury "not to read anything. I think we can assume," he went on, "that they follow your instructions, and I don't think we have to go to each juror."

Judge Farren admitted that he had seen the articles himself, one of which referred to Taylor's allegedly attempting to kill his second wife. But, Farren said, "I feel this jury is sophisticated enough to follow my instructions . . . I will not interview them individually. Anything else, Mr. Venturi?"

Venturi fought to keep his irritation under control. "Well, Judge," he said evenly, "I recall very clearly that this court instructed the jury panel not to read any articles and the very next day there was a man who said he had read an article (on the case) that morning . . . I have to respectfully move for a mistrial . . ."

Farren reacted negatively. "That was prior to the selection of the jury . . . [and the man] had no idea what case he was on—he did not violate any court order," Farren said, ignoring the obvious point that a similar instance of disobeying a judge's instructions could have happened with the impaneled jury.

"I take it, then, that my motion for a mistrial is denied, and also the move to have the jury polled?" Venturi asked, seething.

"Yes, it is," Farren snapped.

"Even though the prosecutor himself has not objected to the group polling?" Venturi pressed.

"That's correct. Anything else?"

Venturi walked into the packed courtroom with a cold feeling that things were not going his way—and the trial hadn't even started yet.

Chaiet expected to call around thirty witnesses during the two- to three-week trial. He started off with forensic witnesses and police officers who testified to finding the body, the layout of the scene, the bloody condition of the corpse, and the evidence of blood splattered and then cleaned up in the Taylor house.

The first important witness, however, was Dr. Richard Bindie. Bindie, a respected pathologist who had performed over fifteen hundred autopsies, delivered the gruesome details of his findings in a quiet monotone.

When the colored photographs of the damaged body were shown, Venturi leaped up to object. Not only were the photos graphic, but he believed they were colored with a "reddish tint" that made them all the more repugnant. He could see the shock on the jurors' faces.

Chaiet ridiculed the idea that the photos were "tinted," and Farren again rejected Venturi's objection. Venturi again asked for a mistrial . . . and again Farren denied it.

Chaiet continued the questioning and Dr. Bindie listed the injuries detail by detail. At one point Chaiet asked, "Now, did you find any more of that Vaseline-like substance?" Chaiet had already led Bindie through a description of it and this time Ken wrote in his trial notes: *"Vaseline,* your ass, Chaiet! What gives with your obsession with Vaseline already?"

"There was a marked amount of Vaseline-like ointment present in the vagina," Bindie went on, "and also the inguinal arc and pubic hairs and the hairs were described, as I said, matted together . . . by this ointment."

"Okay, anything else significant about your general observations of the body?" Chaiet continued.

"There was early signs of decomposition, skin slippage where the skin . . . like, peels off with little pressure, and greenish discoloration at the abdomen, which were signs of decomposition."

Since the start of the trial Ken had lost his passive "I don't care" attitude. He was now fascinated — powerless, but caught up in seeing his fate being manipulated by others. Distraught over watching Chaiet and Bindie, he scribbled in his notes, "That does it. I just bought a thirty-year bid. Slipping skin, green abdomen — turn out the lights, this party's over.

304

This jury is sick to their stomachs. I'm finished."

The jury had indeed, on this first day of the trial, been treated to a montage of decomposing body parts, missing teeth, bloody clothing, fibers, padding, etc. They were inundated with the horror and gore of the crime. Chaiet had been brilliant in his strategy.

At the end of Bindie's presentation, Ken wrote, "What a dreadful start for the first day of testimony."

Chaiet then asked Bindie about alcohol content in the body. Were his findings consistent with the ingestion of alcohol by the deceased . . . or simply the result of decomposition?

Bindie's opinion was that the amount of alcohol found in the body was due to decomposition. Chaiet was clearly sowing doubts in the minds of the jury about Ken's story that Teresa had had some alcohol that night. And if she hadn't had any, then maybe Ken's story about the drugs was also false.

With the Vaseline as a starting point, Chaiet would have loved to prove that there had been some perverted sexual play by a drunken and drugged Ken Taylor that night — even if Teresa had been a willing participant. But there was no evidence of sperm. Sex play mixed with drugs and alcohol would explain a lot of mysteries for Chaiet. He knew that cocaine often intensified sexual urges — but it could just as easily diminish one's sex drive or interrupt one's performance. If that had happened, a frustrated, drugged-up Ken Taylor could have exploded in violence. It was a beautiful theory — but it was all supposition and he couldn't prove it.

Bindie testified that he did vaginal, anal area, and orocavity smears, and "all results were negative." If there *had* been sex, sperm would have been found (unless there was no ejaculation). "Spermatozoa (from male ejaculate) in a dead person," Bindie droned on, "can be found for several days after death because there

305

is no gravity drainage mechanism to rid the body of it."

Venturi didn't want to go over all that gruesome body evidence again, so there wasn't much he could do in his cross-examination of Bindie except to get an admission that the number of blows to Teresa's skull could have been less than "six or seven" instead of nine and still cause as much damage. It was frail help, but it did make it easier for the jury to accept that two, maybe three, blows could have caused nine fractures.

Venturi also got Bindie's opinion that there had been no injury to the perineal and inguinal areas, thereby showing that there had not been any violent sexual behavior—which Chaiet had continually implied by the direction and tenor of his questions.

In his trial notes the next day, Ken wrote, "Rieders is going to be dangerous, potentially damaging. Another scientist, but this scientist is a toxicologist."

Frederick Rieders looked like a typical eccentric scientist with his bow tie, striped pants, checkered shirt, and scuffed shoes. Rumpled and in his late fifties, he had the air of a man who didn't care what anyone thought about him. He had been working at his profession for fifteen years. After serving as chief toxicologist for the Philadelphia medical examiner, he'd become lab director for National Medical Services, a group that assisted medical examiners, coroners, and pathologists across the nation.

Chaiet quickly focused in on whether he had found traces of codeine and cocaine in Teresa's body.

Yes, he had, but the amount was within a "normal analgesic dose between half a grain and one grain."

Chaiet asked whether this amount would produce

"drug-crazed" behavior in someone.

"No," Rieders said. "Codeine is not a stimulant. It is a depressant drug." It was more likely to produce sedation and drowsiness than any type of stimulation," he added.

One down! Chaiet then asked Rieders about cocaine residues in the body.

While Dr. Rieders did not find cocaine itself, he did find the breakdown product of cocaine, benzoylecgonine, showing "that the individual some time prior to her death, which could be many hours, had used cocaine."

But, Rieders added, he didn't know if "there was any active cocaine present in her at the time she was killed."

Again without his own experts, Venturi could do little to alter the effect of Rieders' testimony. Together, Bindie and Rieders made it appear that Teresa had only normal amounts of codeine and the possibility of very little cocaine in her system . . . surely not enough drugs or alcohol to sustain Ken's claim that she had been "drug-crazed."

Ken was shaken by Rieders' appearance. "To this day," he wrote, "I am appalled and confused by this man's testimony."

Ken had already asked Venturi to bring in expert toxicological help of his own. Without it, he groused, Venturi simply seemed outmatched by Chaiet and reduced to asking speculative questions about the possibility of other drugs being present (like heroin) that hadn't been tested for.

During earlier testimony by a forensic chemist on the putrid condition of the blood in the body, Ken became agitated and scrawled in his notes, "It screws up test results . . . for drug analysis. *If* drugs were detected in

307

any amount in a sample of putrid blood, that alone would indicate *a much higher amount than from a fresh sample."*

Now Rieders's testimony was compounding the problem. Furious, Ken argued, "How could Teresa's body have given an accurate reading of the drug levels after decomposition over four days? . . . I believe to this day that another toxicologist, given the same data and told the body had been decomposing for four days, would provide a much different analysis than Rieders."

Ken left the court that day furious with Venturi. Later, Venturi quietly advised Ken that it was useless to get into arguments with medical experts like Rieders and that of none of his tests used "putrid" samples of blood.

The next day's headlines confirmed Ken's prescient fear that Rieders' testimony would be damaging: *Toxicologist Disputes Theory Victim Was Drug-Crazed.*

Chapter Twenty-one

Testimony on June 5, the third day of the trial, moved through a diverse cross-section of witnesses. First came Lucia and Vanderweil, followed by Cindy Diaz, Ken's brother-in-law, and Sheri Delile.

The only significant moment came when Venturi pressed the officers on why there hadn't been any tape recorder present to take down the defendant's statement. All the officers had to rely on notes—and in some cases that was important.

Trying to overcome the impression that Ken was emotionally cold, Venturi leaned toward Lt. Lucia and asked, "Wasn't it a fact that the defendant was very emotional, his lips 'quivering'?"

"Yes, sir," Lucia answered.

". . . And after he composed himself . . . you stated that he said she ran in the room, swung a dumbbell at him, and he got it away and 'gave it to her'—is that correct?"

"Yes."

"Is it not possible," Venturi pressed in, "that he said that she ran in the room, swung at him, and then 'he got away' and gave it to her?"

Trying to remember, Lucia said, "No . . . those were his exact words, what he said to me. I was paying very specific attention at that time. Obviously he was going to tell me something I had been waiting a long time to hear."

"Was a tape recording made of this statement?"

"No, sir."

"Was there a stenographer in the room at the time . . ."

"No, sir."

"So, there is no transcript of the statement?"

"No, sir."

"No further questions," Venturi said, walking away.

Later, Venturi pounded away at the injustice of not having a recording or an accurate statement of his client's confession. The most careful note-taker is only human and can make mistakes, he argued. When he finished, he had left the clear impression that any error could have been made in notes quickly scribbled during such intense, emotion-filled moments—and worse, even later, editing could have occurred.

Lt. Vanderweil recalled Ken using the same words, and again Venturi went after the procedural mistake of having no recording made.

After establishing that Ken was already a suspect in the homicide when he arrived that morning (and the key suspect, after the earring was found in the garage), Venturi said, "There was a lot of activity by a lot of people that morning, isn't that correct? . . . Yet no one got a tape recorder or a court reporter . . . even though they knew he was coming in?"

"That's correct," Vanderweil said.

Chaiet then asked Vanderweil about normal police procedure. First, you conduct a verbal interview with a suspect, Vanderweil said. "You reach a point where you feel you have enough information . . . Then you go back—have either a stenographer or recording device and go over the statement again."

But no matter how Chaiet tried, the question of just exactly what was said when Ken confessed that morning remained unresolved because of the lack of a recording machine. Venturi's implication of police impropriety stuck.

Chaiet needed something dramatic to offset the advantage the defense had gained by the police not having taped Ken's confession. He called Cindy Diaz.

There was going to be another wrangle. The jury was sent out, and Chaiet and Venturi angrily argued over the prosecutor's wish to include a videotape that Cindy's husband had made. It showed Teresa playing with the baby.

To allow such a film that had little or no relevance to the case was simply another dramatic effect of Mr. Chaiet's, Venturi charged.

Not at all, Chaiet countered. The defense itself had made an issue of Teresa Taylor's character. The film went directly to the issue of her character and relationship with the child. The jurors had every right to view her with the child she was alleged to have abused.

Farren rejected Venturi's objection. The tape would be shown.

Again Venturi moved for a mistrial. It was denied by Farren.

The video ran for just under ten minutes, but its impact on the jury was obvious—a few jurors even had tears in their eyes, watching a tape of the pretty, laughing young woman play with her baby so soon after they had viewed the rotting remains of her bloody corpse.

Near the end of the day, Judge Farren asked Venturi if he had decided whether to give Mr. Chaiet the videotape of the Sadoff interview. Venturi was in a bind. He didn't want Chaiet to see Ken admit under sodium amytal that he and Teresa had both oral and anal sex that night while talking with the sex phone services; he'd first said that he'd slept through most of the night. He could see Chalet salivating over this latest change in Ken's story.

"You were to decide by four o'clock today," Farren said. "I know it's five to four, but you don't need the extra five minutes as to whether you're going to use him or not."

In his notes Ken scribbled, "Pompous, fucking asshole."

311

Venturi took a deep breath. Facing the judge, he said, "You would be correct. We have decided not to use Dr. Sadoff."

Farren then announced his own bombshell. If time permitted, after the testimony of Taylor's second wife, Marilyn Bergman, he would begin hearings the next day on whether to admit the Acapulco incident or not.

This was the one Venturi had been waiting for—the single most significant decision of the trial. The admissibility of evidence had always been a complex and even controversial issue. Most states and the federal government allow some evidence prior to the crime a defendant is being tried on to be admitted—within strict guidelines. That's why, to a large extent, Taylor's trial would be at a major crisis once Judge Farren decided whether or not to allow Acapulco—for it was evidence about prior behavior that would clearly have an impact on the jury's emotional attitude toward the defendant. At the hearing, Chaiet didn't even have to "prove" Taylor beat Teresa on their honeymoon, all he really had to do was convince Farren. Then the issue would be presented to the jury.

But first thing in the morning on the fifth day of the trial, June 6, testimony from Marilyn Bergman would begin.

When Marilyn walked into the courtroom, all heads turned. She was indeed a striking woman. Tall, even stately, she was dressed conservatively in a charcoal gray suit and a white blouse, but her face was gray with tension.

Chaiet had wanted that evidence about Taylor chloroforming Marilyn, and he had almost not called her to testify once Farren had disallowed it. But he decided to put her on the stand anyway, if only to establish that Taylor had spent the night in her apartment with Teresa dead in the car outside her front door.

Ken stared at Marilyn as she took the stand, his feelings in turmoil. Since she had not answered any of his letters and had changed her telephone number after their single

312

conversation while he was in jail, he didn't know what to think about her.

But her rejection had hurt, and he was angry. In his notes, he wrote, "Maybe I'll come out of this with a minimal sentence to serve. Then what? You know I'm going to come back to see my girl, my sweet Rhonda. What have you told her? Did you tell her I'm DEAD? SICK? In jail? Ran away? WHAT? What did you tell her? Goddamn you, Marilyn."

Chaiet, ever aware of image and the impressionability of the juror, objected to a Bible that had suddenly appeared in front of Taylor. Farren, after discovering that it was a gift from Marilyn, overruled Chaiet's objection.

It was one of the few brief victories for the defense, but it didn't help Ken's attitude toward Chaiet. In his trial notes, next to Chaiet's objection, he scribbled, "Fuck you, Chaiet, you sniveling, pouting spoiled fuck."

Marilyn's testimony was punctuated by tears. Throughout she broke down and cried. Chaiet was none too gentle with her, even though she was supposed to be the prosecution's witness. He immediately got her to admit that she and Ken had often talked about "getting back together from the very first day we separated."

"What did the defendant say to you, if anything, about the child and about staying with Teresa?" Chaiet went on.

"He wanted to get custody of the child."

"Did he indicate whether or not he wanted to leave Teresa?"

"He wanted the baby started in life and established . . . before he would leave."

"Did he make any comments to you concerning sexual relations with Teresa Taylor?" Chaiet asked.

"Some remarks were made that he wasn't sexually interested, something about the drugs."

"Now," Chaiet said, "during the early morning hours of Sunday, November 18, did you receive telephone calls?"

"Yes."

"And what did you hear? What do you recall hearing?"

313

"Well, mostly what I recall was that they found Teresa's body. She was dead."

At this point Marilyn broke down in tears again and a brief recess was called.

When they resumed, Chaiet still pressed hard. "Were you in a position to see the defendant when he heard that news?"

"I was on the extension phone."

In his notes, scrawled in block letters, Taylor wrote, "Right next to me in bed is more accurate, but thanks just the same."

"Now," Chaiet continued, "did you eventually, I'm sure you did, confront the defendant?"

"Yes."

"And could you describe his emotions at that time?"

"Stoned. He wept some and then stopped and then wept some more and tried to figure out how to get back to New Jersey."

"And on the trip on the plane and driving to Manalapan, did you have discussion with him of what happened to Teresa, or how she was killed?"

"Well, I may have said a lot of things, but there wasn't too much discussion, because Ken would get very upset. And then I just tried to be quiet, because that would upset him more."

"And when you said he got upset in the car, on the plane, would he show that?"

"He was crying," Marilyn said, tears again rolling down her cheeks.

In his cross-examination, Venturi treated Marilyn gently. He directed his questions to establish that Ken liked and respected Teresa, even though they had problems. It was clear he didn't want any hint that Ken wanted to do away with Teresa.

"When he would talk to you about her, he would tell you that she's not a bad person. She just has this problem. Isn't that what he would say?"

"Oh, yes."

"And he was not trying to malign her. In fact, he was very protective of her, wasn't he?"

"I'd say yes. You mean gossip . . . malicious gossip? I don't ever recall Ken doing that about anybody."

"And in terms of her taking care of the baby, when he would say she had problems coping, that was in reference to when she was using drugs? Is that correct?"

"I believe so."

"In fact, there were times that he couldn't make his visitations and you would ask why, and he said it was because Teresa couldn't make it up in the morning and he had to take the baby to the doctor . . . things like that?"

"There were some occasions, you know, he'd leave work."

"And he never said he was definitely going to divorce Teresa, definitely going to leave her, definitely going to go back to you, or anything of that nature, did he?"

"Definitely, specifically? I couldn't say definitely, no."

At the end of Marilyn's testimony, the next edition of the *Freehold Press* headlines blared, *Ex-Spouse Claims Dentist Talked of Leaving 3rd Wife.* The opening lead paragraph read, "Kenneth Taylor considered leaving his third wife, Teresa, but worried about gaining custody of their infant son, his second wife testified yesterday . . ."

"She didn't help me," Ken wrote after Marilyn's testimony, "but she didn't hurt me . . . She could have hurt me. Maybe it's her way of saying, 'I'm sorry' and 'good-bye.' Will I ever see her again? Now there's this bitch Peraino."

The Rule 8 hearing regarding the admissibility of the Acapulco incident was made without the jury present. All else in the courtroom remained the same.

Sorayda Peraino was the first witness, and Chaiet walked her through her memories of meeting the Taylors in Acapulco and her fateful conversation at the hotel desk. It was almost word for word what she had said to McCormick and Fausak.

Venturi was much less gentle. He bore in on her aggressively, trying to confuse her, to break down her story and get her to admit to a faulty memory, a mistake in hearing—anything that would undermine her testimony recalling that moment.

But as nervous as Sorayda Peraino had been originally, she kept firmly to her story that she heard Ken Taylor say that he had had a fight with Teresa and had beaten her.

The next witness was Al Benigno, and Chaiet took him through the emotional turmoil of discovering what had happened to Teresa in Mexico, and of his trip to Acapulco to bring his daughter back. Al remembered that he had often questioned Teresa about her memories of that night. She consistently said that it wasn't Ken who had done it.

A difficult and emotional moment came for Al when Venturi showed him the letter Teresa wrote to Ken while he was in jail and she was in the hospital. At first Al couldn't recognize the handwriting, then Venturi told him that the State had had the letter authenticated as having been written by Teresa. It was too close to a love letter for Al to stomach. "I don't know where you are or what you're doing right now, but I'm in a hospital bed and I can hardly see and that is why I am writing this way. Honey, I don't remember anything. I don't remember what got us here or why we're apart from each other. All I remember is that I went to sleep in my hotel room and I woke up in the hospital . . . All I know is that I want you and love you more than I ever have. As soon as I open my eyes, I ask for you. Please find your way back to me."

Teresa added a postscript to the letter.

"P.S. These doctors don't know how to treat the injured. They keep giving me Valium and all I need is some Pen-Vee K. My front teeth are broken. I told them you could fix them . . ."

After Al Benigno's testimony the hearing was adjourned.

When the hearing resumed on Monday, June 10, Chaiet had Robert Fausak describe his investigative trip to

316

Acapulco. Fausak showed the hotel's security and described that a break-in at the Taylors' *casita* was highly unlikely.

The next witness was Jose Romero, the hotel's assistant manager, whom Chaiet had flown up from Mexico. After describing how he'd taken Ken's telephone call and all that happened that night, Chaiet got him to testify that Ken seemed unhurt by the alleged attack. Romero also described how Teresa Taylor embraced her husband when the Mexican authorities took him to the hospital to see her for the first time. She wanted to be alone with him, Romero testified, and asked the police to release him.

After Romero came Derek Gore, a tall, distinguished, white-haired British executive who was a Las Brisas executive, and who described himself as a "kind of trouble-shooter." He was proud of the hotel's security. They had thirty-two security people on duty at any given time. The *casitas* were surrounded by a 10-foot concrete, reinforced steel fence.

Gore testified that the year of the Taylors' visit in 1983, there had been 193 thefts—none involving any physical attack. Then Gore, in his attempt to protect the hotel, offered the release that Ken and Teresa had signed absolving the management of responsibility for Teresa's injuries, and he claimed to have witnessed the signing of the document.

He also claimed that three days after the incident, on July 17, he had talked to Mr. and Mrs. Taylor around noon. "Mrs. Taylor was obviously very upset and appeared to be nervous," Gore testified. "She didn't answer any of my questions at all. She seemed terribly upset."

Gore, in fact, claimed to have visited Teresa Taylor twice—on July 17, and then again on July 18, at the hotel. This was, of course, impossible, since Teresa was in the hospital from July 14 on.

But Gore's testimony was full of information that conflicted with established facts. His first mistake was in claiming to having drawn up the release and personally witnessed the signatures. Gore had, in fact, never been to the hospital or visited Teresa, and Venturi got him to say twice that he had witnessed the signatures before he pounced on him.

Then Gore testified that he knew of no instance in his fifteen years at Las Brisas where a guest had been assaulted during a robbery. (Jose Romero would testify that two thefts three days after the Taylor incident were reported. And in May and June, two other guests had reported being assaulted during robberies.)

While having a prosecution witness's testimony torn apart was uncomfortable for Chaiet, it didn't bother him too much. Gore was an incidental witness, and not really necessary for his case. Even if all his testimony was thrown out, there was enough with Sorayda Peraino, Romero, and the rest to establish Ken's probable violence toward Teresa.

Ken Taylor was the last witness called. Venturi had advised Ken not to testify because the state had failed to meet its burden of establishing "clear and convincing evidence" that Taylor had attacked his wife. But Ken insisted. He wanted to tell his own story.

Venturi led Ken through the events of July 14: his incarceration in the Acapulco jail, the extortion of five hundred dollars, his going to Teresa in the hospital, and their flight from Mexico.

Chaiet wasn't so accommodating, and throughout his cross-examination the antagonism between the two men was palpable. Each man would snap at the other, each one's tone of voice often bordering on outright dislike. At moments Chaiet was leaning forward toward Ken so the two men were almost face to face.

At one point Chaiet asked, "What did you do when you saw Teresa?"

"Other than my first reaction of horror and shock?"

"I didn't ask you what your reaction was," Chaiet snapped. "I asked you what you did."

318

(In his notes, Ken later wrote, "Chaiet's angry, not wanting to lose his control . . .")

Venturi leaped up to object. Chaiet's comments were not supposed to be directed at the witness, but at the court.

"I took her pulse to see if she was alive," Ken answered finally.

The overt antagonism continued throughout Chaiet's questioning.

In his summary, Venturi pointed out that thirty-two security people were not many to cover 125 acres of hotel space containing 266 *casitas* on different roads. The Taylor *casita* was on the first row and visible from the road. An assault was possible. As for Derek Gore, he was "proven to have made false statements to the court . . . Teresa Taylor never spoke to, never met, never saw Gore . . . Mr. Gore's job, to put it bluntly, is to cover the hotel's rear end."

Both Al Benigno's and Jose Romero's testimony were in agreement and consistent with Ken Taylor's description of what happened, Venturi argued. As for Sorayda Peraino, she was simply confused. "None of these things that Sorayda Peraino [testified] were said to her by Dr. Taylor, but were [in fact] said to her by the police. She's confused about that."

Chaiet, on the other hand, relied heavily on Sorayda's testimony. He pointed out that Sorayda had no motive at all for lying about her conversation with Ken. She was a credible witness, a mother of eight, a woman of character. The security at Las Brisas was simply too good to make an attack by outsiders plausible.

Judge Farren waited out both attorneys. "All right, gentlemen," he said. "We have concluded testimony as required by Rule 8, with regard to the introduction of evidence of a prior act . . ."

In New Jersey, Rule 8 law required that the prosecution, in this case the State, "must establish that this partic-

319

ular incident occurred by clear and convincing evidence."

Farren then reviewed in detail the testimony of all the witnesses, including Derek Gore. However, after reviewing Gore's testimony and noting his misrepresentations, Farren still declared, "I find Mr. Gore to be credible . . ."

Yet, finally, as everyone expected, it came down to Sorayda Peraino's testimony. "I found her to be a very credible individual," Farren said. "She had no ax to grind with this defendant . . . no interest in the outcome of the case . . ."

Farren also found "the testimony of Al Benigno to be absolutely credible . . . He presented himself as a very credible witness with a good recollection . . . but he didn't embellish on statements made to him by the defendant. It could have been very easy for him to say that Teresa 'told me' that Ken did it. Certainly no one could contest that statement . . . because Teresa is now dead. But he didn't say that. He said that Teresa said, 'I don't know what happened.'"

"With regard to Mr. Taylor's testimony," Farren said, "I don't find it to be credible." Farren reviewed Ken Taylor's testimony, ticking off each point, until finally he said, "The one area that jumps out at me is the conduct of this defendant following the alleged attack. We have an individual who is on his honeymoon, allegedly deeply in love with his wife. We also have an individual who is . . . trained in medicine . . . That's his specialty, medicine, taking care of the sick and those in pain. His version is that he got up off the floor, crawled over to his wife. Took her pulse, bearing in mind that she is in a fetal position with her head on the floor and her knees on the floor . . . covered with blood. She was in a very bad condition . . .

"And what does he do? He takes her pulse, then gets up and gets out and looks on the balcony. He claims he fainted, then went inside to take a shower to wash himself off, while his wife is lying by the side of the bed dying. And he never puts her on the bed. He doesn't try to put cold compresses on her head. He doesn't try to stem the

320

bleeding. He doesn't do anything. He goes in and takes a shower."

In his trial notes at this point, Ken wrote angrily, "You Bastard, I did *not* take a shower. I put water on my [legs] . . . Fuck it, it's in."

Farren continued ticking off the more implausible aspects of Ken's story. Finally, he stared down at the defense table. "I find the proposition of the defense that this incident was caused by intruders is a possibility. However, I do not find that it was a probability . . . I will therefore permit the testimony of this incident in Acapulco to be presented to the jury."

There it was. Ken was stunned even though he had expected it. Venturi was furious and jumped up and moved again for mistrial. "It would seem," he said coldly, "that this court had its mind made up after the testimony of Sorayda Peraino, and that was that."

Just as coldly, Farren retorted, "That is absolutely not true."

The hearing had taken two days, and on June 12 the trial began again. The witnesses this time spoke before the open court, essentially repeating what they had said during the hearing. In his instructions to the jury, Judge Farren told them that in listening to what happened in Acapulco, they were to consider only Ken's "state of mind" when Teresa was killed, not whether "if he did it in Mexico, [then] he must have done it in Manalapan." In other words, the judge said, "the issue of Acapulco goes only to the question of intent, self-defense, not to establish that he is a bad person. If you find that this event did occur and he did it, it has nothing to do with trying to indicate to you that he's bad, that he's disposed to commit crimes. You cannot use it for that purpose." The jury's concern was supposed to be with Kenneth Taylor's claim of "self-defense for himself and his son."

In his notes, Ken angrily scribbled, "So, then, how does

321

Acapulco, even if I did it, relate to 11/11/84, 16 months later?"

With barely controlled anger, Venturi rose to move again for a mistrial because of Farren's instructions. Throughout the hearing, Venturi argued, the judge had shown an "anti-defense bias." "Self-defense" was not at issue in Acapulco, and there was no way the jury wouldn't make a connection between Mexico and Manalapan. After hearing about Acapulco everyone on the jury would believe that Ken had "a violent character, a violent personality."

On his part, Farren was equally angry. He denied Venturi's move for a mistrial and said, "There has been no bias, passion or prejudice toward anyone in this case."

Venturi had moved for a mistrial so frequently not only on points of law that truly grated on him, but because he knew that a judge's bias is one of the primary tests of whether a trial can be judged a "mistrial" and whether a conviction can be set aside. The Supreme Court has defined a biased judge as a "structural defect" in a trial, and it can never be considered "harmless." In fact, a biased judge has traditionally been considered as automatically invalidating a conviction and has never been subject to a "harmless error" analysis.

The issue of mistrial arose again soon after the Acapulco testimony was concluded. This time it was over whether Ken Taylor himself would testify in open court before the jury. Venturi thought that during the hearing Ken had come off cold. And in his responses to Chaiet he had even seemed menacing. To be honest, Venturi didn't think Ken would come off too well in front of the jury.

Farren was not pleased when Venturi said that he hadn't yet decided to put Taylor on the stand. The defense, Venturi claimed, wanted more time to review telephone records and prescription forms, some of which Taylor claimed were forged, that were late in arriving from Chaiet.

"I find it difficult, if not impossible," Farren said, "to believe that you have not decided by the seventh or eighth day of this trial whether you're going to put Dr. Taylor on the stand."

Venturi responded, "Judge, without being able to review this information with Doctor Taylor, without being given any time, we can't make an intelligent decision about whether or not he's going to testify."

"We're going to take a five-minute break," Farren said. "When I come out at twenty-five minutes to three, you'll give me that decision."

Ken noted in his transcripts that "Jack is elated! Farren has set himself up for a mistrial."

Five minutes later, when Farren demanded an answer, Venturi rose and said, "Your honor, at this time, with all due respect, I once again renew my motion for a mistrial based on the prejudice of the court . . . [This decision] is in effect putting a gun to our heads in terms of making the most critical decision in the case."

Farren clearly saw that he had been forced into a difficult position. He didn't want it to appear that he had denied the defense adequate opportunity to decide an important issue. Fuming, he finally said, "I don't want to put Doctor Taylor in a position where he cannot tell his side of the story . . . so I'm going to reverse what I have indicated. I will give Mr. Venturi a continuance until Monday morning."

Farren then called the jury back in, advised them of the continuance, and abruptly left the bench.

Over the weekend Venturi tried to convince Ken he shouldn't testify. He knew that with Ken's short fuse, Chaiet would quickly get under his skin. He also argued that the state hadn't really proved its case beyond a reasonable doubt. There was no need for him to testify and maybe make a bad impression.

Ken wanted to testify, but finally he gave in. "Okay, Jack, whatever you say . . ."

When they returned Monday, the defense would rest, and then Chaiet and Venturi would give their summations.

Venturi knew he was in a difficult spot. The way the trial had gone, acquittal was impossible. In his summation notes, he jotted down, "suspicion, speculation, innuendo . . ." to characterize the State's case.

Venturi began his summation by thanking the jury for putting up with all the legal arguments and the delays while they were out of the courtroom. Dr. Taylor had not testified, Venturi went on, because the State had not proved its case beyond reasonable doubt in its indictment of murder. He reminded the jury about the different, "lesser" categories, such as manslaughter in the heat of passion and aggravated manslaughter, all of which the judge would instruct them about.

Venturi tried to have the jury share Ken Taylor's shock upon seeing his wife sexually abuse their son. "Can you imagine the rage of the father?" he said. "Look at the situation through the eyes of the person who was there. Ask yourself whether detached reflection can be expected in view of a raised dumbbell. Whether detached reflection can be expected if that person in her state got past you to your baby. You have to ask yourselves that question through the eyes of a father in fear for his baby."

Venturi continued in this vein, trying to involve the jury emotionally in Ken's experience. Then, he admitted that what Ken did afterward was horrible. "It's obvious the body was wrapped up, taken away, put in a trunk. Things were cleaned up. It's not denied. It doesn't make you like this man. It doesn't make me like him. It doesn't make anybody like him. But it doesn't make it murder."

Walking slowly back and forth before the jury, Venturi

reminded them that it was Ken's effort to buy time, to deliver his son to the safety of his parents.

Ken was weeping at this point, his head and eyes down.

Then Venturi brought up Ken's confession, and how he turned himself in. "What did they [the police] do to preserve what was going to be his statement? Nothing. No court stenographer to take little notes, no tape recorder . . . How different it would be if he had said 'he got away' rather than 'he got *it* away.' He may have said that, but we'll never know beyond a reasonable doubt . . .

"I submit to you that while there is no self-defense and no self-protection of another under those circumstances, the State has still proven nothing more than either reckless manslaughter or manslaughter under reasonable provocation in the heat of passion."

When Venturi switched to Acapulco, he immediately pointed out that none of the Mexican policemen who testified ever maintained that Ken admitted to "laying one finger on his wife." Mrs. Peraino testified that he did. Yet none of her testimony was corroborated by anyone else. "Where did it come from?" Venturi asked. "Why in God's name would he tell her he beat up his wife . . . Does this make any sense at all?"

The State had resorted to simply throwing in Acapulco, the "kitchen sink" sensationalism that he had spoken of at the beginning of the trial.

"This is not a case of murder, ladies and gentlemen," Venturi concluded, "it's the case of a family tragedy . . . Dr. Taylor will always be haunted for the rest of his days by what has happened. I place Dr. Taylor's fate in your hands."

Chaiet wasted no niceties on thanking the jury when he began his thirty-five-minute summary. His deep voice immediately rose in indignation. "Teresa is dead. She can't talk to us. And Taylor is a liar. So when you go into that jury room, there will be some unanswered questions. But there should be no mystery, no mystery at all, that this was a murder, and this defendant is the murderer."

Chaiet quickly brought up Acapulco, and then Manalapan, drawing a clear line between the two. "In both cases Teresa was the victim," his voice boomed. "In both cases the defendant's explanations strain our common sense."

"We heard that he got up . . . came downstairs and observed Teresa having fellatio with the baby. When he saw that, he screamed and she ran to the sewing room. He went after her and she attacked him. Perhaps she was upset that he intruded into her sex play with a five-month-old baby, but he says she attacked him. And when she attacked him, this five-foot-three-inch woman, he took that barbell from her and gave it to her.

"In Acapulco, we heard about intruders. But," Chaiet said sarcastically, "if there was a fight, it was Teresa who put up the battle, not this six-foot, two-hundred-pound defendant. When you use common sense and reason, you don't have to consider the testimony of Mrs. Peraino . . . but what possible motivation could she have to . . . lie to us? How can you be mistaken when you've have a conversation with a man who you've met on his honeymoon and he tells you that he's knocked his wife's teeth out?"

Chaiet traced Ken's bizarre trip to his parents' home, making special reference to the fact that others described him as appearing "normal" during this time, while Teresa's body was still stuffed in the trunk of the car, and before he dumped her body alongside a deserted roadway. "Is this the family tragedy we've heard about?" Chaiet asked scornfully.

Chaiet admitted that Teresa used drugs, but he pointed out that everyone testified that it was a small amount. "She had no difficulty taking care of the baby . . . Where is the 'bizarre' activity?"

His voice rising dramatically, Chaiet was approaching his climax. Ken Taylor, Chaiet said, was a "cold, calculating, devious liar.

"There was no fellatio. There was no self-defense. Why

did it happen? What triggered it? I don't know. Why the Vaseline? I don't know. What time? He says 8 A.M. I say I don't know, because doesn't it seem strange that Teresa was found in the same clothes she had on at ten-thirty at night, with a watch, a bracelet, with earrings, with her necklaces?

"But what do we know? We know that there is no reason in the world for this twenty-five-year-old woman to be dead. For the baby to have no mother. For her parents to have lost a daughter. And if there is no reason for her death, then there is no reason why this defendant should not be held accountable for her murder . . ."

When Chaiet finished the courtroom was hushed. There was only the sound of a few friends and relatives of Teresa's weeping.

Farren's instructions to the jury noted that in addition to acquittal, there were four possible verdicts—murder, aggravated manslaughter, reckless manslaughter, and manslaughter "in the heat of passion" or "under reasonable provocation." With the first, murder, the defendant had to be shown by the State to have killed "knowingly and purposely, beyond a reasonable doubt." With the second and third, there was, Farren explained, an "element of recklessness in both of them." The degree of recklessness, however, is greater in aggravated manslaughter. The fourth, manslaughter in the heat of passion, is when the killing is the result of provocation. "Mere words, looks, gestures alone," Farren said, "no matter how abusive, threatening, or insulting, are never [adequate] provocations. Provocation in law must be such as to . . . probably throw the mind of the average person . . . into a state of uncontrolled rage."

The jury retired at three-thirty, and Ken was taken to a holding cell. A little before six, everyone was called back into the courtroom. The jury was confused and needed more clarification about the categories of murder and manslaughter. Farren went over each again. The jury retired for the night and resumed deliberating the next morning at 8 A.M. A while later the jurors asked for more clarifications. After Farren explained further, the jury retired again at 10:05. But this time it was brief.

At 11:10 A.M., the jury returned with a verdict.

In his holding cell, Ken was told to get ready by his guard, Hopkins. "It doesn't look good, Doc," he said. "I'm sorry."

Ken quickly tied his shoes, adjusted his tie, and put on his suit jacket. Hopkins handcuffed him and led him into the buzzing, overflowing courtroom. Even the aisles were jammed with people.

The court clerk asked the foreman if they had reached a verdict. "Yes, we have," he answered.

"Number one," the court clerk asked, "How do you find the defendant on the charge that . . . he did commit the crime of murder by purposely or knowingly causing the death of Teresa Taylor?"

"We find the defendant guilty," the foreman said softly.

Ken sat rigidly at the defense table, listening, his face pale. The jury was polled, and as each juror repeated "I agree" to the foreman's "Guilty," the words were a damning echo in the giant room. Ken bowed his head as the jurors walked past him on their way out of the courtroom. Then he was handcuffed and led back to the Monmouth County Jail, where he had been held since November 18.

After the verdict, Farren immediately raised the bail to $750,000 and set the sentencing hearing for September 27.

Jean and Zach Taylor were in shock. Zach, his pained face flushed, stared at the floor. Louise sobbed as Al Benigno put his arm around his wife's shoulder. Later, Al told reporters gathered around Paul Chaiet in the hallway that "he didn't get enough. It's crazy. He gets convicted of murder and he can get bail." Louise, still emotionally

328

overwrought, tears choking her, whispered, "I just can't seem to . . . it can never bring her back."

Later, in a press briefing, Jack Venturi said that he would file an appeal. Three things, he said, had created a cumulative effect that had made a fair trial impossible: the Acapulco assault that Judge Farren had allowed; a video of Teresa playing with the baby; and the enlarged, enhanced color photographs of the deceased corpse.

When he heard about Venturi's comments, Chaiet sarcastically responded, "If you were facing thirty years without parole, you'd probably appeal, too."

Chapter Twenty-two

As expected, Judge Farren sentenced Kenneth Taylor to the maximum—life in prison, with a minimum of thirty years served before he would be eligible for parole. In the sentencing, Farren said, "This was a heinous, savage, brutal [crime] . . . He literally slaughtered his wife with a barbell . . . If the statute provided for a fifty-year minimum before parole," Farren went on, "this court would have no problem imposing it."

After the sentencing, Paul Chaiet, who had asked for an eighty-year sentence with no parole for fifty years, said that "the event was so evil, so awful . . . that this defendant should never be released . . . Hopefully he will remain in prison until he dies."

But this wasn't the end of the legacy left by the violence of that night in November. Parts of the drama still had to be played out.

After the verdict, Ken Taylor brooded in jail, trying to contain what even he called "a hideous fury" toward all those who had destroyed him in what he considered an unfair trial. He was also tormented by the fact of his own lack of control and stupidity. "How could I have been so ignorant, so abysmally moronic NOT to have seen what was happening to our lives?" he asked in his diary. "Teresa and I had perpetrated a catastrophe—a tale of drugs, sex, lunacy, and a killing . . . Her death, being in jail, the destruction of our families had all been entirely unnecessary."

The failure to convince others that his had been a crime of passion also continued to gall him. But most of all, he wrote, it was the children.

The joint custody of Philip between his parents and Jeff and Celeste White had been going on for more than six months. It was on December 1, 1983, that Judge Julia Ashbey had made her temporary decision. Since then, the Whites had petitioned to gain full custody. The hearing before Judge Ashbey was originally set for July 2, but the real battle for the child began in August, 1985.

While the elder Taylors and the Whites were preparing for their custody hearings, Kenneth Taylor was figuring out how to escape from jail.

He began to develop a plan in mid-July, when he noticed a damaged window with a roll bar holding it in place. His first problem was to stay close to the room with the roll bar. Feigning continuing pain in his now healed foot, Ken convinced the doctor to let him continue on in the medical wing while his foot was healing. He then managed to exchange cells with a prisoner to get closer to the room with the damaged window. He "bought" an allen wrench from a guard so he could remove the screen over his cell window. Slowly, he also collected a hacksaw blade and arranged for a car, clothes, money, and a pistol. Then he began to work out the details of his plan.

Prior to the August custody hearing, both of the elder Taylors and Jeff and Celeste White were interviewed by doctors and child-care professionals and were even ordered by the family court to undergo psychological tests. One doctor, a court-chosen child psychologist, Michele Rabinowitz, concluded that because bonding was so vital in such a young child, Philip needed "the psychological security of real parents and real commitment . . . In a situation such as this, where there are no 'bad guys,' the decision is difficult." In Dr. Rabinowitz's report, however, she favored

Philip being adopted by Jeff and Celeste White, with extensive visitation being given to the child's natural grandparents.

At the August 27 hearing, Judge Ashbey altered the custody arrangement. She ruled that from September 1 to June 30, Philip would be with Jeff and Celeste White, who had given birth to a baby girl the previous December. From July 1 to August 31 of the next year, he would live with Zach and Jean Taylor. During his stay with the Whites, Philip would have a "monthly visit" with Ken in prison. Ken would also be allowed one collect telephone call a week (on Monday nights) to Philip. Each family had to place a $2,000 bond to guarantee compliance. Both families were "entitled to liberal visitation." It was an arrangement that pleased no one—especially two families with such an antagonistic history.

Because of the custody dates, Philip would be transferred to the Whites on September 1, only a few days away.

Judge Ashbey's order infuriated Ken. It was worse than before. Now Philip was being taken from his parents and would be with the Whites for almost a year.

At this time Ken was still awaiting his sentencing, which had been put off until October 4. With Judge Ashbey's frustrating order, escape became even more pressing.

Ken told the guard who was helping him with the allen wrench and hacksaw blades to go to the Taylor house in Manalapan Sunday night, September 1. Zach and Jean Taylor were leaving for Marion that day, and the key would be under the doormat. He could remove all the furniture and anything else he wanted as "payment" for his assistance.

When the Whites went by the house two days later to pick up Philip's belongings for their "custody" period, they found it empty. They reported the theft to the police. When Zach was called by the police about the robbery, he accused the Whites.

The guard had hidden the hacksaw blades and small wrench in a prison library book by Stephen King, *Different*

Seasons, and he took it to Ken on Friday night, September 13. The next night Ken and another inmate slipped into the empty cell with the roll bar and damaged window. The wrench was the wrong size, so using a piece of metal broken from a plumbing fixture, they loosened the bolts holding the screen. But the real job was sawing through the steel roll bar. They worked at it for hours until the eleven o'clock lockup bell sounded. They were a quarter of an inch from sawing through the bar.

By morning the attempt was uncovered. One of the inmates who knew what was going on talked.

Ken denied knowing anything about it, but he was placed in a basement isolation cell until his sentencing. The guard who had supplied Ken with the hacksaw blades was also fingered by the inmate, but he denied everything as well. Nothing could be proved, but the guard resigned soon after, and, presumably with Ken's furniture, moved to Florida with his girlfriend. Ken had hidden the hacksaw blades so ingeniously that "to this day they remain hidden in the Monmouth County jail."

Ken received more headlines: *Murderer in Escape Try.*

Three weeks after his sentencing Ken was taken in chains to New Jersey's Trenton State Prison, where he was placed in the maximum-security block.

The animosity between the Whites and the Taylors over Philip increased. Little things added up quickly. Jeff and Celeste, ignoring the court's ruling, rejected Ken's Monday night phone calls to Philip. Jean Taylor wrote a caustic letter in November to Judge Ashbey. Not only were the Whites not accepting Ken's phone calls, but they hadn't brought Philip to the prison to see his father. Their request for a Thanksgiving visit had been ignored. But the thing that bothered Jean the most was what she considered Celeste's inadequate care of Philip.

"After Celeste had her [own] baby," Jean wrote Ashbey, "Philip was treated with diaper rash and it was very bad . . . This happened over and over and I had to take him to the doctor and got prescriptions 3e times . . . Sometimes he was so raw the warm water would make him

333

cry . . . we took pictures and I kept records . . . In August Celeste asked me, 'How do I keep Philip from getting diaper rash?' Now that she has both babies, I don't know what the condition is. I am very concerned."

The Taylors also feared that the Whites would not give the "whole truth" to Philip. "They won't tell him . . . what his Mommy was doing to him, that her body contained at least 3 different drugs—codeine, cocaine, and alcohol. That she was attempting to kill his Daddy and was abusing him . . ."

For their part, Jeff and Celeste, and the whole Benigno family, for that matter, almost became physically ill when they thought of Teresa's killer telephoning the house to speak with the baby or Ken having visitation with Philip in jail. They pointed to Dr. Rabinowitz's report that said visitation rights with the grandparents "should not interfere with the natural and normal bonding process."

This fundamental distaste between them gave rise to a spurt of legal actions.

In October the Whites asked a new judge, Walter H. Gehricke, who had replaced Judge Ashbey, to limit the Taylors' visits to the daytime hours.

In November, 1985, the Taylors brought an action against the Whites for not fulfilling the Court's rulings.

Then, in December, the Whites petitioned in New York courts that the controlling jurisdiction move to New York State. The New York decision denying the Whites' motion didn't come down until March of 1986. Philip had not been in New York State long enough to justify any change.

Though the Whites still had custody until July, they dreaded Philip going back to the Taylors and his "visitations" with Ken in prison. According to one account, they even debated fleeing to Canada with the child.

Near the end of May the Taylors filed another action against the Whites. They again listed Jeff and Celeste's failure to abide by the court's ruling. The Whites had consistently denied Ken's phone calls, they had failed to put up the $2,000 bond, they had to be forced by court action to comply with Philip's Thanksgiving visit to the Taylors, and apparently they were even trying to avoid sending Philip to Indiana for his two-month visit in July and August.

A new lawyer for the Whites, Janice Miller, didn't respond directly to the Taylors' charges. Instead, she filed a motion to change the present court-ordered custody arrangement.

A hearing was set on both actions before Judge Gehricke on July 1.

At the hearing all the same arguments were brought up: the Taylors could offer Philip the stable, quiet life in Indiana, they had a house "in a quiet neighborhood" with adequate room to raise a child. From the Whites' point of view, Jeff had a good, steady job, they had just bought a new house near the Benignos', and with their new daughter, they had a solid family environment in which Philip could flourish. They noted that when Philip was ten, the Taylors would be nearly seventy, and, despite "all their good intentions, they would not be able to keep up with him."

The single point that the Whites were strongly against was Philip being allowed to see Kenneth Taylor.

Gehricke put off his decision until August 1. And when it came, it shocked the Taylors. Judge Gehricke had relied heavily on the expertise of Dr. Michele Rabinowitz, whom the Whites had called to testify. Dr. Rabinowitz testified that the original agreement of shared custody "was not in Philip's interest." The child should be allowed to bond psychologically with one set of parents. And, as she had decided earlier, she felt that Jeff and Celeste would be "positive, loving, and nurturing" parents for Philip.

Further, it would not be in the child's best interests to continue allowing any visitation with his father in jail.

As for the Taylors, the doctor could recommend only very limited visitation over the next several years. Visits should be short-term, lasting days, or perhaps as long as two weeks. "Visits with grandparents of one- or two-month duration are highly unusual and interfere with the normal family process," Rabinowitz said.

Gehricke decided that the Taylors would have Philip in Indiana from August 1 to August 16. The Taylors could have a week's overnight visitation with Philip the week after Christmas. The Taylors thereafter had to refer to the Whites as Philip's "mother and father."

Then came the decision that almost sent Ken Taylor screaming against the wall of his cell. "Under no circumstances will Everett [Zach] and Jean Taylor allow any contact between Philip Taylor and Kenneth Taylor. There will be no visits to the Trenton State Prison where he is incarcerated. There will be no telephone communication between Kenneth Taylor and Philip Taylor and no letters read to Philip from Kenneth."

The Taylors had lost. The Whites were now able to begin adoption proceedings for Philip after the custody was final.

But the twists and turns in the Taylor story were not over. In August, during Philip's visit to Marion, the Taylors started adoption proceedings. Their Indiana lawyer, Patrick Ryan, arranged an adoption petition for the Taylors, which involved basically a quick investigation about the Taylors' home (its location and quality), their financial condition and how they related to the child, as observed by a caseworker. All of these conditions were speedily met and the petition was filed before Thomas Hunt, the Grant County circuit judge who would decide whether to allow the petition.

The adoption decree read: "The court, having heard the evidence . . . finds that the natural father has consented to this adoption . . . and that the child's mother is deceased; that a custody proceeding is pending in Monmouth County, N.J.; that the petitioners are the paternal grandparents of Philip Andrew Taylor; that they wish to adopt said child as their own . . ."

On August 7, Judge Hunt signed the decree in his chambers. Philip was now the legally adopted child of Zach and Jean Taylor — in Indiana.

During that same month, almost as the adoption proceedings in Marion were going on, Ken Taylor was planning his second escape attempt, which would take place in late September.

As soon as the Whites discovered what had happened in Marion, they called their lawyer, Janice Miller. On August 7, Miller reacted. She called Marion and talked with Judge Hunt. She wanted the adoption decree voided, explaining that Judge Gehricke had already granted custody to the Whites. Hunt requested a copy of Judge Gehricke's order.

After talking with Janice Miller, Judge Gehricke called Judge Hunt in Marion. Gehricke was furious. He told Hunt that there had been a long, bitter battle over the boy in New Jersey and, as one report describes the conversation, that "those people [the Taylors] have stolen that child in violation of my order."

Judge Hunt replied that if everything Miller and Gehricke was telling him was true, then they should file a petition and he would give them a hearing.

The next day Janice Miller and the Whites flew to Marion, Indiana, where they began a long, tortuous path toward retrieving Philip. They visited other lawyers, the head of the Indiana Bar Association, and even other Grant County Superior Court judges besides Hunt—who had mysteriously disappeared for the weekend on a fishing trip.

Only one person responded to the Millers' pleas for help—Warren Haas, a Welfare Department lawyer. After checking the caseworker's report on the adoption petition, Haas agreed to help Miller. He would issue a CHINS petition, which would claim that Philip was a "child in need of services," on an emergency basis. The emergency was that the Taylors might flee with the child. He filed the petition along with the New Jersey custody order.

Then, along with a social worker and a deputy sheriff, Haas and Miller went to the Taylors'.

Haas explained why they were there, but Zach wouldn't let them in. Even after the deputy sheriff demanded to be let in, claiming that they didn't need a warrant for the CHINS order, Zach blocked their entry. The deputy began pounding on the door, and finally Zach gave up and let them in. The deputy immediately picked up Philip and started to leave, with Zach screaming at

Haas that he was a "no-good, goddamned baby snatcher."

Furious phone calls between Pat Ryan, Judge Hunt, Warren Haas, and Miller burned up the telephone lines over the weekend. Haas and Miller were adamant. They would not return the child. The issue would be determined in court.

With the bad news about the custody battle for Philip, Ken's plans to escape esculated. He had five other inmates going along with him. One of them, a murderer who was in for life, had discovered a window without bars in an attic above the prison furniture shop. The window was almost level with the top of the prison wall. The only problem was that the wall was thirty feet away. The prisoners built a wood bridge in sections, each connected with steel plates and bolts. Once complete, all they would have to do was walk over the plank to the wall, which led to the backyard of the warden's house. Another of the prisoners arranged for a van to be waiting outside the wall near the warden's on October 4.

The plan, however, became ever more violent as the date came closer. A crossbow to shoot the tower guard was created in the wood shop. Molotov cocktails were fashioned, as well as a blowgun that shot sixteen-penny nails. They would firebomb the tower, if necessary. As each item was made ready, it was hidden in the attic.

But again one of the inmates squealed just before the breakout attempt. Those involved were disciplined, and a hearing was scheduled. If any of the prisoners were found guilty, they would receive additional time on their sentences.

The New Jersey headlines treated their readers to another Taylor escapade: *Manalapan Killer, Five Others Await Escape-Try Hearing.*

Ken Taylor, who denied being involved, was found not guilty of the escape attempt at the hearing. But he was immediately transferred to Powhatan Prison in Virginia, and then to the Augusta Correctional Center, a new, tough prison in western Virginia.

For a while Ken was a model prisoner, and he was eventually assigned to tutoring other convicts in getting high school equivalency diplomas. But he was still quietly calculating how to escape.

In Marion, both Judge Hunt and Judge Wright, the judge who had allowed Haas to take Philip, removed themselves from the case—each for his own reasons. Hunt, in particular, was angered by the case. In a later interview in *The Indianapolis Star,* he said, "I was blindsided. I was never completely informed of the New Jersey case. I disqualified myself from the case because I didn't think I could be fair."

With both judges removing themselves, the CHINS order had no effect and Philip was returned to the Taylors.

But back in Staten Island the Benignos and Whites were fuming. Philip, they claimed, had been stolen from them. And they weren't giving up. They gave interviews, talked with lawyers, and held block parties to raise money for further legal action. But nothing seemed to help until Janice Miller suggested that the Whites file a criminal complaint against the Taylors for defying Judge Gehricke's custody order. This was a felony, and the Taylors could be extradited for it.

Even though an indictment and warrant against the Taylors was issued, the Grant County authorities ignored it because there was no judge available to sign the arrest order. They were all attending a judicial conference.

Pat Ryan said that he would fight any extradition attempt against the Taylors. "Adoption proceedings in Indiana take precedence, and the boy was adopted in August . . . The court orders in New Jersey were temporary. Adoption is final."

Once again, however, Paul Chaiet became a thorn in the Taylors' side. On behalf of Monmouth County he sent an extradition request to Indiana governor Robert D. Orr. When Orr authorized service, Jean and Zach Taylor were brought before a judge and released on a $500 bond. A hearing on the Taylors' extradition to New Jersey was scheduled for October 20. The newspapers were having a field day with passionate editorials and letters to the editor mostly supporting the local couple against the Easterners.

As the hearing droned on and each side castigated the other, the issue was suddenly made moot by Govern Orr, who abruptly rescinded his extradition warrant.

All parties were now back to phase one. Philip was still with the Taylors, and the Whites back in Staten Island were trying to get a legal break to go their way.

But Janice Miller was not giving up, either. The original custody order had not been temporary, but had given permanent custody to the Whites. And even though the Whites had no standing in the Indiana courts, they should have received notification of the adoption proceedings by the Taylors. Even Indiana law required such notification.

Another hearing was set for December 2 before Judge R. Alan Brubaker.

In the hearing Pat Ryan argued that the Indiana law at issue, the Uniform Child Custody Jurisdiction Act, didn't apply to adoptions.

After the hearing Judge Brubaker requested that briefs from both sides be before him by February 13. Brubaker would then decide the case within two months. Briefs were properly filed, and all those who had been so passionately involved in the drama of Ken Taylor's son sat back to await Brubaker's decision.

Public opinion in both states was running as expected. Those in Indiana thought the child should go to the Taylors. People in New Jersey thought the child should be returned to the Whites.

When the judgment from Brubaker finally came, an Associated Press headline in Marion on April 13 told it all: *Judge Orders Parents of Wife-Killer to Give Up Boy.*

On April 10, Brubaker found the adoption "invalid" because custody had already been awarded to the Whites and the Whites had never been informed that the adoption was taking place. Brubaker ordered the Taylors to return Philip to Jeff and Celeste White.

Zach and Jean got a last-minute restraining order in an

effort to prevent having to give Philip up. At first the order was upheld, then it was rescinded.

Eventually, Philip was handed over to Jeff White by a silent, subdued Zach Taylor.

Since that traumatic moment, both Jean and Zach Taylor have vowed to keep fighting to get Philip back — which they are continuing to do to this day.

Ken Taylor made other escape attempts within two years. Both were failures, but they landed him in segregation, where he was separated time and time again from the general prison population and its privileges.

Ken Taylor has now spent almost half of his seven years of prison time in isolation cells. By 1989 his appeals to the New Jersey Court of Appeals had been denied. The U.S. Supreme Court had refused to hear his case.

In 1991 he is a calmer man, better adjusted to the fact that he will probably be in jail for many more years. He still yearns to see his children, but he claims that he no longer has any plans to "go to the wall." Even regular prison life is preferable to the gray existence in isolation.

But now, as he looks around him, he sees clearly how the rest of his life has been defined by sex, drugs, and his moments of rage and violence. Once, in his prison diary, he wrote about seeing the future: "I often think about the fact that I am going to be here the rest of my life; I will be sixty-five before even being considered for parole.

"I begin quietly glancing at the older inmates. The gray men. Gray hair, gray skins, gray clothes. Even their eyes seem colorless. Then I notice something odd. Mornings the young men push their way before the sinks to shave. But this time the older inmates don't seem to mind. They watch as the young turks elbow each other, joking, grinning into the steaming mirrors, preening like peacocks with no tails.

"Every morning it's the same. Older inmates are the last

341

to shave, the last to stand in front of the mirrors. I picture myself like them — at fifty, sixty, sixty-five; gray-faced and avoiding seeing what I have become. Thirty-five going on sixty-five. I close my eyes, not wanting to see more."

Afterword

In order to protect the privacy of those tangentially connected to the Taylor case, I have occasionally used pseudonyms — Betty Macdonald (Ken's first high school girlfriend) Katherine "Kay" Mitchell and Marilyn Bergman (Ken Taylor's first and second wives), and Rhonda (his and Marilyn's daughter).

Other pseudonyms used were Dr. Ronald Wheeler (psychiatrist at Ken's naval base),; Jack Lombardi (Teresa's boyfriend when she met Ken), Carrie and Jon (Teresa's friends), and Susie (who helped Teresa get an abortion).

The sources I used were varied. During the seven years he has been in prison, Ken Taylor has written a great deal about his part in this "Roshomon tapestry." Most of the events, dialogue, and internal thoughts attributed to Ken, or seen from his point of view, are from these writings. Other scenes and dialogue are taken from police reports, court transcripts, and interviews (often recalled during police interviews). I have also tried to avoid creating scenes or interpreting someone's thoughts merely for dramatic effect as much as possible.

**PINNACLE BOOKS AND *TRUE DETECTIVE* MAGAZINE
TEAM UP FOR THE GRIZZLIEST TRUE CRIME STORIES
IN PRINT!**

BIZARRE MURDERERS (486, $4.95)
Edited by Rose G. Mandelsberg
The crimes are too shocking to be believed, but they are true
nonetheless:

- The "vampire" who drank his victim's blood
- The hooker who was cooked alive
- The killer who kept his victim's brain as a souvenier
- The murderer who fed his victim's to the pigs

BIZZARE MURDERERS recounts some of the most sensational
slayings in the annals of crime. You won't believe what you
read — but it's all true. And truly bizarre.

CELEBRITY MURDERS   435, $4.95)
Edited by Art Crockett
Some were in the wrong place at the wrong time, others were
the victims of an obssessed fan. Bob Crane, Sharon Tate, Sal Mi-
neo, Rebecca Schaeffer, George Rose, and tohers: stars of the
screen and stage, darlings of the media. All had brilliant careers
cut short by an act of bloody violence. Read the true accounts of
the stars who last roles were played out on a cold, coroner's table.

SERIAL MURDERERS   (432, $4.95)
Edited by Art Crockett
Some of them, like Son of Sam, are known throughout the
world. Others are not well known, like Henry lee Lucas, even
though he killed 176 people. And there are those who are still unknown, their carnage gone unstopped, like the Green River Killer.

They are all serial killers, slaughtering their innocent victims
for reasons known only to themselves. no one knows where they'll
strike, or when. Or *why*. We know only one thing: Once they *do*
start, they will write their stories in blood until someone stops
them.

*Available wherever paperbacks are sold, or order direct from the
Publisher. Send cover price plus 50¢ per copy for mailing and
handling to Pinnacle Books, Dept. 547, 475 Park Avenue South,
New York, N.Y. 10016. Residents of New York, New Jersey and
Pennsylvania must include sales tax. DO NOT SEND CASH.*